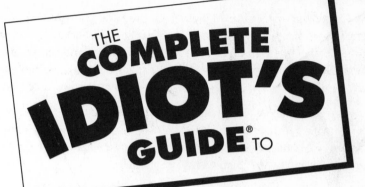

THE
COMPLETE
IDIOT'S
GUIDE® TO

Controlling
Anxiety

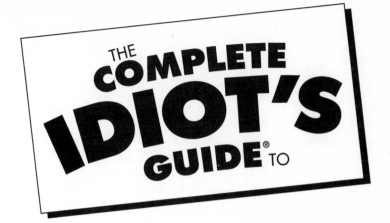

THE COMPLETE IDIOT'S GUIDE® TO

Controlling Anxiety

by Joni E. Johnston, Psy.D.

ALPHA

A member of Penguin Group (USA) Inc.

ALPHA BOOKS

Published by the Penguin Group

Penguin Group (USA) Inc., 375 Hudson Street, New York, New York 10014, U.S.A.

Penguin Group (Canada), 10 Alcorn Avenue, Toronto, Ontario, Canada M4V 3B2 (a division of Pearson Penguin Canada Inc.)

Penguin Books Ltd, 80 Strand, London WC2R 0RL, England

Penguin Ireland, 25 St Stephen's Green, Dublin 2, Ireland (a division of Penguin Books Ltd)

Penguin Group (Australia), 250 Camberwell Road, Camberwell, Victoria 3124, Australia (a division of Pearson Australia Group Pty Ltd)

Penguin Books India Pvt Ltd, 11 Community Centre, Panchsheel Park, New Delhi—110 017, India

Penguin Group (NZ), cnr Airborne and Rosedale Roads, Albany, Auckland 1310, New Zealand (a division of Pearson New Zealand Ltd)

Penguin Books (South Africa) (Pty) Ltd, 24 Sturdee Avenue, Rosebank, Johannesburg 2196, South Africa

Penguin Books Ltd, Registered Offices: 80 Strand, London WC2R 0RL, England

International Standard Book Number: 1-59257-525-0
Library of Congress Catalog Card Number: 2006929094

08   07   8 7 6 5 4 3 2

Interpretation of the printing code: The rightmost number of the first series of numbers is the year of the book's printing; the rightmost number of the second series of numbers is the number of the book's printing. For example, a printing code of 06-1 shows that the first printing occurred in 2006.

Printed in the United States of America

Note: This publication contains the opinions and ideas of its author. It is intended to provide helpful and informative material on the subject matter covered. It is sold with the understanding that the author and publisher are not engaged in rendering professional services in the book. If the reader requires personal assistance or advice, a competent professional should be consulted.

The author and publisher specifically disclaim any responsibility for any liability, loss, or risk, personal or otherwise, which is incurred as a consequence, directly or indirectly, of the use and application of any of the contents of this book.

Most Alpha books are available at special quantity discounts for bulk purchases for sales promotions, premiums, fundraising, or educational use. Special books, or book excerpts, can also be created to fit specific needs.

For details, write: Special Markets, Alpha Books, 375 Hudson Street, New York, NY 10014.

Publisher: *Marie Butler-Knight*
Editorial Director: *Mike Sanders*
Managing Editor: *Billy Fields*
Acquisitions Editor: *Tom Stevens*
Senior Development Editor: *Phil Kitchel*
Production Editor: *Megan Douglass*
Copy Editor: *Keith Cline*

Cartoonist: *Shannon Wheeler*
Cover Designer: *Bill Thomas*
Book Designers: *Trina Wurst/Kurt Owens*
Indexer: *Angie Bess*
Layout: *Chad Dressler*
Proofreader: *Aaron Black*

In memory of Dr. Mary Conrady, who threw the life buoy when I was drowning.

Contents at a Glance

Appendixes

Contents

Introduction

Been There, Done That

At 12:11 A.M. on January 1, 1995, I welcomed my first-born into the world after 22 hours of labor and a C-section. On January 3, I experienced my first panic attack. Just home from the hospital, I had easily fallen asleep, only to be awakened out of a dead slumber a few hours later, gasping for breath and heart racing.

I had no idea what was happening. I remember jumping out of bed, stumbling down the stairs, and throwing the door open. The cold January air seemed to snap me back to reality and help me regain control of my breathing. I spent the next few hours terrified of going back to sleep, afraid of the dark, and wondering if I was experiencing some weird reaction to my anesthesia or if I was losing my mind. Over the next six weeks, as the panic attacks recurred, I began to believe the latter.

There's an irony here. With a family history of depression, I was not unaware of the risk of postpartum complications. I had read up on postpartum depression and was ready to deal with any baby blues that might linger longer than usual. But postpartum panic? During all my years of clinical training, postpartum anxiety was something I had never heard of. Apparently, the psychological landscape hasn't changed that much; just a year ago, I spoke to a well-known psychiatrist who glibly assured me that there's no such thing as postpartum panic disorder.

When I got better, and was able to get some emotional distance, I realized that there had been warning signs during my pregnancy. I had always enjoyed flying; during my nine months of pregnancy, I dreaded boarding any airplane, and the slightest turbulence would have me gripping the arm of the unlucky stranger who happened to sit next to me. Pre-pregnancy, I had once spent a relaxed two hours trapped in an elevator. However, when an elevator door got stuck for a few minutes when I was about five months along, I felt so claustrophobic and panicked that it was all I could do to keep from screaming. On top of that, there were enough little scares during my pregnancy (positive PAP smear, intermittent bleeding, early dilation) that I came to feel as if I were receiving these random electric shocks; just as I was relaxing into expectant motherhood, another worry would jolt me back into a state of alarm.

Before the Tipping Point

Before my postpartum days, if you had ever asked me if I was an anxious person, I would have laughed. So, I'm sure, would any of my family or friends. It drove my mother crazy that I seemed to "thrive under pressure," often waiting until the last minute to get my homework done. My messy room and disorganized approach to life was a testament to the fact that I didn't have a compulsive bone in my body. I had a lot of friends and did well in school.

At the same time, there were early clues that anxiety was a way I responded to stress. I was a nail biter. I always had a lot of "nervous energy" and often fidgeted. During a particular rough patch in my childhood, I went through a period where I stuttered. And I always had a terror of speaking in public, so much so that I became paralyzed with fright when I was supposed to stand up and say a few words to the wonderful classmates who had selected me to be their homecoming queen. Speech prepared, I stood up, walked to the podium, froze—and pretended the microphone was broken.

My mom had a more direct relationship with anxiety. She was a worrier. Throughout my growing up years, she seemed to have a lot of fears and concerns about her health and often developed physical symptoms when under stress; I often wondered if having suddenly lost her father at age 10 was the cause if it. I didn't know it until years after my son was born, but she had also experienced panic attacks after the birth of my younger sister.

A Dark Road but a Bright Future

Fast-forward through a lot of pain, guilt, fear and hard work, and I'm a happy, healthy career woman and (gasp!) mother of four. I am happily married and am lucky enough to have a lifestyle I love. Some of the positive steps I have been able to make so far in my life's journey have been *in spite of* my anxiety. And yet, although I would once have never believed this, I think some of my present fulfillment is also because of it. The personal growth my anxiety "forced" me into has not only taught me to deal with uncertainty and discomfort, it has also helped me be a more empathic parent. I have gained more self-respect, quit procrastinating (most of the time), and given up some nasty mental habits (such as perfectionism and self-criticism).

Am I "cured?" Who knows? I still get occasional blips of anxiety when I'm under stress, but it's been a long time since I've had a full-blown panic attack. We anxiety sufferers learn the hard way not to take too much for granted; symptoms can always rear their ugly head. I can tell you that I don't fear the fear anymore. If it comes, it won't wrestle me to the ground like it once did.

However, this book is about *you*, not me. I share my personal story to show you that I come at this topic from an up-close-and-personal viewpoint as well as a professional one. I am more concerned with helping you make your daily life better than whether or not you fit neatly into any diagnostic category. As such, although the focus of their application is on anxiety, many of the self-help skills in this book are *life* skills that will benefit anyone. And, of course, we also explore anxiety-disorder-specific self-help (that is, what stops obsessive thoughts, how to cope with panic symptoms, and how to recover from phobias). I also used my dual perspective to address the interplay between self-help and professional assistance. In the case of post-traumatic stress disorder, I have steered sufferers to professional assistance because it often *requires* mental-health intervention before there is any emotional relief.

Here's What We Cover

Part 1, "Exploring Anxiety," takes a look at what is a normal amount of anxiety and what is not. In these chapters, you have a chance to evaluate how much worry and anxiety impacts you on a day-to-day basis and learn how mental-health professionals make their diagnoses. We then shift the focus to why some of us are more vulnerable to anxiety, what the path to recovery looks like, and how we can stay on track when the road gets bumpy.

In Part 2, "Fighting Your Way Through the Fright," we build a foundation for tackling our fears by strengthening our ability to manage everyday emotions and stop anxiety-related habits. Anxiety sufferers often have an undeveloped relationship with their everyday emotions, which can lead them to get ambushed by sudden bursts of feelings. This is especially true of anger, which we spend a whole chapter discussing. We also explore how our anxiety and fears can result in a proclivity toward procrastination and assertiveness and how we can get a move on to develop more empowering habits.

Part 3, "Taming Those Alarming Ideas," arms us with the mental weapons to slay negative thoughts and defeat irrational beliefs that have long held many of us captive. Not only do we learn to challenge negative thoughts that fuel generalized anxiety, we also dive down to the core of our beliefs, correcting any myths around our need to be perfect to be loved or our constant need to earn the approval of the people around us. We then explore how these ingrained beliefs can congeal into self-defeating personality traits and how we can begin to build more flexibility and self-acceptance into our lives.

In Part 4, "Boosting the Mind-Body Connection," we capitalize on the inseparable link between our mental health and our physical health. This section explores the relationship between anxiety, exercise, diet, and sleep. We learn how certain foods can rev us up and how others promote a calming effect. We also learn how to prevent anxiety and worry from robbing us of a good night's sleep and how exercise can serve as a buffer from daily hassles and situational stress.

Part 5, "Survive and Thrive Strategies for Diagnosed Distress," takes on the "big boys"—the clinically diagnosed anxiety disorders. Building on the foundation we developed in the previous three parts, we look at state-of-the-art, self-help strategies for panic disorder, obsessive-compulsive disorder, social anxiety, and phobias. We also explore when professional help can boost our personal efforts and what the evidence says is the best anxiety-related treatment for our buck.

Part 6, "Not All in the Family: Keeping Anxiety from the Next Generation" is an empowering section for any anxiety sufferer who is, or plans to be, a mom or a dad. This section starts by exploring one of the best-kept postpartum secrets—postpartum anxiety—and how we can keep anxiety from ruining our joy during pregnancy or after delivery. We also explore parenting traps that can increase tension and worry in our children and how much power we parents have in fostering resilience and hardiness in our offspring. And finally, we explode the myth of the "carefree" childhood, develop ways we can help our children tackle normal fears, and learn how to be the best advocate for our children should they need professional help.

Extras

In addition to the main narrative of *The Complete Idiot's Guide to Controlling Anxiety* are nuggets of useful information designed to cut to the chase about a particular anxiety-related topic. Look for these features:

Anxiety Attack

Quick tips on how to tackle tough situations.

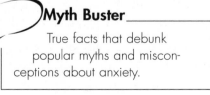

Myth Buster

True facts that debunk popular myths and misconceptions about anxiety.

On the Cutting Edge

Short summaries of the latest anxiety-related research.

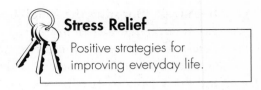 **Stress Relief**

Positive strategies for improving everyday life.

Acknowledgments

"People often say that motivation doesn't last. Well, neither does bathing—that's why we recommend it daily." This quote by Zig Zigler pretty much sums up the process of writing this book—and coping with anxiety. With every new study I absorbed and each story I put down, I was reminded of how life is like writing; it happens a word at a time, we have to show up for it daily, and we have to pay attention to the process. The sentences we "write" on our psyches today, dictated by our actions and our attitudes, eventually become the "stories" of our lives.

How fortunate for me, therefore, to have the opportunity to revisit my own personal values and daily choices at the same time I worked diligently to create a self-help road map for the brave readers who were ready to get back in the driver's seat and take control of their anxiety. *Special thanks* to the people who encouraged me on this journey, including the following:

My literary agent, Evan Fogelman, who continues to exceed all expectations.

My editor, Tom Stevens, for his faith in my writing.

All the mental-health professionals who have been brave enough to publicly share their personal battles with anxiety. You know who you are.

Every anxiety sufferer who has used his or her personal pain to help others. I was continually inspired by the notes of encouragement and self-help tips I found among anxiety sufferers in online communities, chat rooms, and websites.

To the four Z's in my life—Zach, Zhanna, Zane, and Zaylin—who provide all the motivation I need to stay on my path of personal growth. May the lessons I learn make you stronger, wiser, and happier.

To Alex. If consciousness *does* survive after death, I hope I get to spend eternity with you.

Special Thanks to the Technical Reviewer

The Complete Idiot's Guide to Controlling Anxiety was reviewed by an expert who double-checked the accuracy of what you'll learn here, to help us ensure that this book gives you everything you need to know about controlling your anxiety. Special thanks are extended to Sandra K. Trisdale, Ph.D.

Sandra K. Trisdale, Ph.D., is the author of over 30 articles on mental health issues. A former therapist, she is now involved in mental health research in San Diego, California.

Trademarks

All terms mentioned in this book that are known to be or are suspected of being trademarks or service marks have been appropriately capitalized. Alpha Books and Penguin Group (USA) Inc. cannot attest to the accuracy of this information. Use of a term in this book should not be regarded as affecting the validity of any trademark or service mark.

Part 1

Exploring Anxiety

"I'm nervous about that test coming up next week. That phone call sent me into a panic. I'm obsessive about a clean house."

For better or worse, we use anxiety-related words on a regular basis. On the plus side, all of us know what it feels like to have unrealistic worries, knots in our stomach, or a strong desire to avoid a scary or tense situation. On the downside, it can be hard to know how much anxiety is too much or pinpoint when our fears take control of our lives.

That's what this section is about: illustrating the difference between normal anxiety and an anxiety disorder, becoming familiar with the different "faces" anxiety wears, shedding light on anxiety's causes, and predicting what the road to anxiety recovery looks like—and why we should travel down it.

Just the Jitters or Jumping Out of Your Skin?

In This Chapter

- ◆ Meet anxiety's four henchmen
- ◆ Find out when normal anxiety crosses the line
- ◆ Conduct your own anxiety self-assessment
- ◆ Learn who is vulnerable to anxiety disorders
- ◆ Investigate anxiety masqueraders

"Well, Miss Gordon, how are you today?" he [my psychiatrist] asked. I was shocked to hear myself burst into a monologue of almost feverish intensity.

"What's new, Dr. Allen, is that I can't walk the streets of the city I love alone. Unless I'm stoned on pills or with someone. I can't do it. I can't function without Valium. I'm growing too dependent on something other than myself to function. I'm growing too dependent on pills. Why? Tell me why!"

He interrupted. "But I've told you many times, Miss Gordon, they are not addictive. They can't hurt you." And he crossed his legs and sat back in his chair to hear my response.

Barbara Gordon was a talented, award-winning American filmmaker—with an anxiety disorder. She was prescribed Valium and visited a psychiatrist once a week for more than 10 years with no noticeable improvement. Barbara Gordon documented her life with an anxiety disorder in the best-selling book *I'm Dancing as Fast as I Can*, describing in detail her struggle with her anxiety disorder, the Valium addiction she developed when she sought help, and her ultimate recovery. There are at least two take-away messages from this book:

♦ That people from all walks of life develop debilitating anxiety.

♦ No matter how "professional" a mental health professional seems, we are ultimately the best warrior in our ongoing battle for peace of mind.

In this chapter, we talk about what anxiety is and what it's not, when it helps and when it hurts, what's normal and what isn't, and what other illnesses can masquerade as anxiety.

What Is Anxiety?

If someone asked you to define anxiety in 25 words or less, could you do it? Probably, because the odds are you've experienced it. Perhaps you'd say "worrying too much" or "feeling uptight." Perhaps you'd describe a flip-flopping in your stomach or a tightness in your chest. Anxiety involves all of these and more; in fact, it's a combination of four different kinds of components: *physical*, *emotional*, *cognitive*, and/or *behavioral*.

Myth Buster

"Anxiety is a sign of weakness." Wrong! Big, strong, macho guys get anxiety disorders, too. Famous men known or strongly suspected to have suffered from an anxiety disorder include Abraham Lincoln, actor James Garner, football star Earl Campbell, and even Winston Churchill.

Physical Signs: From Butterflies to Goosebumps

Ever had to give a speech? How about asked someone you really liked out on a date, or stood in line waiting to ride Space Mountain for the first time? Then you know firsthand the physical signs of anxiety! These can include the following:

◆ Nausea or indigestion ("butterflies" in the stomach)

◆ Sweating, especially sweaty palms, forehead, or underarms

◆ Shortness of breath

◆ Racing pulse or a feeling like your heart is pounding

◆ Trouble swallowing or feelings of choking

◆ Dizziness or headache

◆ Chills or hot flashes

◆ Muscle tenseness or skin changes ("goose bumps")

◆ Trembling or shaking

◆ Difficulties in sleeping

Emotional Signs: Warning—Fear Ahead

Fear is the main feeling associated with anxiety. And when it starts, it snowballs. First we're anxious about a certain situation. Then we become anxious about being anxious—and afraid that *next* time we're confronted with that situation, we'll get anxious again. Some common fears associated with anxiety in general include the following:

◆ Fear of losing control

◆ Fear of going crazy

◆ Fear of dying

◆ Fear of embarrassment

◆ Fear of being rejected by others due to anxiety

◆ Fear of the future

Other emotions associated with anxiety include feelings of nervousness and irritability. Molehills seem like mountains, and it seems harder to control our tempers. Or perhaps we feel as if we're outside ourselves watching what's happening rather than being involved. In fact, in some anxiety disorders, our feelings can be numbed or blunted; it may be hard to recognize any emotion at all.

Anxiety Attack

Starting to feel nervous in a situation? *Breathe.* Concentrate for a few minutes or even a few seconds on taking slow, deep, regular breaths. When we begin to get anxious, we start breathing quickly and shallowly, which sets up a whole chain reaction in our bodies that can cause *more* anxiety. Stop this pattern before it stops. Try it; you'll be amazed how much difference it can make!

Cognitive Signs: I Think, Therefore I'm Anxious

Cognition is just the fancy term for thinking. What you think very much affects how you feel, and this is never more true than when it comes to anxiety. Depending on the specific type of anxiety disorder (we discuss these more in Chapter 2), many different thinking errors commonly accompany anxiety disorders. Some common ones include the following:

♦ Thinking about fearful situations over and over

♦ Focusing too much on tiny details, not seeing the big picture

♦ Having difficulties concentrating

♦ Overestimating the real danger of situations or exaggerating the risks of everyday activities

♦ Doubting your ability to cope

♦ Worrying that any physical symptom is either the beginning of an anxiety attack or a sign of a life-threatening illness

♦ Overestimating the likelihood of a negative outcome in many situations

♦ Thinking excessively about the possibility of failure or of drawing negative attention

Stress Relief

When speaking or performing in public, some people get so anxious about making a mistake that their anxiety gets out of control. Some therapists who specialize in anxiety disorders actually suggest that performers intentionally make a small error at the beginning of their performance so that they can let go of the internal pressure to be perfect and relax. Try it and see!

◆ Thinking unwanted thoughts again and again no matter how much you try to put them out of your mind

Behavioral Signs: Either Take Charge or Run Away!

The last anxiety henchman involves our response to our symptoms. Because anxiety feels threatening, it's no surprise that, in response to it, we either fight or fly away. Common behavioral responses include the following:

◆ Avoiding situations that have made us anxious in the past

◆ Freezing up

◆ Avoiding situations that we are afraid might make us anxious; refusing to try new experiences

◆ Performing rituals that help control the anxiety

◆ Being unable to perform some normal tasks of everyday life because of fear or anxiety

◆ Engaging in harmful, dangerous, or self-abusive activities

◆ Using drugs or alcohol to try to cope with anxiety

Donny Osmond: A Familiar Face with Anxiety

We started the chapter with filmmaker Barbara Gordon's story. Here's another real-life example of a celebrity who has met anxiety up close and personal. Singer/performer Donny Osmond learned to cover up his anxiety for years until his anxiety got so out of control that he could no longer hide it.

Osmond reported the emotional signs of anxiety, which centered around his escalating fear of performing onstage: "There are times I remember before I walked on stage, where if I had the choice of walking on stage or dying, I would have chosen death."

He has often described some of his anxiety-related thoughts, including pressure to be perfect and the fear of scrutiny: "I knew at least somebody in that audience is looking at me all the time."

He eventually ended up having a full-blown panic attack, with all the physical and behavioral symptoms that accompany them. "I remember shaking in bed, and I just, I couldn't get out of bed. Something was wrong and my wife took me to the hospital."

Through psychotherapy, Osmond eventually learned to cope with his social-anxiety disorder.

Cautious, Nervous, or Dealing with a Disorder?

If you look at all the different anxiety symptoms, you might think we all suffer from anxiety—and you'd be right! There's nothing wrong with a little anxiety. In fact, we need some in order to survive.

For a physical comparison, think about the sensation of pain. No one likes to hurt, but people who are born without an ability to feel it are at chronic risks for serious injuries and tend to die earlier; there has been at least one case of a toddler who could not feel pain who walked into a pretty bonfire on purpose and stayed there. And if pain didn't accompany a heart attack, we wouldn't seek the medical attention we need to survive. So pain isn't much fun, but we need it. In a way, the same is true for anxiety.

> **On the Cutting Edge**
>
> Some people apparently need an anxiety booster shot. Recent research has shown that some people don't feel anxiety even in dangerous or life-threatening situations. These people tend to take extreme risks and are more likely to die in thrill-seeking activities. Apparently, a certain amount of anxiety keeps us on our toes when we need to pay extra attention and proceed with caution.

For example, suppose you need to cross a busy street, but cars are rushing by in both directions. A little jolt of anxiety will motivate you to be extra vigilant and cautious and wait until you can cross safely. If you weren't worried at all, you might just walk out into traffic and get nailed by a car.

In addition, people who don't become anxious in normally anxiety-causing situations may have difficulty learning from mistakes. They may be even more likely than the rest of us to make the same mistakes over and over.

Although not everyone with a chronic anxiety deficit is a criminal, it is true that many criminals have a low ability to become anxious. That may explain, in part, people who make the same mistakes time and time again, even if they are punished for making them. It may also help explain how the presence of anxiety can be an important signal tweaking our conscience, telling us that we are acting, behaving, or thinking in a way that conflicts with a deeply held value or belief.

As discussed previously, normal anxiety can be good for you; it can give your conscience a necessary tug or inspire you to prepare just a little bit harder. There is a continuum of anxiety, and we want to be somewhere in the middle range. So how much anxiety is too much? There are a few ways of telling.

Context and Continuum

First, most people with diagnosable anxiety disorders experience feelings of anxiety, fear, or terror in situations that don't justify it. Either it's a situation (context) in which most of us wouldn't feel anxious at all (such as driving a car), or the level of anxiety is much greater than the circumstances warrant. For example, most of us might feel a little bit uneasy entering a grocery store we've had a bad experience in, but the person who associates panic attacks with a particular store will avoid it no matter the personal or relationship costs.

Of course, the continuum of normal anxiety depends upon the situation, how most people experience it, and your unique personal makeup. So if your palms are sweaty when you stand in line for that new thrill ride at the amusement park, join the crowd! Pretty much all of us are in the same boat. Got a few butterflies in your stomach going in for that important job interview? Perfectly normal. But if you're so terrified of the thrill ride that you refuse to even enter the amusement park, that's not how most people would react. It would be pretty extreme. And if your anxiety gets so out of control that you blow off the interview, or get there and choke, then it's a problem.

Here's a true story: a colleague of mine interviewed at several graduate schools before selecting one. During the interview process, one university conducted group interviews so the staff could see how well potential students handled themselves. In front of the group, this intelligent, articulate woman began to respond to a question, stopped, blushed, and completely froze up. She was unable to answer or even function at all. Although all the candidates had high test scores, high grade point averages, and excellent credentials, this woman's anxiety ended up getting her rejected as a candidate.

Anxiety Attack

Getting back on the horse that threw you can be good advice. When people are frightened by a certain situation, they may start avoiding that situation and others like it. The best thing to do is face the situation again as soon as you can by any means possible—with a friend holding your hand, in gradual steps, through hypnosis, and so on.

State, Trait ... Wait!

Anxiety can be divided into either state anxiety or trait anxiety. *State anxiety* refers to your level of anxiety about a particular situation. Maybe you stay cool during job interviews, but you're terrified of spiders. You're not anxious all the time, just in certain situations.

Trait anxiety refers to our tendency to respond to a wide variety of situations with either too much or not enough anxiety. Those who take high risks tend to have low levels of trait anxiety—even when a higher level might be helpful or appropriate. But people with high levels of trait anxiety tend to be much more anxious in general, even in situations that most of us don't think of as particularly stressful.

Although certain types of state anxiety can be very unpleasant and can impact your life significantly, the high levels of trait anxiety tend to be most crippling.

Can You Handle It?

One way to look at how much your anxiety affects you is by how much it keeps you from dealing with everyday life.

Let's look at three different people with anxiety about the same issue. Betty, Bob, and Brittany are all anxious about heights. But they deal with their fears differently.

> **Myth Buster**
>
> Some people believe that religious faith will overcome anxiety. You might feel that if you're just a devout enough Christian, Jew, Buddhist, Wiccan, Muslim—whatever—you can overcome anxiety. But anxiety disorders are just as real as other medical illnesses. Rather than try to overcome a broken leg (or severe anxiety) through faith alone, why not just bless the doctor who helps you heal?

Betty works on the twenty-sixth floor of a building. Every time she rides up or down the elevator, she closes her eyes and concentrates on her breathing to keep from getting overly nervous. She has a corner office with a great view, but she keeps the blinds pulled because the view scares her. When she and her husband went to Paris and he went up the Eiffel Tower, she decided to stay on the ground and take photos. When she flies on business, she requests a seat as close to the middle of the row as possible. If she sits by the window, she closes the shade and reads a book for distraction.

Bob works in a city on one side of a major river. It's a dead-end job, and he could do better if he were willing to get a job in the city on the other side of the river, but he just can't bring himself to drive across that suspension bridge every day. Once when a job assignment involved giving a presentation on the other side, Bob called in sick. His bosses weren't happy, and the guy who covered for him got the next promotion. Bob met a great woman at a party once. They went out a few times, but she lived across the river. When she found out Bob wasn't willing to drive across the bridge to see her, she called him a "wuss" and dumped him. Bob is sometimes afraid she was right—maybe he is a wuss. His self-esteem is pretty shot, and he hasn't dated anyone in a while.

Brittany is terrified of heights—any heights. When her family went to the Grand Canyon when she was a child, she curled up in a ball on the floor of the family car. Everyone in her family teased her about her fears. She won't get in an elevator, and escalators scare her even more. She has to pay a neighbor's son to come change her lightbulbs because she can't stand on a stepladder. Brittany's husband left her years ago; one of the reasons was that he was tired of his life being so affected by his wife's fears. Brittany's grown daughter lives in Hawaii and is getting increasingly angry with her because she won't fly out to see her new grandchild. But Brittany has never been on a plane—the mere thought makes her shake all over. She walks out of the movie theater if a scene unexpectedly shows a view from a great height or if someone is shown climbing a mountain, driving over a high bridge, or parachuting. She has trouble getting to sleep and often has nightmares about falling. She knows her fears have taken over her life, but she doesn't know what to do about it.

Three people, one fear, and three different outcomes. Betty is anxious about heights, yes, but it doesn't have much impact on her life. She has evolved coping strategies that work for her. The anxiety does not keep her from doing what she wants or needs to do. Brittany clearly has a full-blown anxiety disorder. Her anxiety is impacting her life negatively in a variety of ways. Bob's anxiety is also affecting his life negatively, but it's more subtle. He probably qualifies as having an anxiety disorder, too, but it's not as severe as Brittany's.

Does any of this mean that Betty is smarter, stronger, or somehow better than Brittany or Bob? Absolutely not! Betty has developed some pretty snappy coping strategies. Bob and Brittany need some help in dealing with their anxiety; with treatment, they could both end up doing the things that today seem impossible.

Anxiety Attack

Anxiety makes it hard to look on the bright side. To prepare in advance for anxiety-provoking situations, psychologist Daniel Wegner suggests writing down a list of happy memories, tough times you've conquered, or things you're looking forward to. Keep it in your pocket to review when you get stressed.

Assess Yourself: How Much Is Too Much?

Although different anxiety disorders have their own cluster of symptoms (which we discuss in upcoming chapters), some general signs suggest that your anxiety is severe enough that it's time to take some action. To determine whether your anxiety has crossed the line, ask yourself the following questions—and be honest!

- Does your anxiety cause you to avoid specific places, events, objects, or situations?

- Are these places, events, objects, or situations that other people don't seem to be afraid of or consider normal?

- Does your anxiety interfere with your ability to work?

- Does your anxiety cause problems with your relationships with other people—or prevent you from having relationships at all?

- Does your anxiety keep you from taking care of your responsibilities around the home?

- Does your anxiety cause you discomfort or distress on a regular basis?

- Do things seem to be getting worse over time?

- Have friends, family members, or employers expressed concern over your anxiety and its effect on your life?

- Do you sometimes feel that your thoughts are out of control?

- Do you frequently feel irritable?

- Do other people tell you that you always look stressed out?

- Do you feel like your mind often just goes blank?

- Do you often have trouble falling or staying asleep?

- Do you worry about the same things over and over?

- In your attempts to calm your anxiety, do you engage in activities that other people consider odd (perhaps counting things, or compulsively and repetitively performing the same rituals)?

- Are you highly upset by changes in your normal routine?

- Do you sometimes have unwanted images of disaster or death in your head?

- Do you ever experience actual flashbacks of traumatic events?

In general, the more questions to which you answered "yes," the more likely it is that you have an anxiety disorder.

However, this is just an informal screening. We threw together symptoms from several different anxiety disorders, so even the most anxious person is unlikely to answer yes to each and every question! A person suffering from a generalized anxiety disorder, for example, may not identify with the person who avoids social situations out of embarrassment—and may be completely unable to relate to someone who's developed rituals such as door checking or excessive hand washing. Yet all three of these individuals have anxiety disorders.

Of course, the bottom line, as we said at the beginning of this chapter, is your own experience and perception. If your anxiety is causing you significant pain or is limiting your life—or was enough to make you buy this book—then it's a problem for you. Whether or not you meet the clinical criteria for an anxiety disorder, what matters is that your life gets better—and easier. And it can!

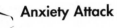 **Anxiety Attack**

By now, most of us are familiar with flashbacks from movies about war. A flashback is a terrifying feeling that one is actually reliving a past traumatic event. But many people don't realize that flashbacks of an extremely stressful situation can be a symptom of an anxiety disorder. If you are having flashbacks, don't try to handle them on your own—seek professional help.

Anxiety ... or Something Else?

So you've read through the chapter so far. You looked at the self-assessment questions. You're sure of it—you have an anxiety disorder.

Well, hold on there, doctor. A number of physical conditions can be mistaken for anxiety disorders. It's important to rule them out first.

General Category	Examples
Cardiovascular (heart)	Mitral valve prolapse and others
Respiratory (lung)	Asthma, emphysema, scleroderma
Central Nervous System	Psychomotor epilepsy/seizure disorder
Metabolic/hormonal	Hyperthyroid, Cushing's disease
Nutritional	Anemia, folate deficiency
Intoxication	Caffeine, amphetamines
Withdrawal	Alcohol, sedatives
Psychological	Depression, ADHD

For instance, several different types of heart conditions can have symptoms similar to anxiety; sometimes a heart attack and a panic attack can be hard to tell apart. The king of heart-triggered anxiety symptoms is called *mitral valve prolapse*; it can cause symptoms almost identical to a true panic attack. This little bulge in a heart valve leaflet is usually not dangerous. Three out of every four people with it will never need treatment and will live as long as the rest of us. In a small subset, though, it can be serious, so it's important to get monitored by a physician if you know or think you might have it. And be aware that it does run in families.

Certain diseases of the lungs can also mirror anxiety symptoms, particularly a racing pulse, inability to catch your breath, or feelings of terror. Any asthma sufferer can tell you that these often occur in the throes of an asthma attack and have nothing to do with anxiety. (Except maybe the natural anxiety of "Where's my darn inhaler *this* time?")

How healthy are your eating habits? If you have a poor diet or difficulty absorbing some critical vitamins or minerals, you could end up with signs that mimic anxiety; in particular, low levels of thiamine, pyroxidine, and folate have all been associated with this, as has iron-deficiency anemia. So take your caring author's advice: swallow those Flintstone vitamins and eat your spinach.

Many illicit drugs can cause anxiety, the most notorious of them being any stimulant, like speed, cocaine, or crystal meth. But another anxiety-inducing intoxicant is perfectly legal. I'll give you a hint: Star + Bucks = What? Although many of us can toss back cappuccinos and lattes with relatively few side effects, some poor souls are very sensitive indeed to caffeine, and a little coffee or tea, even an over-the-counter pain reliever with caffeine, can set off a massive case of the heebie-jeebies. The worst part is that these sensitive people are unlikely to connect the anxiety with the soda or the chocolate bar they had earlier.

Stress Relief

Want to reduce your risk of anxiety? Cut out (or at least cut down) the caffeine. Excessive coffee can make you anxious and jittery. If you suffer from anxiety or panic attacks, even small amounts of caffeine can exacerbate it. How much is too much? It depends. If you have trouble falling asleep, if you find it hard to concentrate during the day, or if you drink more than 5 cups a day, you may be getting too much caffeine.

Other psychological disorders can sometimes look like anxiety. Individuals with attention-deficit hyperactivity disorder, or ADHD, can display the foot wiggling, hand tapping, and other signs that may be mistaken for anxiety. The "drawing a mental blank" symptom—common in anxiety—is also common in depression. In addition, some people with anxiety disorders may have other disorders (depression disorders or substance abuse) that make diagnosis more complicated. Is the substance abuse an attempt to self-medicate for anxiety? Did depression come before the anxiety, or is the person depressed because of it?

When it comes to anxiety disorders, the mind-body connection is tricky indeed. If anxiety is making your life miserable, always get a thorough medical checkup to make sure an underlying physical illness isn't masquerading as anxiety. Start with your primary health-care provider and go from there.

What's the Difference?

What if you're free of any possible physical problem, and you've already been diagnosed with an anxiety disorder? But your cousin has an anxiety disorder, and her symptoms are completely different from yours! Why?

Well, consider a couple of examples. First, a chilling description from *Lucky*, a book by the brilliant writer Alice Sebold. It is an account of her rape, the anxiety disorder it helped create, and her eventual recovery:

> *I had nightmares now even more vivid than before. My sporadic journal of those years is full of them. The recurring image is one I'd seen in a documentary of the Holocaust …. I woke up in cold sweats. Sometimes I screamed ….*

> *I consciously played out the intricate plot of my almost death. The rapist was inside the house. He was climbing the stairs … Far away, near my wall, someone was breathing my air, stealing my oxygen …*

> *I never questioned what was happening to me. It all seemed normal. Threat was everywhere. No place or person was safe. My life was different from other people's; it was natural that I behaved differently.*

> *… I cried in hysterical trills that no one understood, least of all me.*

> *… I loved heroin …. Who wanted to enhance a mood? My goal was to destroy it …*

> *I had post-traumatic stress disorder, but the only way I would believe it was to discover it for myself.*

This is one type of anxiety disorder. The symptoms may or may not be similar to anything you have experienced, because post-traumatic stress disorder (PTSD) is a specific disorder.

Contrast Sebold's reports to that of Amy Wilensky. Wilensky suffered from a much different type of anxiety disorder called obsessive-compulsive disorder, or OCD. This excerpt is from *Passing for Normal: A Memoir of Compulsion*. In it, she discusses how she tried to cope with her fear of an upcoming airplane trip when she was a teenager:

> *As the date for our departure neared, the rituals that had become an integral part of my daily routine tripled. Like fractures, old ones spawned new ones, especially designed to keep the plane from crashing ….*
>
> *At first, I was not allowed to touch any cover—floor, carpet, grass—with my bare feet. After a few days I amended this and decided that I could not have bare feet, so I slept in my sneakers and socks; the sneakers were for insurance. I washed my hair in the bathtub faucet and my body with a washcloth so I wouldn't have to shower or bathe with my shoes or socks on. Through it all, I twitched more than ever, as if I'd stuck my finger in an electric socket and was holding it there …*
>
> *The truth is, even as I followed through with the most bizarre of these rituals—sweating in bed at night in my heavy wool socks—I wasn't truly convinced they would have the intended protective effect. Today, when I occasionally tap the threshold of my apartment door each time I leave and enter, I know more than ever how unconnected the ritual is with anything at all, let alone my personal safety or happiness or success.*

Neither of these accounts sounds very much like the other, and neither one of them sounds much like Donny Osmond's story. Each anxiety disorder shares something in common with the others, but each one is different. These disorders may have different origins and often have different treatments, as we discuss in the following chapters.

The key things to remember with any anxiety disorder are *you are not alone* and *there is hope*. Other people suffer from the same disorder you do; other people have gotten better. *You can feel normal again!*

Having anxiety is nothing to be ashamed of; in fact, the main reason I focused on celebrity experiences of anxiety in this chapter is to show you (and perhaps your doubting or judgmental friends or family) that anxiety is not something anyone *wants* to have; that no one is immune; and that richer, more famous, better-looking, and smarter people than you and I have been down the same road.

In the next chapter, we take a look at the seven sisters of anxiety—and you can find the path you need to take to emotional freedom.

The Least You Need to Know

- ◆ There are four components of anxiety: physical, emotional, cognitive, and/or behavioral.

- ◆ The best way to determine whether your anxiety is truly a disorder is by how much it affects your work, school, social, or interpersonal life.

- ◆ Many medical conditions can be mistaken for anxiety; a physical checkup is always a good idea before deciding that you have an anxiety disorder.

- ◆ Each anxiety disorder has its own set of symptoms; your disorder may not look much like someone else's.

2

The Seven Sisters of Anxiety

In This Chapter

◆ Discover what a diagnosis really means

◆ Meet the seven members of the anxiety family

◆ Understand what they do—and don't—have in common

◆ Learn how to get support from your friends and family

I'm going crazy. I can't breathe. I've got to get out of here. I know the doctors have missed something; maybe I have AIDS! I'd rather die than get up in front of that group. I know I turned off the stove—but what if I didn't? I have to go back and see …. I can't turn off these thoughts racing around and around in my head.

Welcome to the world of anxiety. Unless you've suffered from it, it can be quite difficult to understand how someone's life can be so affected by what may appear quite trivial. Unfortunately, a lot of people have firsthand experience; anxiety disorders plague 40 million people in the United States alone. The number of Americans who suffer from them has more than doubled since 1980.

> **On the Cutting Edge**
>
> A 2004 study found that 25 percent of 9,000 randomly interviewed Americans met the criteria for a mental illness within the past year; less than half of those in need ever get treatment.

However, whereas all anxiety disorders share certain features, there are different members of this dysfunctional family. In this chapter, we take a look at each clinical anxiety disorder, find out what an anxiety disorder diagnosis really means, and learn how to translate a terrifying experience into something your friends and family members can understand.

So What's Your Problem?

Sam goes to his doctor complaining of chest pains, shortness of breath, trouble sleeping, and irritability. His symptoms began after a divorce and escalated after he got a welcome yet stressful promotion at work. His brother, Max, goes to his doctor with an arm injury he received in a flag-football game. Max's doctor does an x-ray and easily diagnoses a broken arm. Ten other physicians could perform the same test and would reach the same conclusion. Unfortunately, this isn't the case for Sam.

Sam's mental state is a changeable collection of thoughts, physical symptoms, and feelings. The doctor can't x-ray his mind. Sam's diagnosis is likely to be done by default; the doctor may do several tests to rule out physical problems and essentially conclude that Sam's problem is "all in your head." How sensitively Dr. Doc communicates this finding will depend upon his or her beliefs about the cause/blame of mental illness.

Read That Label Carefully

When we're talking about diagnoses of psychological problems—anxiety specifically—it's important to keep in mind what they're good for and what they aren't.

For instance, a diagnostic label can provide a useful shortcut for describing (and making sense of) a collection of thoughts, feelings, and behaviors that tend to go together. It can be reassuring to know that there's a name for this terrifying, imprisoning experience, that other people have had—and survived—similar events, and that there are doctors out there who've treated similar problems. You are not alone.

> **On the Cutting Edge**
>
> Anxiety often accompanies depression, and an addiction may accompany a mood disorder. Unfortunately, even though 50 percent of people with one mental disorder also meet the criteria for a second, research suggests that mental-health treatment is often geared toward a single problem or disorder.

On the other hand, although a diagnosis can tell us *what we have*; we should never let it tell us *who we are*. At best, a diagnosis of obsessive-compulsive disorder (OCD) or panic disorder should be regarded as a handy signpost en route to treatment and recovery. When you get an anxiety disorder diagnosis, take all the benefits you can from the structure, clarity, and reassurance it can provide—and take heart in the route to recovery it reveals. But don't let it be a confining and limiting label, or think of it as a precise analysis encompassing everything about your unique experience.

Coexisting, but Not in Peace

Another obstacle to the right diagnosis is the fact that anxiety disorders often coexist with each other; 58 percent of clients diagnosed with one anxiety disorder also meet the criteria for a second. A person diagnosed with panic disorder may also suffer from agoraphobia; he or she may also show signs of depression and social anxiety.

Zeroing in on—and treating—one disorder may bring partial relief but not address the whole problem. For example, an antidepressant may significantly reduce panic symptoms but fail to address the crippling social anxiety that limits careers and puts love lives on hold. In terms of treatment, then, a diagnosis is a great starting point, but ideally the finish line should be clear of any limits our anxiety disorder is currently imposing on our lives.

Physician, Heal Thyself

Another challenge with diagnosing a mental condition is the fact that the source of our symptoms is also the source of information about those symptoms. Max's mind can clearly recall and describe the circumstances surrounding his injury, but how can Sam's mind objectively analyze what is happening at the same time he is suffering? Asking a distressed mind to calmly describe itself is like asking a ball of wool to unravel itself.

Stress Relief

Tracking symptoms (noting time, length, triggers, and so on) on a daily basis can not only help our doctors make better diagnoses, it can help us get some distance on our anxiety symptoms.

Que Pasa?

Finally, cultural differences can be another barrier in our quest to get a clear and objective diagnosis. Although people of all races, cultures, and social classes experience anxiety disorders, there are cultural differences in how individual symptoms are regarded and expressed. As a result, cultural differences can be another barrier in our quest to get an accurate and objective diagnosis.

Cultural differences in emotional expression and social behavior can be misinterpreted as "impairments" if clinicians are not sensitive to the cultural context and meaning of exhibited symptoms. For example, in some cultures, it is normal and natural to channel stress symptoms into physical complaints. In the United States, however, this tendency is frowned upon; who wants to be called a hypochondriac?

On the other hand, serious emotional distress can be overlooked if the person's description or behavior doesn't match what the physician expects. In some Native American languages, there is no equivalent translation for anxiety; savvy clinicians have to rely more on descriptions of stressful events. Similarly, several studies have shown that Asian Americans tend to report feeling more social anxiety in comparison to numerous other groups; however, in these studies, they were much less likely to avoid socially uncomfortable situations or show behaviors that many clinicians would look for in diagnosing a social-anxiety disorder. Absent the anticipated outward signs, the internal turmoil might be missed.

Stress Relief

Choosing a mental-health professional who is culturally similar to you—or who has worked extensively with members of your culture—can reduce misdiagnosis or mistreatment.

Welcome to the Family

Now that we have some perspective on what an anxiety-disorder diagnosis means, let's take a look at the seven anxiety disorders recognized by the *Diagnostic and Statistical Manual IV,* the "bible" of mental-health professionals. You'll see they have a lot in common; for instance, they all involve chronic, uncontrollable fear; numerous physical symptoms; and a strong desire to avoid/escape uncomfortable situations. However, they're also unique; the sudden terror of a panic disorder may be completely unfamiliar to someone with OCD.

Generalized Anxiety Disorder: Thoughts That Go Bump in the Mind

At some point, most of us have worried about a child who's out later than usual, stressed over a dwindling bank account, or imagined that a minor illness was a symptom of a larger one. During times of stress, it's pretty normal to find ourselves stewing over things we can't control.

For the four million Americans suffering from *generalized anxiety disorder,* such worry is a daily companion; even though they realize their anxiety is more intense than the situation warrants, they just can't seem to shake it. Not surprisingly, a constant, low-level state of fear takes its toll, leading to physical symptoms such as headaches, muscle tension, stomach problems, and a disrupted sleep pattern. Over time, these can wear a person down, making life a tiring, uphill series of events. Physical symptoms commonly include the following:

- Restlessness (difficulty relaxing)
- Muscle tension
- Headaches
- Sweatiness
- Nausea
- Frequent need to use the bathroom
- Tiredness
- Trembling
- Difficulty sleeping

Common emotional symptoms include the following:

- Irritability
- Tendency to exaggerate problems
- Ongoing worry
- Difficulty concentrating
- Jumpiness, easily startled

Up to a quarter of people with generalized anxiety disorder (GAD) develop an additional anxiety disorder. GAD sufferers may, for example, choose to stay at home—a place of safety—and develop symptoms approaching agoraphobia. Or they may avoid social contact, developing instead a social-anxiety disorder.

Experience has shown that professional treatment can have a positive impact on GAD. In addition, sufferers can take some action in controlling some of their symptoms, as you will see later in this book.

Anxiety Attack

GAD is diagnosed if symptoms are present for more days than not during a period of at least six months. The symptoms also must interfere with daily living, such as causing you to miss work or school.

Social Phobia: Way Beyond Butterflies

James was always a little shy in elementary school. He described himself as "excruciatingly self-conscious" during his teen years. However, after joining the military, with its built-in social network, he thought his "shyness" was a thing of the past. Until he left the army and his marriage failed.

His civilian job required interaction with new people on a regular basis, and James found it increasingly difficult to put on his "game face." When he was asked to give a presentation, he stressed about it for days and finally called in sick. He began avoiding the lunchroom and felt increasingly self-conscious in meetings. By the time he finally got help, he had passed up at least two promotions and had become so lonely and isolated that he was experiencing fleeting thoughts of suicide.

> ### On the Cutting Edge
>
> A 2006 study found that people suffering social phobia experience increased brain activity when confronted with threatening faces or frightening social situations. This new finding could help identify how severe a person's social phobia is and measure the effectiveness of treatments for the condition.

As you can see, there's a big difference between social phobia—formerly called social-anxiety disorder—and the nervousness many of us feel when asked to speak at a conference or give a wedding toast. With social phobia, the sufferer can become afraid of everyday social interactions such as shopping or going to a party with coworkers. Over time, this anxiety perpetuates itself, resulting in …

- Extreme self-consciousness in social settings.

- A compulsion to avoid social interaction.

- An excessive fear of looking or sounding foolish in front of people.

> ### Myth Buster
>
> *"Social phobia is just shyness."* Think again! Moderately shy individuals don't stress about an upcoming social event for weeks, sweat, tremble and feel terrified during it, or take drastic measures to avoid it.

Although we can all feel shy at times, particularly among strangers or when we are asked to perform a task, social phobia is normally diagnosed when these shy feelings become almost overwhelming, accompanied by physical symptoms of extreme nervousness, and when these symptoms begin to impact a person's ability to function socially.

Panic Disorder: The Tsunami of Anxiety

It's virtually impossible to do justice in describing the terror and fear involved in a panic attack; if you've had one, you know what it's like; if you haven't, you can't imagine it. It is a sudden episode of uncomfortable fear and anxiety. And it's accompanied by at least four of the following little helpmates:

- Racing heart rate (palpitations)
- Sweating
- Trembling
- Feeling of imminent doom
- Feeling of choking
- Inability to breathe (smothering)
- Chest pain (often mistaken for a heart attack)
- Nausea
- Dizziness
- A feeling that things are unreal
- A fear of dying
- Feeling out of control; "going crazy"
- Tingling
- Chills or hot flashes

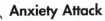

Anxiety Attack

The frightening sensations of a panic attack typically peak within 10 minutes; our bodies can't sustain that level of anxiety and fear for any longer.

Given this bombardment of physical sensations, no wonder a panic attack can make someone feel as if the world is exploding. And it can happen anywhere. Some panic sufferers suffer an attack out of the blue. Others will have attacks every time a specific series of events occur (for example, at restaurants). Others are likely to have panic attacks under certain circumstances, but don't every time.

Anxiety Attack

The physical sensations of anxiety are your body's preparation for danger; it's preparing for fight or flight. Give your body a reason to lower its defenses by making a fist, tensing it so that your knuckles turn white, and then relaxing and releasing the tension.

Not all panic attacks develop into panic disorder. Some people have one panic attack and never experience another one. Some have a few that get better or worse as life stressors change. When a person has suffered at least two unexpected panic attacks—and at least a month of fear and worry over having another one—a clinical diagnosis is likely. Even then, a sufferer may develop coping routines to avoid extreme stress—getting help from family or friends.

For some people, particularly when such support isn't available, the only option is to withdraw from society—which is called agoraphobia.

Agoraphobia: Fear of the Marketplace

Meet panic's twin sister: agoraphobia. Literally meaning, fear of the marketplace, agoraphobia is an anxiety disorder whose sufferers feel that the only safe place is home. Agoraphobia is often misunderstood as a fear of crowds or a fear of open spaces. The clinical definition of agoraphobia is a fear of situations or places "from which escape might be difficult (or embarrassing) or in which help may not be available in the event" of a panic attack. It is a fear of being in a situation or a place from which there is no easy escape.

Often a panic attack can trigger agoraphobia. A person feels insecure, worried about another attack, and even though there may be no evidence that further attacks will happen, or happen anywhere other than a specific place, a person may begin to feel that the home is their only safe haven.

A tendency to develop agoraphobia can run in families. But even if agoraphobia is diagnosed, effective treatments have been found to significantly reduce the symptoms. These include cognitive behavioral therapy, medications, and lifestyle changes, which we discuss later.

Obsessive Compulsive Disorder: The Broken Record

Here's Mark's story:

During my final year at college, I started having unusual symptoms. I couldn't resist having vivid thoughts and images—horrible things such as killing a family member. I worried that I had actually done something terrible, and felt trapped, unable to escape the thoughts. I eventually sought treatment and, with the help of medication and a great therapist, began getting control over my feelings. I was amazed to discover how many other people were suffering from OCD …. OCD was the most terrible experience of my life, but in some ways it has been the best—I am now more confident, and I can really understand how other people feel.

You know how it feels to worry that we didn't lock the door or turn off the stove. You've probably had the sudden impulse to do something out of character or irrational. Although many people can just choose to ignore or override such doubts, more than 2 percent of the U.S. population finds these compelling thoughts or feelings impossible to ignore, ultimately setting in motion a repetitive, energy-draining cycle of behavior aimed at controlling and reducing the emotional discomfort. This repetitive cycle is a series of obsessive thoughts followed by repetitive actions that are geared toward managing or alleviating them.

An *obsession* is an ongoing, repeated concern. A person may become obsessive about upsetting thoughts, sexual images, thoughts about invading germs, or ideas about harming themselves. A *compulsion* is an overwhelming urge to do something, usually in response to obsessive thoughts. For example, repetitive hand washing in an attempt to ward off the fear of germs, or counting objects in an attempt to control obsessive thoughts. The compulsion—or behavior—is a response to the obsession—or concern.

For example, an OCD sufferer may feel compelled to repeat actions, checking things even though rationally they know there is no need. For some, the disorder can take forms that others cannot easily observe. A person may obsessively replay upsetting thoughts, repeat destructive ideas, or conduct mental observations such as breathing awareness, counting steps, or avoiding certain colors.

Unfortunately, although a person may receive a feeling of temporary relief from performing such repeated acts, sufferers report that such relief is short-lived; the person may simply be compelled to repeat further acts, often more complex and involved, as feelings of insecurity heighten.

Specific Phobia: Targeted Fear

Melissa, age 40, loves visiting family on the east coast. Each year she makes the trip from her home in Santa Monica, driving the more than 2,000 miles, making stops on the way to refuel and rest. Though she knows the trip would take a fraction of the time by air, she can't bring herself to even visit an airport. Melissa has a phobia of flying.

Unlike general anxiety, a phobia is a specific fear triggered by an inciting factor—dogs, heights, or the very common claustrophobia, a fear of confined spaces. More than six million Americans suffer from such phobias, and although in many cases a phobia isn't a serious condition (in that it doesn't always interfere with everyday life), some phobias can limit or control a person's behavior.

Remember Indiana Jones, fearless hero and adventurous archeologist? Indy had one chink in his armor—his phobia of snakes. Phobias have nothing to do with bravery or rational logic—the strongest, most intelligent people can suffer from phobias.

Post-Traumatic Stress Disorder: The Endless Movie

Mike can't sleep. He tells his doctor he feels dazed and numb, as if he's in another world. Loud noises make him jump, and he has this constant undercurrent of fear. He starts to cry as he explains how his relationship to his wife and children is becoming strained by his behavior.

Three weeks ago, Mike witnessed his friend accidentally shoot himself in a hunting accident. Two days later, his symptoms began. At present, Mike is suffering with acute stress disorder, an emotional condition that can emerge after a person has either witnessed or experienced death or serious injury. If his symptoms continue for more than a month, his diagnosis will be changed to post-traumatic stress disorder. Its symptoms include the following:

◆ Intense feelings of fear, horror, and helplessness

◆ Reliving the event through flashbacks, nightmares, or, in the case of children, repetitive play that contains the aspects of the event

◆ Dissociation—a shutting down or numbing of feelings or memory

◆ Hyper alertness to danger—easy to startle, trouble concentrating, and a general sense of restlessness and being on edge

◆ Sensitivity to, and avoidance of, anything associated with the trauma

Whereas any of us would be extremely upset following a life-threatening trauma such as a serious car accident, rape, or a life-threatening illness, many of us would not develop post-traumatic stress disorder. Our risk for this disorder goes up or down depending upon the severity of the trauma and our own personal tendencies; in other words, in order for post-traumatic stress disorder to be accurately diagnosed, we would have to have experienced a significant trauma *and* responded with intense, recurrent feelings of horror, fear, and helplessness.

> **On the Cutting Edge**
>
> A 2005 *Journal of Oncology* study found that more than half of parents whose children were undergoing cancer treatment exhibited symptoms consistent with post-traumatic stress disorder.

Anxiety—It's a Family Affair

Because anxiety disorders affect the way we feel, think, and act, our friends and family may be affected by them, too. Maybe we've canceled plans with a friend because of our fears, or our anxiety has made us on-edge and irritable. Now that we know what the problem is, how can we explain our anxiety disorder to others in a way that makes sense and allows us to get the support we need?

Friends and family can only be supportive if they know about a problem. At the same time, no "magic words" can guarantee a positive response; no matter how you say it, some people will be judgmental or skeptical. Most of the people we care about will be supportive of our attempts to get better; they may be less so if they think we're using our diagnosis as an excuse to justify a short fuse or continue avoiding things we're afraid of.

The trick is to prepare in advance, being clear with yourself about why you are telling the person, what you want from him or her, and how you will respond to whatever reaction they might have. For example, before talking to a friend or family member about your anxiety disorder, ask yourself the following:

◆ **Why do I want or need to tell this person?** If you're telling your boss, for example, you should probably stick to how it impacts work, what help/assistance you need, and what you are doing to get better.

◆ **What do I want from him or her?** For instance, do you want emotional support or do you want this person to participate in your treatment?

◆ **How has this person responded to other challenges in the past?** How does s/he handle his or her own emotional bumps and bruises?

Write down what you want this person to know about your anxiety disorder. In addition to telling your own story, it can be useful to find some basic reading material you can recommend they use as a reference. Don't sabotage yourself by sharing with your loved one when you're in the middle of an argument, when either of you are pressed for time, or when either of you are in a bad mood.

Anxiety Attack

Before sharing the fact that you have an anxiety disorder with anyone at work, be sure you know why you are doing it, what the possible consequences are, and what legal rights you have.

Now that we've met the seven anxiety disorders, remember what we discussed about diagnosis. These lists of symptoms represent psychology's best attempt to understand and define real people's experiences. Your experience will be unique, and your path to emotional freedom will be your own; in later chapters, we discuss what the best self-help and professional assistance has to offer.

But before we get to problematic symptoms, let's take a look at the "why" behind the seven "whats." An anxiety disorder diagnosis often raises as many questions as it answers. Why me? Why do some people develop anxiety disorders; is it nature (biology) or nurture? In the next chapter, we discuss the causes of anxiety disorders: the genetics, the biology, the environment, and the internal triggers that either cause them or keep them going.

The Least You Need to Know

♦ Seven anxiety disorders are recognized by mental-health professionals.

♦ All anxiety disorders share an undercurrent of fear, various physical symptoms, and an attempt to avoid unpleasant sensations.

♦ An accurate diagnosis of any mental condition is challenging because it is based on self-report, symptoms often change, and cultural influences may cloud the picture.

♦ Family support can be critical in overcoming an anxiety disorder. Before talking with loved ones, it is helpful to know why you want to share with them and how you'd like them to help you.

Why Me?

In This Chapter

- ◆ Discover who gets tapped to join the anxiety society
- ◆ Explore the biology of fear
- ◆ Understand how we learn to be afraid
- ◆ Investigate how thoughts influence anxiety
- ◆ Recognize what triggers your anxiety

Monica's parents describe her as a happy, sensitive, and eager-to-please child. Sure, in fifth grade, she went through a brief period of what she calls "nervous stuttering" and nail biting, but these subsided as she adjusted to a new school and her parents' separation. High school was fine, even though Monica always felt anxious at parties and was terrified in her speech class. However, she had many good friends. And although she suffered for hours before a speech, she always managed to get through it. In fact, she was valedictorian of her high school class and received an academic scholarship to an Ivy League college hundreds of miles from home.

The first semester away was rough. For the first time, Monica felt "dumb"; academic competition among her peers was fierce, and Monica found herself doubting her ability to succeed. She also worried that she would lose her academic scholarship and let her parents down. Then in November of her freshmen year, she learned her father had prostate cancer. On December 1, walking to class on a sunny-but-cold fall day, Monica had her first panic attack.

All of us experience stress and pressure. Many of us have lost someone close to us or faced the possibility. Yet not all of us develop an anxiety disorder. In this chapter, we look at why anxiety disorders develop and what clues their origins provide to helping us regain control over our lives.

Who Gets Tapped for the Anxiety Society?

Although anyone can get an anxiety disorder, they are twice as common in women as they are in men. Anxiety disorders also show up more often in certain age groups; they can appear at any age, but most people experience their first symptoms in young adulthood.

Anxiety disorders also run in families. If someone in your family has an anxiety disorder, you are several times more likely to develop one yourself; in general, the closer the genetic link between you and your anxious family member, the more your risk goes up. But even if your identical twin has an anxiety disorder, it doesn't mean you will.

Certain life experiences also put us at risk for an anxiety disorder. A childhood history of abuse can increase our odds of adult anxiety, as can childhood parental loss or separation. In addition, children with highly reactive temperaments may be innately more sensitive to their environments and, as a result, more reactive to environmental stressors and the physical cues they generate.

On the Cutting Edge
Recent research identified two genetic factors that create a biological vulnerability to anxiety. One factor creates a predisposition to generalized anxiety disorder, panic disorder, and agoraphobia; the second predicts simple phobias. Social phobia is influenced by both genetic factors.

So where do these disorders come from? Are they psychological or physical? The most commonly accepted model of mental illness is the *diathesis-stress model*. This theory proposes that some people are born with a predisposition for a given illness such as generalized anxiety disorder or panic disorder that may or may not develop, depending on what life throws at them. For instance, a natural worrywart may get along just fine until she is diagnosed with breast cancer. A shy teenager may only develop full-blown social anxiety in response to a humiliating school event or a bully's constant teasing.

The answer, then, is that anxiety disorders often develop for biological and psychological reasons. When they do develop, what we put in our bodies and how we use our minds can make them better or worse.

Psychology and Anxiety

Many years ago, psychiatrists and psychologists believed that anxiety was solely a psychological condition. Psychodynamic theories still focus on anxiety symptoms as an expression of underlying conflicts. For example, the rituals associated with obsessive-compulsive disorder (OCD) are often viewed as a way to ward off unacceptable impulses or internal conflicts. Phobias are interpreted as a use of *displacement*, a psychic defense mechanism whereby a person redirects thoughts, feelings, and impulses from a source that causes anxiety to a safer, more acceptable one. From a psychoanalytic point of view, a boy who develops a fear of horses may really have an unrecognized fear of his father.

Even today, from the psychodynamic perspective, anxiety is usually interpreted as reflecting basic, unresolved conflicts in intimate relationships or hidden anger. Treatment often centers on uncovering these hidden conflicts, impulses, and feelings. Unfortunately, as discussed in Chapter 19, there's not much evidence that this treatment works.

Stress Relief

There is some evidence that women may ruminate more about distressing life events than men, suggesting that learning to monitor and control thoughts and worries may be especially useful tools.

Behave Yourself!

The behavioral model focuses on how we learn to be afraid. According to behaviorists, we learn in three different ways: *classical conditioning*, *operant conditioning*, and *modeling*. All of these have implications when it comes to anxiety.

Classical conditioning is when you learn by automatically associating two different things or stimuli. In particular, the emphasis is on how we learn to pair a normal reflex action with a "neutral" stimulus nearby. If you feed your dog canned food, you can witness classical conditioning firsthand. Watch her drool when she hears the electric can opener running—even if you're opening a can of pineapple! She associates the sound of a can opener (a neutral stimulus) with being fed, and, as a result, is drooling in the absence of dog food.

How can this relate to anxiety? In a famous experiment, social scientist John Watson (1878–1958) intentionally induced a phobia in an 11-month-old boy by pairing a loud noise with a little white rat. (Please note that ethical standards have changed; no university would allow such an experiment now.) Every time little Albert reached for the rat, Watson clanged away. Not only did Albert begin to associate the white rat and the noise, becoming anxious around the rat, he also began to generalize. He became anxious around other white, furry objects, including a rabbit, a fur coat, and a Santa Claus beard.

But this doesn't have to happen in a laboratory. Let's say that when you were little you used to visit Grandma in Tucson, Arizona, an area famous for thunderstorms with lots of lightning and plenty of loud, scary thunder. But all you associated was the reflex (flinching, heart pounding) with a neutral stimulus (Grandma). You might grow anxious even if Grandma came to visit you in your home state, where there was almost never thunder and lightning!

Any parent understands *operant conditioning;* it simply means we learn to do things we're rewarded for and we stop doing things that lead to painful or negative consequences. Although this risk/reward strategy works well most of the time, it can backfire when our avoidance interferes with doing what we love or when short-term rewards lead to long-term problems.

For instance, most of us tend to stay away from things we fear. According to operant conditioning, this avoidance behavior tends to be reinforced because when we avoid (or escape) unpleasant situations, we feel better. An unfortunate side effect, though, is that this strategy reduces opportunities for us to unlearn our fears. An attempt to avoid unpleasant feelings can have life-altering—even life-threatening—consequences. One bad encounter with an inexperienced nurse and a needle could lead us to avoid seeking much-needed medical care for years. Fears of driving after a car accident could adversely impact our careers and our relationships.

Finally, *modeling* is another way we pick up fears. If Mom is terrified of snakes, we may decide snakes are scary without ever coming near one. (If Mom is unlucky, of course, we turn out to be the kid who finds a snake every other week and brings it home, begging, "Can I keep it?") If everyone in the family is anxious about the same thing, we're even more likely to jump on the bandwagon.

So is all anxiety learned? It appears that some anxiety disorders are more so than others. For instance, one study found that more than three quarters of people with a needle phobia had had a bad experience with an injection or blood draw. That sounds like learning at work. On the other hand, a study of children who were terrified of water showed that more than half of them exhibited the fear at their very first aquatic encounter! Obviously, not all anxiety can be associated directly with learning.

Myth Buster

"Stress causes mental illness." In reality, stress may occasionally trigger an episode or cause symptoms such as anxiety or depression, but persistent symptoms appear to be biological in nature. There are probably many things that can contribute to mental illness—the cause is not yet fully understood.

When Twisted Thinking Leads to Anxiety

Cognitive theories of anxiety focus on the way our thoughts influence us. Here's an example: picture yourself about to give a big speech at school or work. Imagine that you're thinking to yourself, "Okay, I can handle this. I'm well prepared. Everyone here wants me to do well. Even if I make a few mistakes, it won't matter."

Now imagine that you're in the same situation, but instead you're thinking, "I can't do this. I'm going to throw up. I'm going to pass out. The speech I prepared is pure garbage. Everyone is just waiting for me to screw up. One mistake and I'll get an F [or get fired]."

It's the same speech! But there's no question about which situation would make you, me, or anyone else more anxious. It's not the reality that matters—*it's what we think* about what happens or what might happen.

- **Cognitive distortions** occur when our thoughts become unreasonable, irrational, or even ridiculous. Psychologists have a whole list of ways we distort our thinking when we become anxious. Some of these probably look familiar to you from personal experience!

- **Catastrophizing** happens when we turn a molehill into a mountain. "Oh my Lord, it's the end of the world—I have to give a talk and I have a run in my pantyhose!" The reality? If your talk is good enough, no one will notice—or care.

- **Dichotomous reasoning** means seeing everything as black or white. You're either a success or a failure, and one mistake means you're a failure. In reality, the world is all about shades of gray, and we all make mistakes.

◆ **Disqualifying the positive** happens when you ignore the good feedback you get. Ten people say you look great today, but you find reasons to discount what they say.

◆ **Emotional reasoning** happens when you decide that what you feel must really reflect reality. You feel like an idiot, so you must really be one. But we all feel like this on occasion, and we can't all be idiots. (Despite the title of this book!)

◆ **Fortune telling** happens when you act as if your worst fears will certainly come true. You're not worried that the worst *might* happen; you're *sure* that it will.

◆ **Labeling** occurs when we give a global label to ourselves ("I'm a failure") rather than seeing something as a single event ("Well, I blew that one, but I'll do better next time").

◆ **Mind reading** is when we assume that others are reacting negatively to us—even when we have no evidence. Always remember the old rule: when you assume, you make an ass out of you and me!

◆ **Minimization** is when you don't give yourself credit for your good qualities or accomplishments. You can tell someone all your faults but can't tell them anything good about yourself.

◆ **Overgeneralization** means taking one event and basing reality on that. He says he loves you at the end of 99 phone calls, but if he forgets to once, it must mean he doesn't really love you.

Stress Relief

One way anxiety can influence thinking is described in a metaphor of a lake. We don't actually perceive things as they really are—we perceive them as they are reflected by our emotions, as in the surface of a lake. If we are emotionally unsettled, angry, afraid, depressed, or anxious, the reflection is distorted, and we cannot see things clearly.

◆ **Personalization** means taking everything personally and ignoring other factors. "She didn't smile; she must hate me!" instead of realizing that her cat just died, or she has cramps today.

◆ **Selective abstraction** happens when you focus on one part rather than the whole; you get five A's on your report card and one B minus—and all you can think about is the B minus.

◆ **"Should" and "have to" statements** can mess up your mind if you go overboard with them. Some 12-step programs refer to overdoing this as "should-ing all over yourself."

Don't Know Much Biology ...

That's the scoop on the psychology of anxiety. What about biology? We discuss this later in the book in more depth, but we'll take a brief look here. You may remember from high school biology that your nervous system transmits information throughout your whole body.

Your nervous system is divided into two parts: your central nervous system (the brain and spinal cord); and the part we're interested in, your *peripheral nervous system*, which transmits information back and forth to your central nervous system.

With me so far? Next let's get more specific. The peripheral nervous system is also divided into two parts: the *somatic nervous system*, which controls our voluntary actions; and the *autonomic nervous system*, which controls our internal organs.

Stick with it—we're almost there! Yes, the autonomic nervous system divides down yet again into two parts: the *parasympathetic system*, which helps us relax; and the *sympathetic system*. The sympathetic system activates our survival responses to perceived threats.

In extreme instances, this is known as *fight or flight*. Your body is preparing you to either run away or do battle. This was probably great for our caveman ancestors. You see that mammoth approaching, and it's time to run like heck or get ready to try to put it on the dinner table.

But it's no help with modern stressors. When it's time to go to the dentist, it's not appropriate to jump out of the chair and run or to challenge the dentist to a duel. It's time to lie back, open our mouths, and cope as best we can.

> **Stress Relief** _____
>
> Learning through rewards and punishments still works, no matter how old we get. But we can reward ourselves, too. Got a stressful event coming up? Depending on how stressful the event (and how much money you've got), a reward might range from a chocolate milkshake to a new dress to that getaway vacation you've been dreaming about.

The Blind Alley—the Pathway of Fear

So what happens in the brain during fight or flight? The startling noise of a mammoth—and every other piece of worrying sensory information—takes two pathways. The first, of which most of are aware, is to the frontal cortex, the reasoning part of the brain, where every perception is analyzed and interpreted with powerful processing tools.

But this processing takes precious time, so there is another route—sometimes called a blind alley or a dirty back road, because it can often lead us to false conclusions. On this route, the perception is rapidly matched by the amygdala against possible threats. The *amygdala* is an almond-shaped structure in the limbic system whose job is to trigger responses to danger. If there is a close enough match, the amygdala will hit the emergency button, raising the heartbeat, changing breathing, and revving up the engines for action. However, because the amygdala's focus is on survival, it tends to err on the side of caution; accuracy takes a backseat to speed and innocuous situations can be misperceived as dangerous. Right or wrong, the amygdala takes a stand long before the rational mind has processed the incoming data.

Of course, sometimes the amygdala serves us well, in getting us out of real danger quickly. But many times this life-saving system activates our panic mechanisms needlessly. Even when the rational mind catches up and concludes there is no threat, it takes a while to calm down the systems that have been alerted.

All the physical symptoms of fear—the shortness of breath, the nausea, the need to use the bathroom, the speeding pulse, the restlessness—are caused by the amygdala's response to a perceived threat. In the case of an anxiety disorder, this blind alley becomes a well-trodden path, a default pattern of response that becomes all too familiar—and we can't stop following it.

Life Experience and Anxiety

We know that biology affects psychology: if your body is pumping adrenaline into your bloodstream, you're unlikely to stay in a calm, peaceful frame of mind. But psychology can also affect biology.

> **Myth Buster**
>
> *"It's all in your mind."*
> Wrong! Anxiety, like all emotions, produces physical reactions in our bodies, too. Sometimes, particularly when the anxiety is extreme, the physical reactions can leave a permanent change, such as a reduced immune system from chronic stress.

People with certain types of anxiety disorders (such as post-traumatic stress disorder [PTSD]) show actual changes in the structure of their brains. They may also produce higher-than-normal levels of stress hormones. So some extreme anxiety-producing experiences can actually change us physically, perhaps permanently.

Ready for an example of how psychology can affect biology? Think about the last vivid dream you had. Was it scary, thrilling, funny, or plain weird? Dreams are perhaps the most dramatic and challenging type of thought we have—and despite the frankly bizarre imagery, we usually completely believe dreams while we're having them. This is because the analytical, fact-checking higher cortex of the brain is largely shut down while we dream. So when we wake up, we are often charged with all the emotions of the dream. The brain and body are responding as if it is real. The sympathetic nervous system accordingly opens up all the channels needed to deal with the apparent "reality." In other words, your body is responding to *nothing but your state of mind*.

In a sense, our brain chemistry changes with every thought. Each time a brain cell makes a connection with another brain cell, a chemical called a *neurotransmitter* is released to jump the gap. And different neurotransmitters are produced for different types of thought. So our state of mind can clearly affect the biology of our brains.

So Who Holds the Smoking Gun—Genes or Environment?

The simple answer, as we've said, is that it's probably a mix of both. There's no doubt that the genetic makeup we inherit from our parents sets a precedent for how we behave—we are all set at different emotional levels, and these levels are largely determined by our genes. However, this does not mean we are genetically doomed. Even if we are more inclined to respond with fear or anxiety to a given situation, learning how to manage emotions and stop irrational thinking from taking hold is a powerful way to manage what nature and nurture have given us.

Take a look at the following table to compare the anxiety risk factors we face from both our biological makeup and what daily life can throw at us:

Diagnosis	Biological Risks	Environmental Risks
PTSD	Some evidence suggests genetic basis for PTSD	Traumatic event
Social phobia	Heightened sensitivity to disapproval; inherited vulnerability possible	Observational modeling—seeing the behavior of others
GAD	Moderately heritable; 20% risk for GAD in blood relatives	Work/life stresses, sleep deprivation, relationship worries
Panic disorder	Moderately heritable; increased risk in blood relatives	Stress—especially recent loss or separation

continues

continued

Diagnosis	Biological Risks	Environmental Risks
Agoraphobia	Research suggests agoraphobia and panic disorder share the same genetic root	Almost half of agoraphobia sufferers report histories of real or feared separation from primary caregiver in childhood
OCD	Moderately heritable; 25% risk for OCD in blood relatives	Increased risk in mothers following childbirth
Specific phobias	Modest genetic influence	Learning phobic responses in childhood

It's clear that biology and the environment can both influence our susceptibility to anxiety disorders.

What Triggers Your Anxiety?

Film actress Scarlett Johansson recently divulged her anxiety trigger: work. She suffered severe panic attacks on the set of one of her movies. "I usually feel nervous before every film, but this time it was a lot worse. I was so nervous that, by the time we were ready for the first scene, I was nearly dead from anxiety."

Understanding the causes of your own anxiety provides a basis for coping and managing your fears. Studies have shown that there are some common causes for anxiety and anxiety disorders, but each person will have his or her own experience and triggers. What are yours? Rate your anxiety level for each of these known anxiety traps.

Stress Relief

Daily hassles are minor irritants—misplacing or losing things, an unreliable car, continuous interruptions by a coworker—that can create wear and tear on an anxious psyche. Dealing directly with these and building a strong support system can significantly cut down on chronic stress.

Anxiety Trigger Checklist

Triggers	Strongly Anxious	Anxious	Not Anxious
Work worries	❑	❑	❑
Relationship dilemmas	❑	❑	❑
Money problems	❑	❑	❑
Recent loss of a loved one	❑	❑	❑
Health concerns	❑	❑	❑
School difficulties	❑	❑	❑
Life trauma such as a road accident	❑	❑	❑

In addition to these common stress inducers, you may also need to think about whether any of the following are already affecting your physical state:

◆ Are you taking medication that can cause excitement, nervousness, or irritability?

◆ Is your caffeine intake too high?

◆ Are you taking illicit drugs such as cocaine or cannabis?

Anxious feelings can spread easily. When we feel anxious, our perspective is altered, and it's hard to pinpoint the source of stress. So it's important to analyze your physical state and anxiety level when you are at your calmest.

You can also discover your own anxiety triggers by completing a stress diary, explained later in the book. Make a note of the situations in which you feel most anxious. Notice when your anxiety levels decrease. This is invaluable information in learning to manage your own type of anxiety.

Now that we've talked about the types of anxiety disorders, and the causes and triggers of your own anxious feelings, what can we do about them? Is it possible to change, or should we accept who we are and live with the consequences? And if we are to change, how do we keep up the motivation when the going gets tough? In the next chapter on what to expect on the road to recovery, we talk about these issues and more.

The Least You Need to Know

- ◆ You are not alone; anxiety is a very common phenomenon.
- ◆ Anxiety has biological and environmental roots.
- ◆ Biology can affect your thinking, and thinking can affect your biology.
- ◆ Understanding your own anxiety triggers helps to form the basis of recovery

4

What to Expect on the Path to Recovery

In This Chapter

- ◆ Find out what to expect on your journey to calm
- ◆ Avoid emotional potholes by anchoring your values
- ◆ Discover the secrets of staying power
- ◆ Develop a winning attitude in the war against anxiety

As a young girl, Eleanor Roosevelt developed a terror of water after the steamship she was traveling on was involved in a midsea collision with another vessel. She and her father barely managed to get in the same lifeboat. Afterward, she refused to go on another boat trip and, as a result of her fear, never learned to swim.

After her husband contracted polio, he could no longer play as actively with their children. Eleanor found herself taking over many parenting tasks—and, once again, came face to face with her water phobia. This time, though, she wasn't willing to give in to it. Out of her love for her children, Eleanor also found the motivation, and the strength, to break free of her phobia. She took swimming lessons and gradually regained her comfort in the water. In fact, overcoming her fear of water gave her so much courage that she decided to conquer another personal challenge: she learned to drive.

Eleanor's motivation didn't make her fears go away. Instead, Eleanor found her way *through* her fear. In fact, her lifelong motto became, "You must look fear in the face. You must do the thing you think you cannot do."

Tackling anxiety, whether it's a temporary state of mind or a chronic problem, is a journey. It's common for us to feel afraid, to have ups and downs, and, at times, to have to do things that are the opposite of what our instincts tell us. To keep ourselves on the path to peace, let's explore what to expect and how we can overcome our initial fears, rally our motivation, gain momentum, and bounce back when things don't go as we planned.

The Value of the Beaten Path

Anxiety and worry drain our energy and sap our motivation. So how do we muster the strength to take it on when it's already taking its toll? How do people ever make changes? These are good questions.

> **Myth Buster**
>
> *"Change is just a question of willpower."* Not always. Determination is key, but we also need the skills and the resources.

Identifying and focusing on our values can be one source of strength and motivation. A value is a belief, a mission, or a philosophy that is important to us; hard work, independence, concern for others. These serve as the inspiration for our goals; if honesty is value, for instance, I probably won't aspire to be a bank robber or con artist. A concern for others might lead me to do volunteer work or choose a helping profession.

We're happiest when the way we live our lives is consistent with our core values. Unfortunately, anxiety, worry, and fear can keep us from doing so by either tempting us to *avoid* activities that would fulfill our values, or *doing* things that are contradictory to how we see ourselves. If Eleanor Roosevelt had let it, her fear of water could have prevented her from being the courageous, involved parent she valued. A person with extreme social anxiety might find herself lying at the last minute to get out of a work talk, violating her personal value of honesty and keeping commitments.

Core values can help us stay committed to conquering our anxiety by keeping the "big picture" in mind. It gives us something to move *toward* in the struggle to move *away* from our fear. It can also help us tolerate temporary discomfort by keeping in mind the payoff at the end of the road, much like an expectant mom is willing to go through labor pains to get that bundle of joy.

So what are your personal values? What core beliefs form the bedrock of who you are? What's your basic philosophy or personal mission statement?

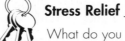 **Stress Relief**

What do you want to be remembered for? How would you want your closest friends and family to describe you at your funeral? Writing your obituary can be a dramatic way to help clarify your personal values and make contact with what you care about.

Consider some of the following values, and determine which of these are most important to you.

Adventure
Calm, quietude, peace
Commitment
Communication
Community
Concern for others
Creativity
Discovery
Faith
Family
Friendship
Fun
Goodness
Gratitude
Hard work
Harmony

Honesty
Honor
Independence
Inner peace
Innovation
Integrity
Justice
Knowledge
Leadership
Love, romance
Loyalty
Meaning
Money
Openness
Pleasure
Positive attitude

Which of these would be your top five? How do you act them out in your everyday words and actions? Write them down and put your list in a place where you can readily see it. Let it serve as a quick measure by which you evaluate your everyday decisions and choices.

The Anxiety Price Tag

Now that you've got a clearer picture of what values are closest to your heart, take a close look at how anxiety clouds the picture. Because anxiety is an attention grabber, it can take our focus away from the very things we treasure most.

For instance, if we obsessively worry about harm befalling someone we care about, we may not give our child the growing room to explore the world on his or her own. Our fear of flying might prevent us from attending a cherished friend's wedding or loved one's funeral. Unmanaged stress might cause us to snap at people we care about, alienate coworkers, or abuse drugs or alcohol.

As painful as it is, getting a snapshot of how anxiety limits our lives is critical, especially when there's so much immediate relief in *giving in to* what our anxiety or fear is telling us. Yes, maybe we can avoid a panic attack if we don't get back behind the wheel of our car, but think of what this costs us. Think of our dependence on others to take us places, our child's confusion over why mom or dad can't carpool, and the secret shame and guilt we feel about it.

How does your anxiety affect you? What personal costs have you had to pay? What about the lifestyle changes and relationship issues caused or made worse by your anxiety?

Here's an exercise designed to help you see on a daily basis how costly giving in to your anxiety really is. For the next seven days, make daily recordings of situations or events that trigger your anxiety, concerns, or worries. Write down how you experience that anxiety; this should include your physical symptoms, feelings, thoughts, and concerns. Then record what your coping strategy was, what emotions your coping strategy produced, and what were the lost-opportunity costs. Here's an example of what your log might look like.

Situation: *Asked to give a talk at work.*

Anxiety: *Afraid of being embarrassed, scared my anxiety would cause me to lose my train of thought.*

Coping strategy: *Tried to talk myself into it but called in sick at the last minute.*

Emotional impact: *Felt like a failure, felt guilty and ashamed, frustrated.*

Opportunity cost: *Boss was irritated, lost chance to impress the sales group.*

A warning: this exercise takes courage. Many people who initially commit to this exercise wind up avoiding it or "forgetting" to do it. Don't let yourself be one of them. If it helps, remind yourself that taking stock doesn't commit you to making any behavior changes; it's just a look-see. It's also a reminder that avoiding anxiety comes at a price, one that ultimately might be higher than going through it.

Settling the Account

Getting clear about anxiety's costs can be a powerful motivator. Another ally is developing the right attitude—toward ourselves and toward our anxiety symptoms. I'm not talking about looking on the bright side; I'm talking about the deliberate cultivation of some healing beliefs that can help us put our anxiety symptoms in perspective and show respect to ourselves.

Let's take a look at five attitudes that can get your mind, your heart, and your willpower working together.

I am not ashamed of myself or my symptoms.

If people knew how I really felt, they'd think I was crazy. I must really be a loser if I can't even control my own feelings. I can't tell my husband; he couldn't handle it.

There are valid reasons why many of us keep our anxiety a secret, such as the very real stigma society still puts on mental-health challenges, or the common confusion between everyday worry and a clinical disorder. Whether you decide to tell others about your anxiety is less important than having the *emotional option* to tell them. If, out of our fear of rejection or sense of shame, we *have* to keep our anxiety a secret, we are making decisions based on what will protect us from the rejection or scrutiny of others, not what will help us heal.

Anxiety is my teacher. What can I learn?

Ever tried a Chinese finger trap? It's a tube of woven straw about 5 inches long and half an inch wide. You slide both index fingers into the straw tube, one finger at each end. If you then attempt to pull them out, the tube catches and tightens. The only way to regain some freedom and space of movement is to push the fingers in first and then slide them out. I once gave them out as party favors at my 5-year-old's birthday and can still picture a frantic mother running down my driveway, fingers stuck in each end, shouting, "I can't get out!"

Anxiety can be like that. If, at the first uncomfortable physical sensation, we tighten up and try to fight our feelings, more often than not, they will get worse. We are now adding anxiety about our symptoms to our initial fear. See how this can snowball?

On the other hand, rather than pushing against our anxiety, what if we add something to it? Perhaps we add a scientific observation, almost like we're describing the sensations as if they belong to someone else: "Hmm, for me, anxiety seems to start with a flip-flop in my stomach, almost as if I'm riding a roller coaster." Perhaps we rate it: "That's about a three on the anxiety scale." "Wow, that was a big wave; I'd give it an eight." Or perhaps we adopt an attitude of curiosity: "I wonder what these feelings are trying to tell me."

By going with our anxiety, rather than fighting it, we are much more likely to flow through our discomfort rather than make it worse or get trapped by it. And whereas it can be a mean teacher, anxiety does sometimes have important lessons for us; it has helped me take better care of myself, set better limits with others, and get more in touch with all my feelings.

> **Myth Buster**
>
> *"I should never feel anxious."* Anxiety is a normal human emotion—we all feel it at times! In fact, trying to avoid anxiety can just make you feel more anxious.

Symptoms are an opportunity to practice—not a test.

"You only fail when you stop trying." Uh-huh. Not in the competitive United States! We're born and bred to win, win, win—every time, no excuses, and no mistakes. Which is a good thing if we're trying to win a competition on the outside; perhaps not so good if the struggle is within.

If you've decided to tackle your anxiety, I can assure you that you *are* going to take steps forward and get knocked back. Perhaps we find ourselves "relapsing" into obsessive thoughts and worry after our mother dies, or can't control our terror in anticipation of a visit to a new dentist. Maybe we promise ourselves we'll stay at the party until 8:30 and then flee at 7, or leave the grocery store during a panic attack even though we promised ourselves we'd ride it out.

Okay, so you didn't meet your initial goal. Let that experience be feedback to you as you take corrective action. What can you adjust? Perhaps you need to visit the dentist's office before your appointment, to make it a more comfortable place. Maybe you need to get some help with your grieving, or join a self-help group. Maybe it'd be easier to stay at the party if you planned some ice-breakers and conversation starters.

Talk to yourself about setbacks in the same way you would talk to a child who is having a tough time learning a new skill. You'd encourage her. You'd put temporary setbacks in perspective. You'd problem solve with her when she faced glitches and bumps in the road. And you'd *never* call her a failure.

> ### On the Cutting Edge
>
> People who suffer from anxiety disorders may be more likely to experience relapses following attempts to quit drinking, suggesting that anxiety treatment may be a necessary component—and great benefit—to individuals who self-medicate with alcohol.

Anxiety is uncomfortable, but it's not dangerous.

Anxiety is uncomfortable. It's unpleasant. It can feel overwhelming. As a result, when anxiety hits, our instincts tell us to *do* something. Move. Get out of there. Make it stop!

How ironic it is; going against the flow may ultimately result in smoother sailing. Allowing ourselves to get used to wading through moments of emotional discomfort can do wonders in building up our confidence to deal with the really tough times. Internal messages such as "I'm feeling anxious, and that's okay right now" can go a long way toward defusing our fear's power to blackmail us.

> ### Stress Relief
>
> When we feel we've hit a roadblock in reaching a personal goal, seeing our journey from a third-person perspective—as if looking at one's past self in a movie—can help us appreciate the progress we've already made and give us the strength we need to keep going.

I don't have to like my feelings to be able to handle them.

I can't stand it. I've got to get out of here. What if it gets worse?

Every time we allow those thoughts into our head, we are creating a picture of ourselves as vulnerable and weak.

In addition, uncertainty is especially distasteful for those of us who crave control. Trying to anticipate, avoid, or escape pain can put you in a tense state of vigilance, constantly monitoring your environment for signs of threat. To overcome anxiety, you need to be willing to lower your defenses and tolerate some uncertainty. By accepting the risk of a negative outcome, you are lessening your need for certainty, and anxiety will reduce.

With these five attitudes as your base, take a look at some additional ways you can keep yourself steady on your self-help journey.

Keeping the Engine Running

We've already mentioned several ways we can keep on keeping-on as we work to control our anxiety. We've talked about defining and living according to our personal values, keeping track of what our anxiety costs us, and developing a healing perspective.

Let's take a look at some other top tips for keeping those motivational engines running:

◆ **Reward yourself.** Praise yourself for every baby step you take in the right direction. In addition, if you've taken a big leap, by staying in a tough situation or breathing through some scary symptoms, reward yourself with something you enjoy.

◆ **Build a skills base.** If you're nervous in social situations, work on your communication skills. For chronic tension or worry, learn meditation or take a course in biofeedback. For performance anxiety, try visualization or self-hypnosis. These life skills can help anyone, anxious or not, lead a better life.

◆ **Don't go it alone.** Don't make becoming anxiety free a solo effort. Find people you can share your struggles with, whether it's an online support group or close circle of family and friends.

Stress Relief

Need another motivator? Reducing anxiety can improve relationships, and recent research confirms that people involved in committed relationships are generally happier than others.

On the surface, making the decision to deal with anxiety seems like a no-brainer. Who doesn't want to feel better? Yet in reality, taking charge of our emotional freedom requires some up-front commitment; we've got to be clear about our goals, develop helpful attitudes, and suffer through some emotional bumps and bruises. Just as labor pains and sleepless nights are part of the new-parent package, we may have to go through some rough spots before we get to the prize.

This chapter examines the mixed feelings so many of us have when we start on the path to recovery from anxiety. On the one hand, we're sick and tired of anxiety taking up so much of our valuable time and energy; on the other hand, what if nothing we do makes any difference? *What if we feel worse?*

In the next chapter, we look at how we can build our emotional reservoir by strengthening our emotional intelligence. We explore the value of emotional self-awareness as well as basic strategies for managing our emotions. We tackle the whole issue of emotions—what they are, what they do, and how anxiety impacts them.

The Least You Need to Know

- The journey from anxiety to peace is never straightforward or discomfort free, but it is worth it.

- Being clear about our personal values, and honest about anxiety's costs, can be powerful motivation to plow ahead.

- Developing healthy attitudes about the recovery process can buffer us from setbacks and potholes.

- Anxiety often creates a paradox; if we fight it, it gets stronger. On the other hand, if we flow through it, it lessens.

Part 2

Fighting Your Way Through the Fright

Fear is perhaps the most primitive emotion we have. Because of its survival focus, it quickly takes over our thoughts and drives our behavior.

This section looks at how we can build up our emotional intelligence to better manage our everyday emotions and use difficult emotions, such as anger, to our benefit. From there, we talk about the role of anxiety in avoidance behavior and how we can give up self-defeating behaviors such as passivity and procrastination that ultimately make our anxiety worse.

Listen to Your Teachers Before They Yell

In This Chapter

- ◆ Understand the role between emotions and anxiety
- ◆ Discover the feelings underneath your worries
- ◆ Evaluate your emotional intelligence
- ◆ Find out how to better manage your emotions

How are you? It's a common enough question, one we hear every day. But honestly, how do you *feel?* Feelings are, after all, responsible for much of what we think about and do, so it's a very important question.

Ideally, our emotions are our teachers, telling us what's important about our needs, our wants, and how the world around us is treating us. They serve as an early-warning system when our internal needs aren't being met by our external reality. Even when they seem counterproductive—like the fear accompanying a panic attack or the chronic worry that underlies general-ized anxiety—they can teach us some important lessons about ourselves.

But what if we've lost touch with them? What if we ignore them? And what happens when our emotions start shouting? Emotional mismanagement could be said to be at the heart of every conflict the world has ever known. In other words, becoming "in tune" with how you feel, responding appropriately to your emotions, like responding to your teachers, takes a little skill and practice.

In this chapter we discuss the role of our feelings in managing anxiety, how emotions affect us, and what it means to be emotionally intelligent.

What Are Feelings, Anyway?

Artists often trumpet their feelings as being responsible for their art; William Wordsworth described poetry as the spontaneous overflow of powerful feelings. Picasso once said the artist is the receptacle for the emotions that come from the world around. For the rest of us, our feelings make us human, allow us to fall in love, tempt us to get even, and motivate us to climb the corporate ladder.

Feelings have often taken a back seat in the field of psychology. In fact, it was long believed that our thoughts were the major force behind our actions. But as a good car salesperson knows, our feelings have a much more persuasive influence on the choices we make. How many of us chose a mate based on a careful analysis of that person's strengths or weaknesses; it's more likely we jumped into the flames of love *in spite of* our logic. Often our thoughts come into justify getting what our feelings want!

Emotions are produced by the brain in response to the balance between our needs and wants and what the outside world is offering us. Falling in love is a combination of internal needs for intimacy and closeness coupled (hopefully!) with the right timing and chemistry with another person. The correspondence of needs/wants and the outside world produce feelings.

Setting the Emotional Thermostat

Although we all share the same basic feelings—love, sadness, happiness, guilt, and so on—we differ in the particular feelings we experience at any given time and how strongly we feel them. Some of us are more "high strung," often prone to strong feelings, whereas others seem more emotionally cool. Some of us easily express our emotions, whereas others prefer a poker face.

Individual differences in emotional sensitivity and expressiveness are an interesting interplay between nature and nurture. It probably comes as no surprise that we inherit much of our emotional tuning from our parents. Some of this inheritance shows up in the temperament we're born with.

For example, from birth, children differ in how sensitive they are to different stimuli in their environment and how intense their response. My oldest son has always been extremely aggravated by shirt tags, tight hugs, bright lights, and loud noises. On the other hand, one of my younger kids could probably wear a shirt made out of Brill-O pads and could enjoy a TV show while a marching band played in our family room.

Intensity of reaction refers to the energy level of a person's typical response. For example, a child who has a low threshold of responsiveness but a high intensity of reaction may respond to a bad tasting medicine with a very loud, "Yuck!" and lots of facial grimacing and spitting. On the other hand, another child with the same threshold of responsiveness but a low intensity of reaction may only wrinkle his nose in distaste.

Honey, you don't really feel that way. How can you say you were mad that I missed your birthday party; don't you know how hard I work? Snap out of that bad mood, young man, and quit being so selfish.

Whereas some characteristics are no doubt genetic, research is casting light on the patterns of emotional behavior we learn while growing up. It seems that not only do we get our emotional setting (high strung or laid back) from our parents, we also learn our patterns of dealing with our feelings from watching them.

Were you able to blow off steam in your house without upsetting anyone? How comfortable were your parents in expressing their emotions—both positive and negative? Children from homes in which family members are expected to express feelings, whether in shouting matches or calm conversation, are more likely as adults to do likewise, whereas children from homes where emotional expression is taboo are more likely to be emotionally reserved (or repressed) as adults.

One fascinating study compared parents of anxiety-disordered children to parents of children with no mental-health problems to see how these families coped with emotional challenges. Specifically, their habits in dealing with or discussing their children's feelings were

> ### On the Cutting Edge
>
> While human emotions are universal, the culture in which we are raised gives us "rules" about when and where our feelings can be expressed. A child raised in a typical Italian family, for example, may be more emotionally expressive than one brought up in Finland.

recorded to see whether there were any differences in parenting style. The results? Parents of children with anxiety disorders were less inclined to talk to their children about feelings. In some cases, parents of anxious children tended to discourage emotional discussions by ignoring the child's attempts to do so or by changing the subject.

Learning to understand and express emotions is an important developmental experience through which children develop emotional competence. Children look to parents for guidance on how to deal with their own feelings. Some treatments for young anxiety sufferers now include a family component, in which parents are helped to better manage their own stress and anxiety and model more effective emotion management by openly discussing emotions with their child.

Pay Me Now or Pay Me Later

Let's pretend your 17-year-old sister calls you up because she's upset. She's just broken up with her boyfriend, and she's got a ton of college applications due out in a few weeks. She still hasn't gotten her SAT scores back and is imagining the worst. You love your sister, but, to be honest, you're not in the best frame of mind yourself. You've been working 14 hours a day and you've just heard rumors about a work layoff, which, because you've just bought a car you can barely afford, worries you even more than it usually would. Plus this is only the nine hundred ninety-ninth time your sister has broken up with her boyfriend, who, in your opinion, is a class-A jerk.

So you respond with something like, "Oh, Sis, quit being so dramatic. You've aced every test you've ever taken, you'll probably get accepted to Harvard, and as for your ex-boyfriend—the jerk—I'm glad you broke up and I'm sick of hearing about it."

> **Stress Relief**
>
> One way of letting go of fear is to allow yourself to feel afraid—even for a moment. In other words, rather than trying to think it through, just feel it through. By letting the feeling do its job, it can then stop alarming you, allowing your higher-reasoning powers to process the information and make a secure judgment.

Whether what you're saying is true or not, the odds are that this response is going to get you the opposite of what you want. You're trying to get your sister to be less emotional and more rational; by discounting her feelings, however, the odds are she's going to become more emotional and less rational.

Feelings, ours and anyone else's, are like that. Like them or not, we are best advised to accept them, listen to them, and understand why they are there. We don't—and shouldn't—give in to them or use them as an excuse to justify our behavior. But they are important signals and, if we ignore them, they're likely to get louder until we stop and listen.

Listen Up and Let Go!

Okay, I want you to be calm right this minute. Do you hear me? I'm talking to you. In fact, I'll give you 60 seconds to be perfectly calm and anxiety free or I'm going to call your boss and get you fired. Or hold your dog for ransom. If you succeed, I'll give you a big prize.

I'll bet you that big prize that this command failed miserably. No matter how much we try, there are some feelings we can't control. The primary emotions—fear, anger, happiness, sadness—are hard-wired into every one of us; they're the feelings that kept our ancestors alive. And yet many of us think we should be able to avoid or control negative feelings, and that we've failed if we can't.

Did you know that by not listening to your feelings, you are actually telling yourself that you are not important enough to listen to? Ignoring how you feel can really shake your self-esteem. Pretty soon you'll be carrying around lots of unexpressed and unaddressed feelings, which can damage mental and physical health.

> **Myth Buster**
>
> *"Ignoring feelings makes them go away."* Wrong! In fact, it is more likely that your feelings will shout louder to get your attention—by raising your heart rate, releasing stress chemicals, and slowing down your rational thought, making it hard to concentrate—in other words, by inducing feelings of anxiety.

> **Stress Relief**
>
> Music is a great mood modifier. Start off with a tune that closely matches your mood and gradually work your way to something more relaxing. Your brain will readily accept the mood-matched music, and by gradually introducing something more soothing, you'll transition into a calmer state.

I'll Pass on Those Seconds

Anyone who has had a panic attack can feel panicked at the thought of having another one. This fear of the fear is a "secondary" feeling; it's based largely on the things we're telling ourselves about the first feelings. "I couldn't stand to feel that bad again" can quickly turn discomfort into terror. "Dan's not home and I've got that bad feeling; maybe it's a sign that something terrible has happened" can turn concern into crippling anxiety.

These secondary feelings cause us the most psychic problems. Often the original feelings aren't as big and hard to manage as the secondary feelings make it seem. It takes practice to distinguish our original feelings from the thoughts and feelings we have about that feeling. Yet this process frees us to focus on building our mental muscles to accept our primary feelings—which we can't directly control anyway—and eliminate the secondary feelings that we're feeding with our scary thoughts. (See Chapters 8 and 9).

Welcome to Emotional University

Learning how to handle everyday emotions not only builds up our strength for handling the "big guns" of an anxiety disorder, it is perhaps the single best predictor of how successful we will be in life. You may have heard the term *emotional intelligence* bantered around at a company meeting or in a magazine article on relationships. Those who can effectively manage emotions—both their own and those of the people around them—are thought to have a high level of emotional intelligence, or EQ.

Take a quick snapshot of your emotional intelligence. For each item that follows, circle the answer that best describes you. Although informal, it can give you an overview of your emotional strengths and weaknesses. The first half will help you evaluate how intelligent you are about your own feelings; the second half is geared toward your awareness of, and sensitivity to, the emotions of others.

1. **I stay relaxed and composed under pressure.**
   1 = Very true
   2 = Mostly true
   3 = Sometimes true
   4 = Mostly not true
   5 = Not true at all

2. **I can identify negative feelings without becoming distressed.**
   1 = Very true
   2 = Mostly true
   3 = Sometimes true
   4 = Mostly not true
   5 = Not true at all

3. **I calm myself quickly when I get angry or upset.**
   1 = Very true
   2 = Mostly true
   3 = Sometimes true
   4 = Mostly not true
   5 = Not true at all

4. **I can pull myself together quickly after an unexpected setback.**
   1 = Very true
   2 = Mostly true
   3 = Sometimes true
   4 = Mostly not true
   5 = Not true at all

5. **I am aware of how my behavior impacts others.**
   1 = Very true
   2 = Mostly true
   3 = Sometimes true
   4 = Mostly not true
   5 = Not true at all

6. **When I'm in a bad mood, I know what or who is upsetting me.**
   1 = Very true
   2 = Mostly true
   3 = Sometimes true
   4 = Mostly not true
   5 = Not true at all

7. **Even when I do my best, I feel guilty about the things that did not get done.**
   5 = Very true
   4 = Mostly true
   3 = Sometimes true
   2 = Mostly not true
   1 = Not true at all

8. **When I am upset, I can pinpoint exactly what aspect of the problem bugs me.**
   1 = Very true
   2 = Mostly true
   3 = Sometimes true
   4 = Mostly not true
   5 = Not true at all

9. **I am able to get over guilt about little mistakes that I made in the past.**
   1 = Very true
   2 = Mostly true
   3 = Sometimes true
   4 = Mostly not true
   5 = Not true at all

10. **I am able to stop thinking about my problems when I want to.**
    1 = Very true
    2 = Mostly true
    3 = Sometimes true
    4 = Mostly not true
    5 = Not true at all

11. **I will do whatever I can to keep myself from crying.**
    5 = Very true
    4 = Mostly true
    3 = Sometimes true
    2 = Mostly not true
    1 = Not true at all

12. **People who know me tell me that I overreact to minor problems.**
    5 = Very true
    4 = Mostly true
    3 = Sometimes true
    2 = Mostly not true
    1 = Not true at all

13. **No matter how much I accomplish, I have a nagging feeling that I should be doing more.**
    5 = Very true
    4 = Mostly true
    3 = Sometimes true
    2 = Mostly not true
    1 = Not true at all

Now add up all the numbers to the questions; your total score should fall somewhere between 13 and 65. To get your average score for managing your own feelings, just add the total of your score and divide by 13. If your total falls between 2 and 3.5, then you are fairly average in managing feelings. Below 2 means you are above average. Higher than 3.5 means there is progress to be made on getting a better grip on those emotions!

Now answer the following questions about managing other people's feelings:

1. **I am not satisfied with my work unless someone else praises it.**
   5 = Very true
   4 = Mostly true
   3 = Sometimes true
   2 = Mostly not true
   1 = Not true at all

2. **People who are emotional make me uncomfortable.**
   5 = Very true
   4 = Mostly true
   3 = Sometimes true
   2 = Mostly not true
   1 = Not true at all

3. **I need someone's push in order to get going.**
   5 = Very true
   4 = Mostly true
   3 = Sometimes true
   2 = Mostly not true
   1 = Not true at all

4. **It seems to me that people's reactions come out of the blue.**
   5 = Very true
   4 = Mostly true
   3 = Sometimes true
   2 = Mostly not true
   1 = Not true at all

5. **I panic when I have to face someone who is angry.**
   5 = Very true
   4 = Mostly true
   3 = Sometimes true
   2 = Mostly not true
   1 = Not true at all

6. **Some people make me feel bad about myself no matter what I do.**
   5 = Very true
   4 = Mostly true
   3 = Sometimes true
   2 = Mostly not true
   1 = Not true at all

7. **I pay attention and listen to others without jumping to conclusions.**
   1 = Very true
   2 = Mostly true
   3 = Sometimes true
   4 = Mostly not true
   5 = Not true at all

8. **I can receive feedback or criticism without becoming defensive.**
   1 = Very true
   2 = Mostly true
   3 = Sometimes true
   4 = Mostly not true
   5 = Not true at all

9. **I am sensitive to other people's emotions and moods.**
   1 = Very true
   2 = Mostly true
   3 = Sometimes true
   4 = Mostly not true
   5 = Not true at all

Use the same scoring suggestions as the first half of the quiz.

So how comfortable are you with the emotions of the people around you? How does your own self-awareness compare with your sensitivity to others? Are you better at listening and understanding other people's feelings than your own, or are you better able to interpret and cope with what's going on inside you but find other people a mystery? Ideally, of course, we do well on both.

Stress Relief _____

Increase self-awareness by taking your emotional temperature several times a day. Rate yourself on a 1 to 10 emotional scale, jot down your score, what was happening at the time, and how you responded to your feelings. Taking notice of your feelings in this way can diffuse stress because you are listening to your inner self rather than trying to ignore it.

Pitfalls on the Way to Graduation

Developing our emotional intelligence can be tricky. As with any skill, there are old habits to break and pitfalls to avoid. There are also a few myths about what it means to be more emotionally intelligent; for example, a high EQ means "I should always be able to control my moods" or it means "I should be more emotional." As we become more aware of, and respectful toward, our feelings, the following are some emotional potholes to watch out for.

Feelings are Faster—and Stronger—Than Thoughts

Our thoughts are always playing catch-up to our feelings. Consider this; the limbic system, the center of our emotions, operates at speeds of a thousandth of a second. In contrast, the rational mind, the neocortex, operates at about one tenth of a second. The helpful part of our emotional edge is that our feelings can help us react quickly in life-and-death situations, before we've even had time to think about the danger. The downside is that we can become ambushed by them.

Strategy: Pay attention. Feelings rarely jump right into shouting mode; they usually build up to it, so we have time to become aware of feelings as they build. When feelings first arise, ask yourself, "What is this feeling? What is it telling me?" Processing it in this way will usually put your feeling on hold while you process it—stopping it from snowballing out of control.

Feelings and Thoughts Can Get Tangled Up

Strong emotions can cloud our thinking; when we feel angry, we think angry thoughts and feel even angrier. Perhaps we conjure up angry memories from the past. If we go the next step, we then behave angrily—by shouting, slamming a door, or giving the target of our anger the "cold shoulder." Conversely, if we're emotionally repressed, we may find ourselves thinking critical or judgmental thoughts, or acting vengefully, without "feeling" angry.

Strategy: Don't make any important decisions (or pronouncements) when you have strong feelings. Instead, buy yourself some time and get some perspective on them; talk it out with a friend or write down your thoughts, feelings, and options (in three separate categories) in a diary or journal. In other words, listen to your feelings but only respond to them *once you understand them*. Only then can you make the best judgment about what to do.

> ### On the Cutting Edge
>
> Recent research suggests that self-control is like a muscle and, when we use it, we need some time to regain strength. Following a period of self-control in the face of tempting food, alcohol, or tobacco, people were found to have less physical stamina, reduced problem-solving ability, and less impulse control. But take heart; the more we use it, the stronger it becomes.

Self-Medication for Bad Feelings Can Backfire

Lots of things can temporarily chase away negative feelings; drugs, alcohol, food, sex, gambling ... The effects, however, are predictably short-lived, not only because we haven't listened to the original feelings, but now we've added other feelings (guilt, shame, embarrassment) on top of them. We may have even made our real circumstances worse. A short-term fix with a long-term price tag.

> **On the Cutting Edge**
>
> When we're anxious or stressed, we're less capable of giving ourselves the mental boost we need. If you can't see the bright side on your own, find someone who can! Talk to an upbeat friend or go to a place associated with fun, such as a park or a party.

Strategy: If you find yourself reaching for an outside solution to uncomfortable feelings, build in delays. Put that dress on hold or go for a walk before you eat that second piece of cake. Unless they're ingrained habits, most impulses will subside within 15 minutes if you remove yourself from the temptation and give yourself a breather.

Judging Our Feelings Doesn't Help

Although it's worthwhile to evaluate our emotions and decide how to respond to them, we shouldn't just dismiss feelings as being bad. The chances are that they will only raise the noise levels next time to get your attention.

> **Myth Buster**
>
> *"All uncomfortable emotions are bad."* Not true! Emotional discomfort can signal us to pay attention to real danger or threats. Research found that carefree individuals were more likely to ignore signs of cancer than those who showed moderate levels of anxiety.

What Worry Can Do

Worry is what happens when we transfer our fears into our head. Instead of *feeling* our anxiety, we channel it into anxious *thinking*. In fact, it's just another way to avoid our true feelings. More often than not, we wind up with the worst of both worlds; there's still that undercurrent of tension and our thoughts become less unproductive and irrational.

Because our thoughts play such a critical role in anxiety, we spend two whole chapters (7 and 8) learning how to recognize and remedy self-defeating or fear-producing thoughts. For now, start to explore some of the possible fears underneath those worries and investigate in what life events you have felt similarly. For instance, any parent is terrified at the thought of losing a child; however, a parent who lost his mom to cancer at age 14 may have a much harder time stopping the "what ifs" in response to his child's bout with the flu.

Fine-Tuning Our Alarm System

We human beings are wired with some pretty amazing alarm systems. Our emotions are one of them. Ideally, we listen to them when they beep, we investigate why they're beeping, and we decide whether we need to take action or wait and see.

Sounds pretty simple, but it's not. Some of us have an extremely sensitive alarm system. Some of us have learned, either through life experiences or early socialization, to either ignore our feelings or fight whatever triggers them. And, of course, if we have an anxiety disorder, our alarm system can malfunction. Anxiety can develop in response to an overly active alarm system, and anxiety can send our everyday emotions into overdrive.

This is particularly true when it comes to anger. The Greek philosopher Aristotle rightly said, "Anyone can become angry—that is easy. But to be angry with the right person, to the right degree, at the right time, for the right purpose, and in the right way; this is not easy." In the next chapter we explore the relationship between anger and anxiety, how we can use it as a motivator, and how we can prevent it from sabotaging ourselves and our relationships.

The Least You Need to Know

- ◆ Emotions are signals that our goals, needs, and wants are not being met.
- ◆ Babies come into the world wired with different levels of emotional sensitivity and with differences in how intensely they are likely to respond to the world around them. These can be heightened or suppressed by our environment.
- ◆ Emotional intelligence is the ability to effectively use your feelings and to be aware of, and positively influence, the feelings of others.
- ◆ Primary emotions are those that our ancestors relied on for survival—such as fear and anger. Secondary emotions, on the other hand, are a result of our interpretation of the primary-emotion triggering event.
- ◆ Anyone can boost his or her emotional competence. It starts with self-awareness or paying attention to early emotional signals.

Chapter 6

Making Friends with Anger

In This Chapter

- ◆ Discover the link between anxiety and anger
- ◆ Explore the effects of anger on you and your relationships
- ◆ Find out how to manage anger and aggression
- ◆ Learn some techniques for dispersing anger and frustration

How can I be angry at you? Let me count the ways. I can be afraid of my anger, stuffing it down and lying to you about how I really feel. I can deny my anger—to you and myself—and let it come out sideways, by "forgetting" to do things you ask me to or making snide remarks. I can blow in like a thunderstorm, releasing all my anger in a sudden, uncontrolled outburst. I can use my anger to feel in control by threatening or bullying you. I can use my anger as a mask to hide the fear, shame, and uncertainty I really feel.

In the preceding chapter, we talked about the purpose and value of our emotions. In this chapter, we focus on one particular—and often problematic—emotion: anger.

Why pick out this particular emotion for a whole chapter? Well, anger is a natural part of the human condition, but few of us are friends with it. Many of us spend too much time either trying to squash it or clean up the aftermath after letting it loose.

> ### Myth Buster _____
>
> *"Anger isn't a problem for me—I don't shout or get aggressive with people."* Think again! Anger can show itself through open confrontation, but also through quiet ways such as resentment or lack of communication or through veiled methods such as sarcasm.

Anxiety makes it that much harder to cope with anger; on the one hand, feeling afraid and on-edge can make us irritable and more likely to lash out when we get annoyed. And on the other, some of us may be so frightened by our anger that we literally panic at the thought of getting mad at the people we care about. Let's take a look at the many faces of anger and how we can use these feelings to make our relationships—and our lives—better.

Joined at the Hip

Bill is worried about his job. There have been layoffs recently, and there are rumors about more. He can't sleep; he wakes up at all hours thinking through every comment his boss made the previous day to see whether there's some sign that he's about to get the ax. He's becoming increasingly competitive with his colleagues and is snappy and defensive when anyone makes even constructive suggestions. As a result, his co-workers avoid him whenever possible, and his boss is giving him fewer assignments because she thinks Bill is under too much pressure. When his boss hands yet another plum assignment to a colleague, Bill loses his temper, calls his boss several names, and storms out of the office, slamming the door.

Michelle, on the other hand, has a different scenario. After the birth of her second child, she suffered a serious bout of post-partum panic disorder. With her internal alarm system already maxed out, she found it harder and harder to be patient with her 2 year old, who was naturally responding to a new sibling with temper tantrums and increased clinginess. Even her newborn's cries set her teeth on edge. The shame she felt over her anxiety made it that much more difficult to accept that she was *angry* that life was so tough right now. Instead of using these feelings as a signal to get the help and support she needed, she felt increasingly depressed.

Am I more or less irritable when I feel anxious? Your answer to this question is a valuable clue in understanding the link between your anxiety and your anger. For most of us, anxiety leaves us feeling sensitive and irritable—emotions which are foothills on the pathway to anger mountain. Recent research, for example, found that individuals with generalized anxiety disorder (GAD) are twice as likely to experience anger-related relationship problems in comparison to nonsufferers, with 7 out of 10 suffers confirming that their anxiety created relationship problems, from having arguments to problems with sexual intimacy.

Typically a person who suffers from anxiety can feel anger because they …

- ◆ Feel a lack or loss of control.
- ◆ Think it is not appropriate to discuss negative feelings with someone, allowing these feelings to build up.
- ◆ Feel frustrated about being anxious.
- ◆ Worry about rejection.

A feeling of losing control is usually at the heart of anger. Some people may, for example, be angry about anxiety itself, feeling that they are powerless to change their condition.

Take Cynthia's experience. Cynthia developed symptoms of obsessive-compulsive disorder (OCD) shortly after her mother died. She panicked if she didn't double-check the house alarm, and she repeatedly cleaned the kitchen and the bathroom. During this time, she was also starting a new relationship with a loving, considerate new boyfriend. There was no way, though, that she was going to tell him about her obsessions or compulsions; why risk ruining a good thing? Instead, she tried to control her impulses whenever he was around.

These efforts took more and more energy. Cynthia began to resent her new beau, blaming her lack of disclosure on him; couldn't he see that something was going wrong? How could he be so clueless? If he really cared about her, he would make more effort to really understand how she was feeling about the loss of her mother and what she was going through now.

What Is Anger?

Anger starts with frustration, the feeling we experience when we don't get what we want. Our goal, whether it's to be happy, feel good about ourselves, or get to work on time, has been threatened or blocked. Then we start looking for someone or something to blame.

If our frustration is strong, and the goal important enough, we feel anger. We experience an urge to take back some control. Sometimes our anger pays off; most wrongs that have been righted in the world have started with a deep sense of outrage that spawned an unwillingness to tolerate unacceptable or abusive circumstances. On a personal level, think of a time when your anger helped you protect yourself or get to a better place, perhaps by leaving a bullying boss or finally letting go of an energy-draining friend.

Anger can also be seductive. Call it getting our own back, settling the score, an eye for an eye. Being aggressive toward someone who has hurt our feelings or treated us unfairly makes us feel better. But it also makes us more likely to hurt that person even more later on. It can give a person who feels out of control a sense of being back in the driver's seat. When we're angry our pulse rises, breath quickens, blood flow speeds up the delivery of oxygen to the muscles, pain relieving chemicals are released, and the pupils dilate. Sound familiar? The list of physical responses looks very similar to what happens when a person is passionately making love!

No matter how seductive, though, letting loose or feeding anger can make matters worse. Anger can easily lead to aggression, the intentional act of harming someone. Experience has shown that it is very difficult to control our responses when we are aroused by anger. It can be a dangerous state of mind.

Myth Buster

"The best way to get rid of anger is to vent." No way! Research has shown that expressing hostility gets easier with practice, a fact that calls into question the wisdom of getting rid of aggression by beating up a punching bag. It's best to find out what triggers your anger and then develop strategies to keep those triggers from toppling you over the edge.

Stress Relief

Assertiveness is a planned, constructive use of anger that gets us what we want without losing control or damaging relationships.

Getting to Know Your Anger

For many of us, anger is a chameleon. Your experience and expression of it will depend upon your beliefs, your views of yourself, and the situation and source of your frustration. It may be easier to control anger at your boss than to suppress your frustration with a sibling, with whom you have little fear of losing.

So if anger can take on different forms, how can we detect it in ourselves? What clues do we look for? Here are some of the signs and symptoms that suggest our boiling pot is about to boil over.

Physical Cues	Behavioral Cues	Mental Cues
Clenching your jaws or grinding your teeth	Raising your voice, screaming, or crying	Exaggeration: "You always," "I never," "You idiot!"
Chronic shoulder and neck tightness	Losing your sense of humor or using sarcasm	Blaming: "It's not me—it's this damn system," "If only you were more reasonable"
Stomachaches or headaches	Hurtful: malicious gossip, stealing, trouble making, unforgiving, judgmental (holier-than-thou)	Characterizing: "Men are lazy," "Women are stupid," "Doctors are idiots"
Sweating, shaking, or trembling	Rebellious: antisocial behavior, defiance, refusal to talk or cooperate, jeopardizing plans, disruptive, distrustful, sulky	Suspicious: "If you really loved me you would …," "You cheated!"
Increased heart rate	Withdrawal: quiet remoteness, silence, lack of communication.	Fantasies of revenge or getting even

If it's too threatening to come in the front door with our anger, we can always come in the back. This indirect expression is often called *passive-aggression*, a pattern of sabotaging the source of our anger by doing the opposite of what he or she wanted. We drag our heels after making a verbal commitment, make constantly critical remarks, verbally agreeing ("sure, whatever") but inwardly remaining defiant, leading to being "sick" or frequently late or procrastinating. Although not as outwardly hostile, this way of expressing anger is just as real and, at times, just as damaging.

At the extreme, there's the perpetual victim, those who have developed the habit of accepting their powerlessness, resigning themselves to

On the Cutting Edge

Good friends aren't good at everything! Studies at the University of Virginia have shown that hidden anger is more easily noticed by mere acquaintances than close friends, perhaps because friends don't want the relationship to be threatened by anger or viewed in an unflattering light by their pal.

their emotional discomfort and pain. The flip side is the need to avoid responsibility and blame; after all, through no fault of their own, they have been mistreated. Those stuck in the victim role are hard to cheer up or help; they won't cooperate. They are more likely to sulk or lay a guilt trip on someone rather than get openly angry—and they reject the helpful suggestions offered them.

A Few "Anger Targets" and Their Scapegoats

When we feel angry, we may choose to avoid the risk of expressing anger at a person, by storing it up for someone with whom we feel "safer." For example, a person may have a bad day at the office and come home and argue with their spouse or partner. It has long been believed that repressed anger, hidden in the mind, will leak out—displaced—causing rifts with innocent scapegoats. In this sense, the scapegoat is in fact our closest confidant, the person with whom we feel safest, or who we feel unlikely to lose. So how do we avoid hurting the ones we love?

> **Anxiety Attack**
>
> Anger often masks our deepest fears. In an anger-making situation, ask yourself what deep fears it might be stirring in you.

Charging the Account: The Personal Cost of Anger

What about the personal cost? Anger can disrupt our mental health; in fact, many people believe that chronic depression can be caused by anger turned inward.

From a physical standpoint, chronic or frequent anger puts pressure on the cardiovascular system, leading some experts to claim that chronic anger kills. And the effects are even more serious for people who already have heart or blood-pressure problems. In addition, research has shown that when we are angry, the blood prepares to clot in anticipation of a wound. This can prove fatal to people who have narrowed or blocked arteries.

> **Stress Relief**
>
> It's not easy to see things clearly when we are emotionally charged. If it's not possible to walk away and take a "time out," take yourself away in your mind, using visual imagery to give yourself the mental space that will allow you to reapproach the problem with a wider perspective.

Human nature, it seems, designed our anger response for emergencies only, and not for our daily routine. From this perspective, anger is like a bank account with limited funds. We can't keep making withdrawals without going bankrupt; our physical system is simply not designed to be constantly angry.

Stress Relief _____

Giving people a "heads-up" when challenging emotions are wreaking havoc on your self-control can help minimize the relationship damage. For instance, an "I'm sorry I'm having a really bad day today, please excuse me if I'm rude" can prevent others from taking your remarks so personally. Similarly, giving others this option by saying, "I'm sorry you're having a hard time," rather than reacting to their grouchy behavior can take the sting out of the situation.

The Anger Balance

So what has anger ever done for us? A lot! The feelings of control and righteousness that come from anger can motivate us to challenge and change difficult interpersonal and social injustices. If handled correctly, our anger can motivate others to help us. Anger can help us overcome feelings of vulnerability and vent tensions and frustrations. It can provide the energy and resolve necessary to defend ourselves when we've been wronged or threatened.

On the other hand, obeying our angry feelings without questioning them or choosing from a range of carefully considered responses, will leave us with few friends and big heart problems. The aim is to allow anger to do its job and let the rational mind do its job. A negotiation between anger and rational thinking will give you the best balance available.

Anger is an emotion designed to alert us to something that *may* require attention. Don't make the mistake of assuming your anger is a key witness that *must* be listened to and obeyed. Instead, view it more as a weatherman, trying to see clearly through the fog.

Another way of looking at anger is to liken it to a crying baby. We should acknowledge the noise, and think carefully about the best way of proceeding, gently holding the baby and calming it down, while we check to see what the real problem is and tell ourselves, "It could be nothing, or there may be a real problem. Let's see."

On the Cutting Edge

Anger—in moderation—does have an upside. It seems anger can be better for us as an emotional response to short-term frustrations than fear. In studies, people who respond to challenging circumstances with fear suffer more stress as time passes than those who react with anger.

What Do I Do with These Feelings?

When it comes to anger, balancing the ability to recognize and respect, on the one hand, with corralling and controlling it, on the other, is no easy task. This becomes even more complex when we consider that anger management not only involves responding appropriately when anger rears its head, but structuring our everyday life so we up the odds that our background climate is calm. On a daily basis, lower your emotional temperature by …

- Dealing with irritating daily hassles so that they don't build up over time.

- Avoiding anger fuel like aggressive movies or TV, hostile or resentful company, or negative self-talk.

- Developing calming habits like meditation or yoga.

- Stopping destructive thoughts and fantasies. Don't go back over old ground.

- Keep a daily gratitude journal; write down five things you're grateful for each day.

- Reward yourself for staying in control of your anger and keep track of any negative consequences for outbursts.

- Use humor.

- Learn to monitor your thoughts to keep your rational mind from feeding your anger.

But what about the times when angry feelings rise up suddenly? What about unfair situations that need to be addressed, limits that need to be set, verbal abuse that needs to be stopped? In the next chapter, we look at the art of assertiveness and how we can express our anger in a way that will maximize the odds that we will get what we want.

For now, the trick is to give yourself enough space to keep your emotions from leading you down the path of self-destruction. The first step, of course, is becoming aware when your anger alarm goes off; the sooner you hear it, the less likely it will become so loud that it takes over. And the best way to do this is to start connecting the dots between what happens, your thoughts about it, how you feel about it, and what you do.

Anxiety Attack

Imagine that anger opens an options menu dropping down over your eyes, like on a computer screen. We can then select the best option in response to our feelings, rather than automatically using the defaults that our feelings urge us to do.

Anger Diary

An anger diary or journal is one of the best ways to keep track of our relationship with anger. To get the most bang for the buck, make daily entries into a diary that documents the following information for each anger-provoking event:

- What happened?

- What was provocative about the situation?

- What thoughts were going through your mind?

- On a scale of 0–10, how angry did you feel?

- What did you do?

- What were the consequences of your behavior on yourself and others?

- Were you already keyed up or stressed about something else? If so, what?

- What physical symptoms did you have?

- What was your first impulse? Did you want to flee from the pressure or throw something?

- How did you feel immediately after the episode?

- How do you feel about it now?

After recording this information for 14 days, look back through it and see what recurring themes or "triggers" make you mad. For many of us, the themes will look something like this:

- Other people doing or not doing what you expect them to do (spouse not listening, customer taking up too much of your time)

- Situational events that get in your way (repeated interruptions at work, traffic jams, car problems)

- People taking advantage of you (boss requesting too much from you, family member asking to borrow money again)

- Being angry and disappointed in yourself (acting in ways that you're ashamed of, failing to get an assignment or promotion)

Also look for anger-triggering thoughts that recur. You can recognize these particular thoughts because they will generally involve one or more of the following themes:

♦ The perception that you have been victimized or harmed.

♦ The belief that the person who provoked you meant you deliberate harm.

♦ The belief that the other person was wrong and that he or she should have behaved differently.

♦ The belief that life is "not fair," i.e., another person is getting more of his or her share in life while you are getting less than you deserve.

Use your anger diary to identify instances when you felt harm was done to you, why you thought the act was done deliberately, and why you thought that it was wrong.

Tracking your thoughts will also help you begin to see the underlying assumptions that guide those automatic thoughts. We discuss assumptions—and how to deal with them—in Chapter 9. For now, here are some examples of underlying assumptions that lead to angry thoughts and negative feelings:

♦ People don't care about me.

♦ People demand/expect too much of me.

♦ People try to take advantage of me.

♦ People think only of themselves.

♦ People don't treat me the way I should be treated.

♦ People don't give me the help I need.

♦ People try to control or manipulate me.

And here are some situations in which these assumptions are likely to occur:

♦ When stating a difference of opinion

♦ While receiving and expressing negative feelings

♦ While dealing with someone who is being uncooperative

♦ While talking about something that irritates or annoys you

♦ While disclosing sensitive information

♦ When saying "no" or standing up for yourself

- ◆ While responding to undeserved criticism
- ◆ When asking for cooperation

Most people find a few thoughts that frequently trigger their anger. Look for situations that trigger your anger and see whether you can't identify the particular set of triggering thoughts that really send you over the edge.

The purpose of your diary is to help you identify patterns of behavior and specific recurring elements that really "push your buttons." The more accurately you can observe your feelings and behaviors and the more detailed your anger diary, the more likely you will be able to identify anger triggers and how you react to them. Of course, the bigger goal is to use this insight so that we can plan more productive strategies for responding to these feelings; in other words, so we can put a "safety" on those anger triggers.

Put a Safety on That Trigger

As you've discovered, anger-triggering thoughts occur automatically and almost instantaneously. It takes some conscious work to identify them and to substitute something more to your liking.

For example, you ask your spouse how his day went and he snaps at you. It's hard to step back and take notice of your physical reaction when your first impulse is to pull his hair out. However, by taking a deep breathe and noticing your stress symptoms, it gives you some perspective on the situation and allows you to look at the situation more objectively rather than going with your first impulse to attack. Instead of automatically assuming your husband is deliberately torturing you (which might be your first thought), you can consider all the possible explanations for his outburst; perhaps he had a bad day, maybe he's got some leftovers from the argument you had this morning, and so on. It doesn't mean you excuse his behavior or justify his actions; considering all the possibilities just gives you the freedom to seek more information— and take care of yourself in the process—before reacting.

In this chapter, we have examined the emotion of anger, what it is, how it affects us, and what we can do about it. For better or worse, anger is a powerful motivator; at its best it can help eliminate a sense of vulnerability and motivate us to take much-needed action. In the next chapter, we take a look at two "actions" that are often paired— procrastination and assertiveness—and how we can get a move on to make our lives better.

The Least You Need to Know

◆ Anger is a powerful motivator that we can use to our benefit or to our detriment.

◆ Anxiety can make it harder to control our anger, and being afraid of our anger can make us anxious.

◆ How we experience—and express—our anger is a combination of our inborn temperament and what we've learned.

◆ Effective anger management requires us to investigate our triggers and how we respond to them.

◆ Daily monitoring of our frustration level can be a powerful tool in anger management.

Chapter 7

Speak Up and Move On!

In This Chapter

- ◆ Find how fear of conflict feeds procrastination
- ◆ Discover the link between procrastination and anxiety
- ◆ Learn how to stand up for yourself
- ◆ See how shrinking your to-do list can shrink your stress

Some of us anxious folks are so ultra-responsible you wouldn't think we'd have any trouble getting things done. Often, though, we're too good at getting *other people's* things done. I'm not about to suggest that you ditch everyone in your life and start over. But I am suggesting that you learn to act assertively when faced with other people's agendas so that you can move forward with your own life.

In this chapter, we take a look at conflict avoidance and procrastination and the role they can play in aggravating anxiety. We also focus on how we can be more proactive and assertive, reducing the risk that last-minute emergencies (either self-created or proclaimed by our crisis-riddled neighbor) will disrupt our peace and sabotage our priorities.

Doing Good—and Doing Yourself In

How often have you found yourself in one of these situations?

◆ You've just agreed to baby-sit your niece's children—again—even though you have a stressful work project due this Friday.

◆ Your neighbor drops in uninvited several times a week and spends hours telling you her personal problems. As a result, you're behind in your writing deadline.

◆ Your husband is going through a rough patch at work and constantly takes his frustrations out on you by being rude, picking fights, or silently fuming. Even though you know it has to be done, you find yourself "dragging your feet" when he asks you to finish paying the bills.

What themes emerge when you look at the above scenarios? Procrastination? Lack of assertiveness? Resentment? By not saying "no" to your niece, your work project is now delayed. If you were able to set limits with your neighbor, you'd send her on her way—maybe with the phone number of a good therapist!—and get your writing done. If you refused to be your husband's emotional garbage disposal, you might be more motivated to get those bills paid.

Isn't This a Book About Anxiety?

All three scenarios show how we can avoid conflict with others at the expense of getting our own needs met. However, the more we do that, the more anxious (and angry) we are likely to feel. The more anxious we feel, the more we are likely to put challenging or stressful things off, and the more chaos we invite into our lives to justify putting things off.

Of course, things do happen that are beyond our control. We can learn, however, to be discriminating about what is and is not our responsibility. Passivity and procrastination do not cause anxiety disorders. In fact, we can think of them as misguided attempts to manage our anxiety by avoiding unpleasant confrontations or tasks. However, in the long run, procrastination, whether in setting limits because we don't want to deal with conflict or in tackling a must-do, adds to our stress level. If procrastination or conflict avoidance becomes a habit, we can aggravate any anxiety we already have.

Crossing off every item on your to-do list won't cure an anxiety disorder—but it'll sure lighten your stress load. And sometimes, remedying bad habits that can lead to worry and stress can ultimately help us manage our anxiety.

Just Say "Yes!" (to Yourself)

If you've ever "put up" with a situation until you "blew up," you know what it's like to go from passive to aggressive faster than the speed of light. Many of us who declare our limits by losing our cool learn the wrong lesson. Either we feel so guilty about losing it that we try even harder not to say anything the next time, or we feel so much better that we give ourselves permission to do it again.

It is possible, though, to say "no" before we reach the point of no return. In fact, saying "no" with calm and confidence is a sign of healthy assertiveness. It's not an insult or a rejection. It's just a piece of information.

"Is it raining outside?" "No."

"Will you baby-sit for me today?" "No."

Can you imagine being able to say "no" without tagging on a litany of excuses? It's hard. And yet, in the English language, the word *no* makes up a complete sentence. So why does "no" seem mean, selfish, or incomplete, when it's really the right answer?

One reason is simply that many of us were taught *not* to say "no." When a teacher or parent asked you to do something, "no" wasn't really an option. How would your third-grade teacher have responded if you'd politely declined her request for you to write an answer on the chalkboard? The normal socialization process encouraged us to be "nice" and accept birthday party invitations from kids we didn't like.

In other words, we learned that it's not okay to say "no" just because we don't want to do something. As an adult, all this early learning can make it difficult to tell the difference between "have-to's" and "want-to's." It can also lead us to the main reason that we have trouble with saying "no": fear.

There are the "little" fears, of course. There are fears of being judged selfish, lazy, or incompetent. There's the fear of hurting someone's feelings. There's the fear that the other person won't be able to cope if we say "no."

But all of these fears and more are just mini-versions of the giant fear of abandonment. "If I say no to my friend's request, she won't like me any more." "If I tell my husband I need more help with the kids, he'll be mad at me." "If I talk to my boss about the work overload I'm experiencing and ask him to prioritize, he'll think I can't handle the pressure."

Myth Buster _____

"Being assertive is about being selfish." Wrong! Being assertive is about being honest. Assertiveness is about acknowledging *all* opinions as important. It conveys the message "I matter, and you do, too."

More often than not, there is no real substance to this fear. Our friend may prefer that we say "yes," but it probably isn't going to jeopardize our relationship. People may sometimes try to control us with their disapproval; if we can learn to see this for what it is, however, it loses its power. And consider the likely consequences of *not* talking to your boss about too much work—missed deadlines, sloppy work, focusing on the wrong assignment.

It's More Than Saying "No"

The ability to say "no" gracefully is a skill that can be easily learned, but true assertiveness comes as much before we open our mouths as when we do. It's first and foremost an attitude, a stance toward oneself and the outside world that says "I matter, and you do, too."

For example, let's pretend that one of your pet peeves is being late. You believe it's disrespectful to be late because it communicates to the other person that you don't value his or her time. In your mind, timeliness is linked to trust; you want to be able to count on it when a person says, "I'll meet you there at 7." Occasional glitches aside, if someone is frequently late, you think it suggests a lack of discipline.

Here's the problem. You've just fallen head over heels over Mr. Wonderful-but-Laid-Back. Because you're so crazy about him, you try your best to overlook the fact that he's half an hour late for every date you make. He always calls if he promised to, but it might not be *when* he said he would. Try as you might, you're starting to realize that this quirk or habit of his is becoming a *big deal* to you.

An assertive attitude starts from the perspective that you both have legitimate viewpoints, that your new beau might not have the same beliefs about time, and you have the right to express your feelings and ask for what you want.

An assertive attitude would include the following:

◆ Confidence that you can handle conflict. ("Resolving this issue will prevent me from feeling resentful.")

◆ A positive, optimistic outlook. ("I think we can figure out a way to improve this situation.")

◆ Clarity about what you need or want. ("It's important to me to be on time.")

◆ Calm communication without attacking the other person or giving in. ("I hear you telling me to 'lighten up.' I realize being on time may not be as important to you.")

◆ Negotiation, if it turns out the two of you want different things. ("I can see where you might be running a few minutes late. I'll tell you what; if you're not here by 6:45, I'll meet you at the movie theater.")

◆ Sticking to clear boundaries. ("If you're not ready to leave by 7:30, I'll go ahead and see you when you get there.")

In all of these examples, nonverbal communication is at least as important as what you say. Tone of voice and body language make a difference in how your words are received. An open, relaxed stance and a calm, low voice convey confidence and respect.

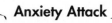

Anxiety Attack

Some research suggests that women, in particular, are likely to feel anxious when they have to say "no" because it threatens our need to stay connected by pleasing others. However, saying "yes" when we want to say "no" is dishonest and ultimately disconnects us from other people and ourselves.

No Passive-Aggressive Play Allowed

When we don't trust ourselves to directly ask for what we want, it's tempting to do it in sneakier ways. Giving our mom the "silent treatment." Sulking when our spouse forgets our anniversary. Instead of talking to our boss about our excessive workload, we let it pile up on our desk and hope she'll notice we have too much to do. These are all ways of trying to communicate indirectly and regain a sense of control. The problem is that our communication can be easily misinterpreted or overlooked or, worse, be used as justification for someone to continue treating us unfairly.

Assertiveness, by contrast, is not about controlling people or situations. Truly assertive people give others the same rights they give themselves. They are willing to communicate what they want and leave other people free to say yes or no. If the needs of other people don't mesh with their own, assertive people don't panic or fume.

Stress Relief

Research shows that, in business, 20 percent of success depends on technical skill and 80 percent depends on an adaptive, positive personality.

They are willing to negotiate toward a solution that best meets everybody's needs. This creates a relationship and environment that invites creative solutions and allows everyone to get their needs met.

Get Some Skills!

When we realize that assertiveness is as good for the people we care about as it is for ourselves, we can choose to let go of the false beliefs and fears holding us back and adopt an assertive approach to life. When we make that commitment, it's time to take an honest look at where our relationships are right now and what we can expect as we move up the assertiveness ladder.

Our first step—painful as it may be—is taking responsibility for the way other people are treating us. If your life is full of people who impose on you, it's because *you've been giving them the results they want.* (Ouch!) And they may not like it when you decide to change the rules of the game.

In fact, the rewards for saying "no" and sticking to it are often delayed. That is, people who've gotten what they want because of our lack of assertiveness aren't likely to jump for joy when we decide to speak up. It's pretty common for people to initially react with anger and disbelief—and do *more* of whatever has worked in the past. For example, a spouse who has used guilt to get you to back down is likely to use more guilt when you start to set limits. That's a normal reaction from anyone who is facing a new set of rules; we don't have to judge this and we certainly don't want to give in to it.

However, over time you'll reap many rewards for asking for what you want and setting limits about what you don't. People will respect you more. Those who truly care about you will adjust. If someone leaves, then so be it; they didn't care about you, they just cared about what they were getting from you.

In addition to anticipating some resistance, we can also bone up on how to say "no" with grace and confidence. Here are some of my favorite guidelines.

How to "Just Say No"

Say, "No." Say, "I'm sorry, I can't." Say, "No, thank you." But however you say it, don't elaborate. Get comfortable with the word *no* through practice and use it as a complete sentence whenever you can. Don't volunteer a reason, especially when dealing with people who chronically impose on you. To these folks, offering a reason is like raising a target for them to shoot down.

If it's too uncomfortable not to give a reason, just give one deal-killer rather than a bunch of little ones that can water down your resolve. "I have other plans" and "I've decided not to take any more projects until June" are examples. "I don't want to" is another one; no one can logically argue that one away.

When dealing with an especially persistent person with whom you don't have an ongoing relationship (for example, a telemarketer who keeps calling or an overly enthusiastic salesperson), adopt the Broken-Record Technique. In a calm and pleasant tone, keep repeating what you have already said. It won't take long for them to realize they've hit a dead end.

Let them have their feelings. People are allowed to be disappointed and frustrated when you tell them "no." You are not responsible for making them feel better; don't even try.

When the Ball Is in Your Court

What if *you're* the one asking for something? The first step is to prepare yourself mentally. Remember your assertive stance: "I matter, and you do, too." You have every right to ask for what you want, and the other people have every right to answer however they please.

Before you speak up, be very clear in your own mind about the difference between how you feel and what you want. These are not the same things. For instance, I might feel overwhelmed by all the things I have to do today. However, if I just talk about my feelings, I may get sympathy but no offer of assistance. On the other hand, if I'm specific about what kind of relief I need, I might get some real help. Think about

how differently you might respond to my venting ("I'm so stressed about all the kids' Valentine's parties") versus my request ("Will you go to one of the kids' parties tomorrow? I've got a proposal that needs to be out by the end of business Wednesday.")

If the attitude is right but you still aren't sure about the skill part, practice with a friend or in front of a mirror. You can use the mirror to practice relaxed, confident body language. And your friend can help you create a realistic conversation. In this conversation …

> **Stress Relief**
>
> Post a list of your strengths in a prominent place. Organize them into three categories: *I have* (strong relationships, structure at home, role models); *I am* (a hopeful person, a caring person, proud of myself); and *I can* (ask for help when I need it, solve problems). These words can constantly remind you that you have what it takes.

◆ State your problem and what you need from the other person. ("I'm distressed because of X, and I would like you to do Y to help me solve that problem.")

◆ Deal effectively with distracting responses. ("If you'd like for me to take out the trash more often, I'm happy to talk about that later. Right now, I need to address X. Are you willing to do Y?")

◆ If you meet objections, listen to the other person's point of view with respect. See whether you can work out a solution that works for both of you.

◆ Stay focused on clear, honest communication.

◆ Agree to get the help of a third party if the two of you can't come to a happy solution.

◆ If what you need to ask for is non-negotiable (for example, fidelity, nonviolence, or fair pay), be polite but clear about what the consequences are if the need is not met. Say what you mean, and mean what you say.

Then There's Preemptive Assertiveness—Delegation

Many of us with anxiety sufferers have a grandé-sized sense of responsibility. (We talk more about anxiety-prone personality traits in Chapter 10.) No one can do it better than we can. We've got to oversee everything to make sure it's done right. Why delegate when we'd wind up worrying so much about it anyway that we might as well just do it ourselves?

> **Stress Relief** _____
>
> *"We are what we read?"* True or not, it sure doesn't hurt to borrow courage and inspiration by reading biographies about people who've faced obstacles and been successful.

Because we wind up shooting ourselves in the foot. If we feel compelled to do everything ourselves, our to-do list will always be endless. Dangling to-dos create stress and worry, which can exacerbate anxiety. With some advanced preparation, we can delegate tasks such that we don't wind up obsessing endlessly about how well it's getting done.

The following guidelines can be useful in knowing when, to whom, and how to delegate effectively—and peacefully:

◆ **Develop some delegation "rules of thumb."** *Don't* delegate tasks that are enjoyable and meaningful to you. *Do* farm out tasks that someone else can do better, that you dislike the most, or are overly time-consuming in comparison to the value they bring you.

- **Choose and train the right person.** A 7 year old is probably not capable of successfully cleaning the bathroom; most 11 year olds can. Skills and abilities also vary with adults; even if it's a task any large animal could do, take nothing for granted and spend the up-front time interviewing and training.

- **Alleviate worries (and glitches) by creating feedback loops.** Set mini-deadlines if the situation warrants. Create a proactive system for handling the unexpected; for example, put the responsibility on the delegate to come to you with any problems or questions well before the agreed-upon deadline.

- **Delegate the authority, not the methods.** If your husband agrees to comb your daughter's hair, keep your mouth shut if it's not in a French twist. Focus on the bigger goal (getting help from your spouse) rather than the immediate out-come (a Halloweenesque hairdo). Otherwise the "you're not happy with how I do it anyway" excuse can rear its ugly head.

You can't—and wouldn't want to—delegate everything. When you're first starting out, delegate to the edge of your comfort level and no further. When you gain confidence in your ability to manage tasks—rather than always do them—you'll feel freer to tackle more important items. Such as the activities that you've been procrastinating on.

A High-Priced Strategy

Procrastination isn't a bad word. It's simply the act of putting off doing something until later. Sometimes procrastination is appropriate and even valuable; for example, you have a job to do that will take a couple of hours, and you're starving. Putting off work until after you've eaten is probably the best decision, especially if you want to think clearly while you work.

The reason "procrastination" has a bad rep is because it can become a way to avoid any task that is stressful or anxiety inducing. We need to prepare for that business talk, but just the thought of getting up in front of those people gives us the heebie-jeebies. So instead of pre-paring extra hard for it—which would be a great anxiety-relieving strategy—we avoid even the

> **On the Cutting Edge**
>
> Researchers studied the effects of procrastination on health and stress levels among college students. Although those who procrastinated began the semester with lower stress levels than nonprocrastinators, they ended up with worse stress levels and health by the end. Also procrastinators' overall stress levels and health rated worse than nonprocrastinators'.

thought of it. As time gets closer, and we're still unprepared, our anxiety escalates. And we've still got to give that darn speech!

Procrastinators can look different on the surface. There is the Scarlett O'Hara type, who seems brave and confident, but always says, "I'll think about that tomorrow," when faced with anything unpleasant. Then there is the type of procrastinator who seems more timid and prone to put off tasks due to low self-esteem or self-doubt.

In fact, both types of procrastination are often rooted in fear, which can manifest in several ways. We may …

◆ **Fear failure.** This can be paralyzing for anyone with an anxiety disorder. It's so easy to believe that failing at even a small task would be devastating. "If I fail at this, I could lose my job, spouse, friends …."

◆ **Fear success.** For those of us prone to anxiety, success just ups the ante. "What if they expect me to do it right every time?" "What if I do so well I get a promotion and I don't like that job as much as I like this one?"

◆ **Fear imperfection.** Your motto might be "If something's worth doing, it's worth doing perfectly." The problem with that is that perfectionism is a tyrant that won't allow you to let go of a task after you start. In an effort to avoid the trap of perfection, you avoid the task.

◆ **Fear being overwhelmed or trapped.** There's nothing like seeing the entire list of semester assignments on the first day of class to get the old adrenaline flowing. Anxiety can make it difficult to see that you can break down large tasks into smaller, easily managed ones. As a result, you wind up thinking you have to swallow the elephant whole rather than taking it one bite at a time.

◆ **Fear abandonment or isolation.** Getting things done can mean giving up our hypervigilant attention to people and relationships, and feeling disconnected from others raises our anxiety level.

◆ **Fear being controlled by someone else.** If you resent someone's authority over you, you may find it hard to get going on projects assigned to you. Unfortunately, you only punish yourself by procrastinating.

> **Myth Buster**
>
> *"When I feel better, I'll do it."* Nine times out of ten, our feelings change *after* we take action, not before. You may need to take very small steps, but don't let that keep you from taking any steps at all.

Face the Music by Writing It Down

Fortunately, some powerful tools can help us overcome procrastination and address the fears underneath. Start by taking inventory of all the undone tasks and unresolved matters that clutter your mind and stress you out. This is not a to-do list! This is just an exercise in self-exploration.

Start with a piece of paper split into two columns with the following headings:

<u>Action</u>   <u>Anxiety</u>

On the left, list every task that needs doing or that you find yourself putting off. Write down small tasks such as household errands as well as big goals you've always had but never accomplished. Just get it all down on paper and out of your head.

On the right, across from each task, write down any obstacles, fears, worries, or other negative stuff that come up. For instance, maybe you've promised to do something for someone you feel resentful toward; the promised action would be on the left and the anger and resentment would be on the right.

Nothing should be considered off limits. Your procrastination may have nothing to do with the actual task, so just write what comes to mind. When you finish, look for any patterns that emerge. Do you put off things that you're afraid of? Angry about? Ambivalent toward? As you become acquainted with the thoughts and feelings that feed your procrastination, you can choose the most workable methods for dealing with it.

Most often, these strategies involve better use of our mental space or wiser use of our time.

Mental Space: Overcoming the Fear Factor

Perhaps as you perused your list you noticed that your feelings get in the way of your accomplishments. Every time you sit down to do the put-off task, you feel anxious and nervous and wind up finding reasons to delay it again. The following tips are some ways we can create "space" between ourselves and our anxiety symptoms:

◆ **Do calming activities first.** We discuss specific relaxation techniques in the self-help chapters in the next section. For now, though, try listening to calming music or take a leisurely walk before you tackle that daunting task.

◆ **Give yourself an "out" that allows you to stay "in."** Give yourself as much control over the process as possible but don't let yourself quit. For example, if you feel anxious, take a break and focus on your breathing; inhale deeply while counting five heartbeats, and then exhale as you count five more. Make deals with yourself; work on it for 15 minutes, and then stop for a little while.

Stress Relief _____

Dr. Steven Covey's *The Seven Habits of Highly Effective People* is still the best book I've read in terms of "putting first things first." Consider checking it out—or rereading it if it's been a while.

◆ **Bookend the scary stuff.** When you feel afraid to face a task alone, call up a friend right before you do it. Tell her what you're about to do and that you'll call her right after you do it. You'll get support and feel more accountable at the same time.

Time, Precious Time

"Dr. J, you're not living in the real world. It's not mental space I need, it's an extra hour in the day." If those were your thoughts reading the above section, take heart. There's time-management help, too!

Specifically, here are some logistical tools that can help you plow your way through a confusing, undifferentiated mass of to-dos. Here are some logistical tools that can help you make time your ally, not your tormentor. Use only those tips that seem doable. If a system is too complicated, it's difficult to stick with it.

◆ **Prioritize your to-do list.** List items either by their importance or the date they are due.

◆ **Jog your memory.** Get yourself the right "tickler" system, such as a calendar that has room for notes, a planner, or a simple spiral notebook. Your tasks will go into the calendar.

◆ **Get a quick fix.** Schedule one or two quick tasks to be done every day. That will give you some relief and get the ball rolling.

◆ **Be disciplined.** Tackle one piece of a larger task each day. If you're trying to plow through the closet from Hades, schedule 30 minutes a day to chip away at it, preferably at the same time each day. Be just as diligent about not overdoing it as you are about sticking to your commitment. If we start out with too much of a bang, we can fizzle out or become overwhelmed before we get to the meat of the task at hand.

◆ **Schedule breaks.** Make room for pleasurable activities such as hobbies or outings with friends. Schedule them as seriously as you would any other item; these daily uplifts are what helps us stay balanced and focused.

◆ **Under-schedule.** Leave spaces in your calendar for the unexpected. When asked to do something next week, ask for a day to think about it. Assume you will be as busy next week as you are this week.

On the surface, procrastination and the lack of assertiveness seem like two unrelated problems. However, as we've seen throughout this chapter, they both involve avoidance, either of conflict or of tasks. They also both have a complicated relationship with anxiety; fears can underlie passivity or procrastination and either of them can cause us to feel anxious. We've also talked about how we can "get a move on" to stand up for our rights and get the job done.

 **Anxiety Attack**

If you find yourself automatically saying "yes" to every request (and later regretting it), start saying, "Let me think about it and get back to you." This delay will buy you some time to evaluate whether the task or activity is really in your best interest.

But what if the problem can't be dealt with out there? What if our struggle is internal, in the form of negative thoughts or chronic worries? In the next chapter, we take a look at how we can take control of our thoughts and use them to soothe—rather than feed—our anxiety.

The Least You Need to Know

◆ Conflict avoidance fuels procrastination by overloading our schedules and tempting us to use others as an excuse for putting things off.

◆ Procrastination and interpersonal passivity are often used to avoid discomfort but actually make us more anxious in the long run.

◆ Assertiveness is both an attitude and a skill. It carries the message "I matter, and you do, too."

◆ Delegation is a way to be responsible without getting overwhelmed.

◆ Procrastination can be a result of mental barriers or poorly used time.

◆ Mental aids in the war against procrastination can include getting support and encouraging others to hold us accountable; time boosters can include prioritization, under-scheduling, and balanced to-do lists.

Part

Taming Those Alarming Ideas

Behind every painful emotion is a dysfunctional thought. We generalized-anxiety sufferers, in particular, are susceptible to thinking errors that magnify uncomfortable feelings and physical sensations.

This section explores the iceberg of cognition, starting with the negative automatic thoughts that surface every day and moving deeper to uncover, and correct, dysfunctional core beliefs. Finally, we look at the relationship between anxiety disorders and personality traits, detailing how we can embrace our natural temperament and still relinquish self-defeating habits.

Chapter 8

Tackling the "What If" Syndrome

In This Chapter

- ◆ Discover how actively we produce our inner dialogue
- ◆ Investigate the relationship between thoughts and feelings
- ◆ Discover how to correct the thinking errors that fuel anxiety
- ◆ Learn how to make pessimism work in your favor

My aunt stockpiled water and canned goods in what she called a "survival room." The husband of a friend of mine withdrew all of his money from the bank, convinced that the Y2K bug would wreak havoc on his finances. Others greeted the new millennium with wild abandon, seeing it as a fresh start and the dawn of a new age.

How did *you* ring in the year 2000? At 11:59 P.M. on December 31, 1999, many of us held our breath as the culmination of months of fear mongering and uncertainty about the Y2K computer bug were about to come to an end. Many people had talked themselves—and each other—into a state of real anxiety about the world as we know it suddenly ending (or at least our control over it suddenly vanishing). In reality, we didn't know exactly what would happen. And yet in response to the same circumstances, some people prepared for the worst-case scenario while others acted as if nothing was happening.

Everyday life can be like this, too. Some of us seem to have an inner monologue stuck on alert, constantly monitoring our environment for threat and having "what if" conversations in response to the slightest worry. Without question, being prepared for trouble can be helpful. However, when our inner voice is too quick to jump to conclusions, we can find ourselves plummeting deeper and deeper into an anxious state of mind. Small fears can become huge catastrophes merely in response to what we tell ourselves.

In this chapter, we discuss the relationship between our thoughts and our feelings. Specifically, we investigate thinking styles that have a calming effect as well as some common thinking styles that magnify anxiety. And you'll find out how to escape when the what-if trap grabs you.

I Think, Therefore I Am

In many ways, it's hard to think about thoughts. By the time we're adults, they happen so automatically that they seem to be a central part of who we are. How often do you think of yourself as the maestro of your mental concerto? If you're like most of us, we often feel more like an audience member watching an internal dialogue.

In reality, though, we are the directors of our internal play. We write the script and develop the characters. More and more, psychologists consider thoughts to be mental behaviors, perhaps to emphasize how actively we participate in them and how much we can change them. Just as we can quit a bad habit such as smoking or overeating, we can get rid of self-defeating or counterproductive mental habits.

But how can we tell whether a thought is "bad" for us? Often our feelings provide the clues. For example, the pre-millennium doomsayers may have had thoughts such as "The end is near, and only the prepared will survive. Water and food supplies will collapse. Financial chaos will make it impossible to get access to your money or to buy needed supplies." If these beliefs prompted us to make a few extra shopping trips or withdrawals from our ATM, no harm done. On the other hand, if these thoughts resulted in sleepless nights and crippling anxiety, perhaps we were making a mountain out of what turned out to be a molehill.

Many anxiety sufferers have a habit of making mountains out of molehills, getting so caught up in what ifs that we lose the ability to enjoy the here and now. For example, pretend that you just found out that you didn't get accepted to your number-one college choice. Here's your reaction: "Oh, my god. I didn't get into NYU. This is *terrible!*

I was sure I would be accepted—the admissions director told me I was just the kind of student she was looking for! What if I don't get into *any* of the colleges I applied to? I bet I won't. I should have applied to more! Why was I so lazy?"

As you can see, negative thinking can take hold and snowball. What starts as a simple disappointment can turn into a cascade of worry and defeating ideas. Imagine the anxiety and panic we might feel—rather than the normal sadness or disappointment—if we view one incident as a sign that all is lost or the future is doomed. Our thoughts have a profound effect on our anxiety.

Stress Relief

Keep a journal! Research shows that people who write down their anxieties in a journal are healthier and better able to cope with stresses. As an experiment, write for 20 minutes a day for 4 consecutive days about your deepest thoughts and feelings concerning the most stressful aspects of your life.

Thinking Glitches That Cause Trouble

In the above example, we turned disappointment over one college's rejection into worry and fear by imagining the worst-case scenario—that we might not get accepted by *any* college. This is an example of a *cognitive distortion*, a faulty thinking pattern that distorts the reality of a situation. Cognitive distortions are logical but not rational. They can also create a lot of unnecessary anxiety and worry. In fact, by learning to identify the distortions or mistakes in our thinking process, we can combat anxiety by recognizing that what we are afraid of is unlikely and the reality is not that bad.

For example, you have to give a presentation to a group of potential customers next week. You're presenting on a new product line, so the content of your talk is new to you. Cognitive distortions could make your life miserable before ("I'm not a good presenter, I know I'll bomb this"), during ("Look at that guy's frown; I know he thinks I'm an idiot"), and after ("I can't believe I forget to show that last slide"). And the irony is that our anxiety or stress level may have no connection to the reality of the situation.

Almost everyone automatically generates cognitive distortions at times. They are particularly rampant in those of us who struggle with anxiety. On the bright side, they're so prevalent that psychologists have made tremendous strides in identifying them and devising ways to overcome them. We briefly covered some of these in Chapter 3; let's take a closer look at how we can prevent them for impacting us on a daily basis. Some of the most common cognitive distortions are as follows:

- **Catastrophic thinking** happens when we turn a molehill into a mountain. Individuals with panic attacks often believe they are dying, having a heart attack, or going "crazy." Although panic symptoms *feel* dangerous, they aren't dangerous. *Believing* they're dangerous, though, makes them a lot worse.

- **Black/white thinking** is when we think thoughts such as "If I'm not perfectly safe and totally free from harm, then I'm in utter danger and completely vulnerable to harm." This kind of thinking operates in extremes; it's all or nothing. In reality, the world is all about shades of gray.

- **Disqualifying the positive** happens when we reject the positive experiences we've had (they don't count) or ignore the good feedback we get. "He only said I did a good job on that presentation because he feels sorry for me."

- **Emotional reasoning** happens when you decide that what you feel must really reflect reality. "I feel like I'm going to crack up!" means I'm really out of my mind. Reality: feeling like a failure does not make us one.

- **Fortune telling** happens when you act as if your worst fears will certainly come true. "I just know I'll have a panic attack while I'm driving—I'll have a wreck and maybe kill someone. So I don't drive." Reality check: plenty of people drive while they're anxious, and panic attacks don't usually cause wrecks.

- **Labeling** is a form of all-or-nothing thinking applied to ourselves. It occurs when we give a global label to ourselves ("I'm a failure!") rather than seeing something as a single event. ("Well, I blew that one, but I'll do better next time.")

- **Mind reading** is when we assume that others are reacting negatively to us—even when we have no evidence. ("Everyone can see how nervous I am at this party.")

- **Magnification/minimization** happens when we distort the significance of particular events. For example, we focus on all our minor mistakes but ignore our accomplishments/successes.

- **Overgeneralization** happens when one negative event means that nothing will go well. ("I had another panic attack. I'll never get better.")

- **Personalization** means relating negative events to oneself even when there is no basis. For example, the CEO doesn't speak to us when we encounter her in the hall, and we automatically interpret this as a lack of respect. In reality, she may have been preoccupied about something else or not felt well.

- **"Should" statements** are when we tell ourselves that things should be the way we hoped or expected them to be rather than accepting what is. ("I shouldn't feel so anxious and afraid; no one else feels this way." "I shouldn't have made so many mistakes.")

Having conversations with ourselves is pretty normal; in fact, we all do it. Where we start to interfere with our lives is when we let these conversations take on a life of their own. If we let our thoughts take on an unhealthy attitude, one that is working against us rather than for us, it's time to turn our internal conversation back to reality rather than let it engage in a running, negative commentary.

Warning! Restructuring Ahead!

So how do we catch those negative thoughts and turn them around? Obviously, we have to start paying attention to the thoughts that fly around in our head. Thought awareness is the first step in managing negative thoughts: you cannot manage thoughts that you are unaware of.

The words that we use to talk to ourselves can provide valuable clues about how productive—or not—our thinking is. For example, "what if?" is often the first sign that we are making negative predictions about the future. One what-if thought can quickly lead to another, resulting in a spiral of worry. Other examples of negative thoughts involve putting ourselves down, doubting ourselves, expecting failure, or criticizing our mistakes. The accompanying self-talk involves phrases such as *you should, you never,* or *you always.* Negative thinking damages confidence, harms performance, and paralyzes mental skills.

Catching negative thoughts takes conscious effort. In fact, in the beginning, it helps to write them down. By logging our negative thoughts for a reasonable period of time, we can start to identify negative thinking patterns. This process also slows down automatic thoughts and allows us to take the role of observer (or investigator) rather than participant. It can also help us see the link between our moods and our thoughts; in fact, when we start tracking our negative thoughts, we may initially start with "bad" feelings and work our way backward. It can be surprising to find that negative thoughts lead to upsetting feelings rather than the other way around.

When we start analyzing and understanding our counterproductive thoughts and their sources, the real work begins. We have to put them "on trial," gathering evidence that both supports and disputes these thoughts. Sara, for example, lost her father to cancer when she was 10. As an adult, she is terrified of getting sick; whenever she has *any* physical symptoms, she finds her thoughts spinning out of control. "I feel dizzy. Maybe it's a brain tumor."

She's diligent about getting it checked out, but finds it hard to accept her doctor's reassurance. "Maybe she missed something. Maybe the CAT scan is wrong." Not surprisingly, her worry and anxiety actually increase her physical symptoms, which, in turn, increase her worry and anxiety.

For Sara, doing a reality check meant taking an objective look at the evidence. Her dizziness, she found, increased when she was under stress. It got better when she sat down. This pattern is not, of course, likely in someone who has a brain tumor. Over time, Sara began to see the role her misinterpretation of anxiety symptoms had in perpetuating her fear and was able to substitute more realistic thought processes. She also became better at observing her thoughts, much like a friend would listen to someone's fears and concerns. "There are those anxiety thoughts again," she would tell herself, rather than interpreting those thoughts as real or letting them control her mood.

Cognitive restructuring requires us to develop a greater awareness of our thoughts and our moods. It also involves replacing counterproductive thinking with realistic thoughts. This is not a "look on the bright side" panacea. It's impossible for most of us to go from fearful to optimistic thinking. Sara couldn't just tell herself, "There's no way I have brain cancer." But she *could* take a realistic look at the evidence and begin to replace her catastrophic thoughts with balanced ones. Often this requires us to get at the core beliefs underneath our worries. In Sara's case, she believed:

If her father had cancer, she was destined to have it.

Reality: Heredity is not destiny. Although some illnesses have a genetic component, the fact that a parent has a life-threatening illness does not automatically mean a child will get it.

Physical symptoms are always a sign of serious illness.

Reality: The average person experiences about two or three inexplicable twinges, pains, aches, or odd symptoms every day.

If she did have cancer, it was sure to be inoperable and fatal.

Reality: Many cancer patients recover. In fact, overall, 50 percent of cancer patients eventually die of something else.

> **Myth Buster**
>
> "What-if thinking is always bad." It's true that getting stuck in what ifs is counterproductive; however, imagining worst-case scenarios can be useful if we then switch into planning mode and take action to prevent it.

If her doctors couldn't find anything wrong with her, it was because they missed something.

Reality: The odds of a neurological exam, MRI, and complete physical workup missing a brain tumor are astronomically in your favor. In this day of proactive medicine (and malpractice lawsuits), doctors are more likely to rule out any diseases that can kill the patient first, and then work their way down to less serious diseases.

By discovering the basic belief that underpins the negative thought, and then challenging that belief, thinking can return to a more objective, reasonable style. One way to uncover these beliefs is to ask yourself questions such as "Where does this thought come from?" In fact, we can use our what-if thinking in our favor. Try this technique to find the core beliefs underneath your worries. Write down your what-if thought. Then ask yourself, "What if that did happen?" Write your answer. Then ask again, "What if that did happen?" Write it down. Keep going until you find your core belief, the belief that is at the root of your fears. For most of us, we uncover a deep-rooted fear of being rejected, hurt, or unloved; and our core belief protects us from this possibility. (We discuss how to deal with these in the next chapter.)

Anxiety Attack

Having trouble telling moods from thoughts? Moods can usually be expressed in one word: happy, sad, mad. But thoughts are more complex, needing several words to express them (I'll never get that promotion; he's saying that because he knows it gets to me).

Defensive Pessimism: Preparing for the Sky to Fall

Cognitive restructuring, as discussed previously, involves challenging negative or counterproductive thoughts and replacing them with more rational, less anxiety-producing ones. Certainly, always seeing the dark clouds instead of the rainbow can take its toll on our mental disposition and, according to some studies, our physical health; new research suggests that pessimists are more likely to have a propensity for certain diseases such as Alzheimer's and Parkinson's disease. However, according to Dr. Julie K. Norem, not all pessimists are created equal. Those of us who use our what-if thinking to *prepare for* upcoming events, for example, are just as successful as the-glass-is-half-fullers.

What a relief! If I had a dollar for every time my grandmother said, "Joni is a pessimist to be an optimist," I'd be lying on a beach in Tahiti drinking margaritas. What she was describing is a long-standing coping strategy of mine—the tendency to imagine every possible worst-case scenario and then make a plan to avoid or prevent them. If I had to give a speech, I would automatically conjure up dire straits: *perhaps I won't be able to see my notes, what if I forget my opening lines, what if I suddenly lose my train of thought in the middle?* In response to these anxiety-producing thoughts, I would over-prepare and memorize my opening lines; I even had a joke prepared just in case I drew a blank.

Myth Buster

"Seeing the glass as half empty means you can't enjoy life." Although it's great to see things in a positive way, there are some advantages to seeing life's problems and challenges. Society needs people who know how to use caution in judgment—as long as your view of things leads to a positive outcome, such as safer driving or carefully planned business decisions.

Anxiety Attack

One way of controlling the amount of worry is to set aside a daily worry time. Give yourself 20 minutes a day to worry about any and everything. When worries hit at any other time, tell yourself "stop" and remind yourself that you can deal with it at worry time.

Dr. Norem calls this strategy *defensive pessimism* and says it's a common strategy for anxiety sufferers who can't for the life of them see life through rose-colored glasses. It's an adaptive way of going with our natural flow, by putting our worries to good use. In other words, by imagining potential problems, we can develop relevant strategies for dealing with or preventing negative outcomes.

For *strategic optimists*, people who like to psych themselves up for a challenge, this routine would produce more anxiety, not less. But for those of us who are natural worriers, this strategy can give us a sense of control over uncomfortable circumstances. We use our thinking to prompt creative problem solving, rather than cause an anxiety buildup. By lowering our expectations and being prepared for the worst, we can then begin to tackle potential challenges without feeling the stress of high expectations.

Defensive pessimists take *action* to keep anxiety from leading to avoidance or self-sabotage. An avoider does not figure out how to plan for and control something that makes him feel anxious. As a result, he does not learn how to reduce his anxieties except by avoiding people and situations that lead to anxiety. Self-handicappers tend to procrastinate in response to anxiety; they are least likely to work on what is most important. Nor does defensive pessimism simply mean having a bad attitude, such as "This job sucks."

So how do you know whether you're a defensive pessimist? Think about how you tend to approach a new situation or challenging situation. Do you naturally:

◆ Lower your expectations to protect yourself from disappointment?

◆ Make a point of not being overly confident in case you miss something or under prepare?

◆ Prefer to prepare up until the last minute rather than relax or do something else?

◆ Automatically imagine all the things that could go wrong?

- Think through every possible glitch or problem?

- Develop contingency plans for these glitches?

- Drive optimistic friends batty with anticipatory troubleshooting?

If you find yourself chuckling as you read these, the odds are you have developed a defensive coping strategy. Congratulate yourself! You've developed a way to manage your anxiety in a way that keeps it from interfering with what you need to do. You've learned to tolerate anxiety in order to get things done. When we look at defensive pessimism in this light, it looks like a pretty positive form of negative thinking!

Look on the Bright Side

This is not to say that optimism is all bad. In fact, optimists tend to experience less stress, experience more positive emotions, and live longer than their pessimistic friends. Arguing *for* negative thinking as a way to manage anxiety and prepare for worst-case scenarios is very different from arguing *against* positive thinking.

Some of us, it seems, are born optimists. To some degree, optimism seems to be an inborn trait, a hidden but important part of some lucky people's genetic code. It runs in families, although research has yet to shed light on what gene or brain chemistry is responsible.

Still, the thinking habits we learn are a far more important influence, most psychologists agree. For instance, when faced with challenge or novelty, optimists set high expectations and they actively avoid thinking about unpleasant possibilities; in fact, when forced to do so, their

> **On the Cutting Edge**
>
> Aiming for a high self-esteem? Research seems to suggest that perhaps we should strive for a happy medium. Although low self-esteem can be linked to depression and anxiety, a high self-esteem is more common among people who treat others badly, such as in violent crime and fraud.

anxiety goes *up*. Optimists and pessimists also tend to explain problems to themselves in different ways. Optimists usually think of problems as temporary, external ("It's not my fault"), and impacting a relatively small part of their world. Pessimists, on the other hand, more quickly conclude that problems are their fault, that they're irreversible, and that they will have a major impact on their day-to-day life.

There's a trade-off with each viewpoint. We pessimists may have a more accurate view of situations and a clearer picture of our strengths and weaknesses. However, our realism may cloud over our willingness to reach for the sky. The optimist is more likely to persevere in the face of defeat and ultimately overcome the problem. In addition, in situations where we have to "fill in the blanks," or where there's more than one possible explanation, pessimists may naturally gravitate toward the most devastating and the most personal story. Relationship breakups are but one example where there are often multiple causes and different perspectives; if we automatically assume blame and feel devastated every time a relationship ends, we may be less willing to jump back into the dating game.

So which is the best strategy? Do we accept our defensive pessimism and applaud ourselves for the productive avenue into which we're channeling our anxiety? Or do we keep striving to be more upbeat and positive?

The best solution may be somewhere in the middle. First of all, optimism may come more easily as we get better control over our anxiety; as long as we're caught up in our symptoms, looking on the bright side may feel like trying to swim upstream without a paddle. At the same time, we *can* watch carefully to make sure our pessimism is *strategic*, that we're using our what-ifs to make a plan, limiting our negative thoughts to events or situations (not ourselves), and controlling the amount of time we spend worrying about things.

Here are some guidelines that might help:

- Don't beat yourself up over negative thoughts; instead, mine them for useful information.

- *Stop* critical thoughts about yourself. When you find yourself putting yourself down, argue as forcefully against those thoughts as you would while defending a friend who was under verbal attack by your worst enemy.

- Separate the feelings about a setback or mistake from the thoughts about it. Allowing yourself to feel the feelings (disappointment, worry, sadness) can help prevent the catastrophic thoughts that often happen when thoughts and feelings get mixed up.

- Practice interpreting setbacks or mistakes as temporary events that can be overcome.

- Immediately after a disappointment, do something pleasurable. Wait to think about your problems until you're in a more positive frame of mind.

In this chapter, we've discussed the role our thoughts play in shaping our feelings and guiding our behavior. We've seen how automatic thoughts can fuel our anxiety without us even being aware of it. We've also investigated common thinking errors that tend to plague anxiety sufferers and how we develop more realistic, and useful, thoughts.

Changing "bad" mental habits is hard. However, by paying attention to our inner conversations, we can become more aware of the power and evaluate the truth in what we tell ourselves. What can be harder to detect are the core beliefs that provide the map of how we view ourselves and the world. It's this map that leads us down certain daily thinking paths. In the next chapter, we examine the core beliefs we developed in childhood and evaluate how closely our mental map matches the peaceful territory we want to live in.

The Least You Need to Know

- ◆ Our thoughts are mental behaviors that we can learn to control.
- ◆ Certain thinking habits distort reality and raise anxiety levels.
- ◆ By paying attention, we can learn to replace negative thoughts with realistic alternatives.
- ◆ Defensive pessimism can work for us if we use it to control our anxiety and make a plan to avoid worst-case scenarios.
- ◆ Optimism seems to run in families but can be developed through practice, especially when we're relaxed or anxiety free.

Mental Myths

In This Chapter

- ◆ Discover your hidden assumptions
- ◆ Get to the core of your "self"
- ◆ Find out how believing is seeing
- ◆ Identify dysfunctional beliefs that cause anxiety
- ◆ Reset your core belief system

A second spouse should be better than his predecessor. Individuals in a remarriage are less committed to making their relationship last. A new spouse should be able to step right into the role as parent to her stepchildren.

Imagine the pressure I would put on a remarriage if I automatically expected it to be better than the first, or assumed a step-parenting role should be effortless. Odds are this attitude would make it much more likely we'd wind up in divorce court, like the 55 to 60 percent of remarriages that dissolve. On the other hand, if I expected it to take some time for everyone to adjust, or recognized that my past relationship history is less important than building a strong relationship with my new partner, we'd be off to a better start.

The same is true when we look at our view of the world in general. In the preceding chapter we discussed how our everyday thoughts can get off track and raise our anxiety level. However, these mental behaviors are shaped by our core beliefs about ourselves and the world around us. At an early age, we develop theories about how life works and what it takes to survive and thrive. In this chapter, we examine mental myths that can make life harder than it has to be—and how we can replace dysfunctional assumptions with empowering ideas.

Oh Yes, I Believe!

A belief is something that we *assume* to be true. It's different from a fact, which can be objectively verified. For instance, if I drop an apple from a tree, it will fall to the ground. This is a fact that can be observed and repeated any number of times. It doesn't matter what kind of tree I have climbed or the size or color of the apple. On the other hand, I could have different *beliefs* about why this is. I could subscribe to the most popular explanation—gravity—or I could be creative and come up with a theory of my own.

Beliefs come from two sources: our own experience and reflections, or from what other people tell us. Either way, they serve an important purpose. They anchor our understanding of the world around us, giving us a sense of predictability and control. They drive how we behave and influence how we feel. By the time we're adults, we have an entire map in our heads of what we assume to be true. This map becomes our reality. If I believe that people are basically good, then I am likely to be trusting and trustworthy. This may make it easy for me to develop friends and close relationships. On the other hand, if I assume that this is *always* true, I may be naïve and easily taken advantage of.

> **Myth Buster**
>
> *"Beliefs are sacred and shouldn't be changed."* Of course! Whereas some beliefs are sacred, others, such as a person's political views or beliefs about themselves and their capabilities change, with time. In fact, it's natural to modify your beliefs whenever you receive more information.

On the downside, when we form a belief, we tend to stick with it even in the face of contradictory evidence. For example, in one research study, subjects were told to find certain letters (B, E, R) and certain numbers (5, 6, 8). In phase two, they were told to find certain letter-number combinations with the caveat that B and 6 would never occur together. When questioned later, 40 percent of the subjects said they had doubted the honesty of the researcher's caveat. These subjects were significantly more likely to report seeing the "B-6" combination *even though it was not there*. Seeing isn't just believing; apparently, believing is seeing.

From this perspective, the visible aspects of our daily lives—the things we think, the feelings we feel, the things we do—are the 10 percent of the iceberg that is above the surface. What lies below our thoughts, feelings, and actions are our core beliefs. Whether they are stated or unstated, whether we are conscious of them or not, our core beliefs are the principles we live by that dictate our thoughts, feelings, and actions.

Stress Relief _____

Ask yourself, "What do you believe is true even though you cannot prove it?" That's a good way to get at some of the core beliefs that serve as a radar in everyday life.

A Map of "Me"

I have to be perfect in order to be loved. I must be liked by everyone I meet. I can't take care of myself. If I show vulnerability or weakness, I will get rejected.

Imagine the anxiety-filled life these beliefs can generate. And yet many of us have at least one of these lurking in our psyches. Just as we develop strong beliefs about the world around us, we develop some pretty fixed ideas about ourselves. A child whose parents are overwhelmed may feel like the only way to get approval is to be "strong" or "tough." Another who faces frequent criticism may come to doubt her ability to make sound decisions, ultimately concluding that she can't trust her own instincts or judgment.

Unfortunately, as we've seen, we can fail to challenge or reexamine assumptions about ourselves or the way the world works, even when they are causing us worry and anxiety. Instead, we may continue to draw false conclusions about ourselves and selectively tune in to any data in our environment that supports these assumptions—however negative or self-defeating they may be. A great first date doesn't call us for a second, confirming our belief that we're unlovable, when in reality he may have gotten back together with his old girlfriend.

On the Cutting Edge

Studies suggest that some of our beliefs are influenced by our culture. For example, American culture values uniqueness and individualism; not surprisingly, Americans tend to take personal credit for their successes and to see themselves as the exception to the norm. In Asian countries, on the other hand, loyalty to family and relationships is vital; as a result, individuals are more likely to believe personal success comes through strong affiliation with one's group, teamwork, and collaboration.

Examining our core beliefs about ourselves is perhaps the most important first step in reducing anxiety and leading a happy life. Dysfunctional self-beliefs cause us to misinterpret what happens to us, block us from achieving our goals, create extreme emotions, and can lead to counterproductive behaviors. In fact, my definition of a dysfunctional belief is any belief that makes life harder, limits your options, and/or exaggerates negative emotions.

Anxiety Attack _____

Want to discover your basic beliefs about yourself? Write out your life story. What are the themes in your story? What kind of "character" are you? Were you competent or incompetent, trustworthy or untrustworthy, lovable or not lovable?

Those of us with anxiety often have core beliefs about perfectionism, approval, and control. Based on these beliefs, we've developed a personal code of conduct, unwritten rules that we must live by in order to be loved and accepted by ourselves and others. Although these probably served us well at some point in our lives, it's all too easy to get stuck in them and live by them long after their use has expired. See whether any of these beliefs resonate with you:

- I must worry about things that could be dangerous, unpleasant, or frightening; otherwise, they might happen.

- I must always have the love and approval of those around me.

- I must "earn" the love of others through success and accomplishments.

- I cannot make a decision without the approval of the people around me.

- I should be upset by other people's problems.

- It is better to avoid conflict or tension than face up to it and risk rejection.

Another problematic belief system that plagues many anxiety sufferers has to do with our beliefs about our feelings. Beliefs that negative emotions are bad, destructive, or intolerable often have a boomerang effect. Rather than help us avoid unpleasant feelings, these beliefs can cause them to run amok. Believing that *feeling* out of control means we *are* out of control can quickly turn anxiety into panic.

One clue that our core beliefs about emotions are working against us is when we find our emotions snowballing in response to our thoughts. We have anxiety symptoms, worry about the anxiety, then feel more anxious. Some of the most common dysfunctional beliefs about emotions include the following:

- ◆ Feeling fear is a sign of weakness.

- ◆ It is wrong to feel angry at the people I love.

- ◆ Feeling bad means my life is out of control.

- ◆ I *can't stand* feeling uncomfortable or anxious.

- ◆ If I feel guilty, I must be guilty.

- ◆ I should always be in control of how I feel.

Just as we discussed in the last chapter, changing core beliefs requires insight and realism; it's not a Pollyanna approach to life. For example, everyone feels fear, anger, and guilt; the trick is to use them as signals to make our lives better or take a different path. We can start reducing their power by reframing beliefs as preferences. It would be *nice* to never feel angry at the people we love. We would *prefer* to always be in control of our emotions. It would be *great* if everyone always loved and approved of us. *But it's okay if things don't always work out that way!* Because they won't.

> **Myth Buster**
>
> *"I can't change who I am."* Not true. We can always change what we do. In fact, many people find that changing their behavior results in unexpected side benefits, including calmer emotions, higher self-esteem, and more positive thinking.

What core beliefs do you have about yourself? Are they working for you? If you find yourself often bogged down by disappointment or self-criticism, perhaps it's time to bring out the mirror and take a close look at what's beneath the looking glass.

Seeing the Big Picture

Two core beliefs about ourselves, in particular, are big predictors in how happy and how successful our lives turn out. These beliefs have to do with how lovable and how capable we believe ourselves to be. Clues about these core beliefs can often be found in early childhood, especially when we examine how we learned to gain acceptance and attention. What were you taught about being lovable? Did you get it through self-sacrifice or by denying negative or painful emotions? What messages did you get about being powerful and responsible? Were you encouraged to gently take ownership for mistakes, to blame others, or to crucify yourself for minor glitches?

For better or worse, these early messages often solidify into core beliefs and can virtually guide the way we approach every situation. For example, here's how beliefs about competency and ownership might lead to very different attitudes, feelings and behaviors.

Seeing ourselves as competent, for instance, is likely to lead us to take on new challenges, to try new things, and to have confidence in ourselves. On the other hand, seeing ourselves as less capable is likely to lead to a self-defeating approach whereby we either avoid new situations or quickly give up when faced with a setback or challenge.

Pleased to Meet You?

We've already seen how core beliefs about ourselves can either wreak havoc on our state of mind or buffer our psyches from the ups and downs of everyday life. So, too, can our core beliefs about others.

For instance, support from friends and family can play a critical role in recovering from an anxiety disorder. And yet many anxiety sufferers have core beliefs about relationships that prevent them from getting the support they need. We may hide our symptoms for years, putting on a false front that hides our loneliness and pain. We may lie to avoid a threatening situation because we don't trust the other person to "handle" the truth or accept us for the way we really are.

Or we may go to the other extreme, depending upon our support person so much that we never have the chance to work through our fears and recognize our own strength. Relying exclusively on one person to support our recovery is likely to lead to disappointment on our part and resentment on the part of our support person. We may pull our family into spending too much time trying to help us, failing to see any progress. We may blame ourselves instead of realizing that we have picked a person who is unavailable or unwilling to accept us; a good support person is someone who will help us in a productive way while also encouraging us to be responsible for our own emotional well-being.

As we begin to examine how we see other people, bear in mind that our beliefs, even those that are deeply held from infancy, are only beliefs. They are assumptions we work with until we know better. Then we can change them.

Ms. Uncertainty Meets the Control Freak

Arguably, the deepest need we humans have is the need for control. We long for consistency, understanding, closure—anything that will give us a feeling of predictability. In fact, feeling out of control is one of the scariest experiences anyone can have; as a former panic-attack sufferer, I will swear to it. When we think about life stressors, it's the feeling of powerlessness, of being unable to do anything about what's happening, that is often the most difficult part to handle.

However, for those of us who are anxiety prone, the need to be in control can mask a deep-seated fear of losing control. This fear can take many forms; fear of losing control to illness, a fear of being dominated or controlled in a relationship, or a fear of acting weird or embarrassing oneself during a panic attack. It's amazing how skillful some of us can become at *acting* in control when our inner world is in utter turmoil.

What kind of core beliefs might contribute to these fears? Most often, I think, they relate to beliefs about our vulnerability. Deep down, we question our ability to handle life's curveballs, in spite of evidence that we have done so on many occasions. "I couldn't handle that," we think as we worry about some possible catastrophe. "I would just die," we think as we imagine ourselves screaming and running out of a place where we've just had a panic attack. "I don't know what I'd do," we think as we imagine someone ridiculing our social discomfort or laughing at our public-speaking anxiety.

Underneath are core beliefs that tell us 1) we are vulnerable, and 2) the world is dangerous and we have to be on our guard. Challenging these core beliefs is an important part of increasing our sense of personal safety. As anxiety sufferers, we can—and we have—handled tougher times than many people ever will. We don't have to put up emotional roadblocks to protect ourselves from the possibility of rejection or from being dominated by others; we can set limits or reevaluate our relationship status at any time. We also need to remind ourselves of all the things we have accomplished at the same time we have been riddled with anxiety; a friend of mine told me recently that during her worst bouts with generalized anxiety, she threw two of her sons' birthday parties, was room mom for both boys, and had a successful part-time business!

Challenging these core beliefs may mean rethinking our ideas of what "handling" means. For example, it doesn't mean we don't have painful feelings about problems or upsetting events. Few people sail through life without some degree of emotional pain; perhaps "handling" should mean we continue to do the things we need and want to do *in spite of* how we feel.

Stress Relief

For those of us who have a need for control, anger can be seductive because it's the one feeling that can make us feel powerful. Take some time to look underneath the anger; the feelings and thoughts you uncover can provide valuable information about your core beliefs.

Warning! Dangerous Beliefs Ahead!

At the beginning of the chapter, we reviewed some core beliefs about remarriage that could make it harder to stick with a new partner during normally tough times. We also saw how hidden these core beliefs can be, superficially revealing themselves through painful feelings or negative thoughts. And yet if we focus solely on changing the surface, without addressing the 90 percent of the iceberg below, we're likely to develop new versions (thoughts, feelings, actions) of the old problem (fundamental beliefs about our lack of worth or capability).

Paradoxically, those of us who suffer from anxiety have an advantage when it comes to investigating negative core beliefs because they're most likely to pop to the surface when we're feeling the worst. For example, what are the things you tell yourself when you're feeling the worst? I'm not looking for the things you think you *should* believe about yourself, but what you really do believe about yourself when things look darkest—things such as *I'm never going to be a success. No one will ever love me. There's something wrong with me. I can't seem to do anything right. People will take advantage of you if you don't watch them very carefully. Men always leave me in the end. No one cares about me. The world is dangerous and unpredictable.* These statements are big clues to what these negative core beliefs are.

Another shortcut in mining these beliefs is to look at what is happening in your life. What results are you getting in your life? If every boyfriend leaves you, the odds are that you have a core belief about the opposite sex that is clouding your judgment about who you get involved with or how you handle relationships. If you put off getting professional assistance even though you've tried every self-help strategy known to man and anxiety is still ruling your life, you probably have negative core beliefs about asking for help and/or trusting others. Remember, we're often attracted to people and situations that will confirm that our core beliefs are true.

> **Anxiety Attack**
>
> Another way to get at our core beliefs; complete the following sentences: *I am _____. People are _____. The world is _____.*

Diary of a Worrywart

Being able to change our thoughts and our responses to them is perhaps the very essence of being in control. No one can take that away from us. No matter how hard it is to believe, we do choose our beliefs and, at some point in our lives, they served us well. They protected our self-esteem and they provided a sense of predictability and certainty. Now they contain the essence of our conscious and unconscious insecurities.

However, until named, negative core beliefs are often experienced as "feelings." Worriers, for instance, are often responding to a number of beliefs that wreak havoc on our peace of mind. *"If I think it, then it must be true"* is a common belief in response to a frightening thought or scary possibility. In reality, of course, all of us have irrational thoughts occasionally. And that's all they are—just thoughts.

"I have to be in control to be safe" is an underlying belief that exacerbates fear in the face of unpredictability or uncertainty. Again, in reality, how we play the hand we're dealt with is the best predictor of happiness and success. We aren't the ones dealing the cards.

> **Stress Relief**
>
> Ask questions that cause you to rethink your assumptions. Is the problem really a problem? Is what I am doing or thinking working for me? What should I stop or start thinking or doing to change my situation?

Get With the Belief Correction Program!

Core beliefs weren't born yesterday, and they won't go away tomorrow. It takes a lot of energy and work to challenge some fundamental assumptions about ourselves and the world around us. In the midst of our anxiety, we may not have the internal resources to tackle a longer-term project such as this one; what we can do, though, is to start paying attention to the core beliefs that rear their heads during our toughest times.

As we feel calmer and more secure, we can begin to actively challenge them. We remind ourselves that our beliefs are merely assumptions we have made about the truth. We acknowledge that our core beliefs have helped us make sense of our world and realize that their use has run its course. We look at what we want out of life and come up with core beliefs that would help us get it. *I am worthy of love. I deserve to be treated well. I am a strong, capable person. I can make my own decisions. I can handle tough times and unpleasant emotions.*

There are several strategies we can use to tackle dysfunctional core beliefs; many of them are discussed in this book. Keeping our values up front (Chapter 4) can give us the motivation to keep at what seems like a daunting task. We can use the restructuring tips we discussed in Chapter 8 to help us

> **Anxiety Attack**
>
> When you feel a negative emotion rising, ask yourself, "What could I be telling myself that causes this feeling?" When you identify the self-talk, ask, "What assumption or belief would have to be in place to support this kind of talk?" You can then begin to tackle the core belief.

replace negative core beliefs with more realistic ones. And in the next section, we take a look at core beliefs that underlie specific anxiety disorders, such as social anxiety and panic disorder.

The overall message in this chapter is that we do have control over what's really important—our thoughts and our actions. No matter how firmly entrenched our thought patterns, or how deeply ingrained our behavior, we can steer ourselves in a different, more peaceful direction. In fact, new research shows that even personality traits, once believed to be "set" by an early age, are more malleable than we once thought. In the next chapter, we take a look at the anxiety-prone personality and how we can let go of perfectionism and the need for approval.

The Least You Need to Know

- ◆ Beliefs are assumptions we assume to be true.

- ◆ Everyday thoughts, feelings, and actions give us clues about our core beliefs.

- ◆ Dysfunctional beliefs limit our options and cause unnecessary stress and anxiety.

- ◆ Anxiety sufferers often have negative core beliefs about our self-worth and our ability to handle life's ups and downs.

- ◆ We can learn to identify negative core beliefs by paying attention to what we tell ourselves when we are feeling down and by examining counterproductive patterns of behavior.

10

Improve the State of Your Personality Traits

In This Chapter

- ◆ Take a look at the new view of personality
- ◆ Define the "panic-prone personality"
- ◆ Find out whether you're a highly sensitive person
- ◆ Discover strategies for tackling perfectionism and the need for approval
- ◆ Learn how to gracefully handle criticism

Apparently, it was written in the stars: I was born to be an emotional, sensitive person. Born October 29, I'm a Scorpio. Check out any of the lists of "Scorpio" personality traits and you'll likely find "penetrating insight, emotional sensitivity, and intensity of emotions" among them. A great combo for being both a psychologist and an anxiety sufferer.

In reality, I don't know of any research linking anxiety to my astrological sign. However, considerable research suggests that anxiety and certain personality traits often go hand in hand. These personality traits—our unique patterns of relating to the world around us—are a combination of genetic predisposition, life experiences, and learned behavior. And depending upon the circumstances, they can work for us or against us.

This chapter takes a look at the link between anxiety and personality. We cover how certain personality traits can predispose us to tension and worry. You'll have the chance to see whether you're a "highly sensitive person." And we cover some strategies for tackling two of anxiety's frequent companions: perfectionism and the need for approval.

The "Person" Behind the Personality

"It's just in her nature to help others." "We have such different personalities." "He's just a difficult person." Many of us have made these statements, and it shows how aware we are that we each have a collection of unique attributes. This collection of behaviors, temperament, and emotional and mental qualities make up our "personality." They are the thoughts and feelings that drive our interactions with the world.

Each personality is made up of several *traits*, stable characteristics that influence an individual's thoughts, feelings, and behavior. A "difficult" personality, for example, might be a catchall used to describe someone who is stingy, argumentative, close-minded, and unstable. Of course, this person might also be ambitious and self-reliant. Furthermore, each personality trait might be more or less pronounced depending upon the person's history.

A detail-oriented personality trait might choose an accounting profession and reinforce his or her attention to detail at work. This trait may help that person excel in the workplace. But what if this same attention to detail makes it hard to make everyday decisions in a timely fashion or results in a rigid interpersonal style? What works in one situation may not work in another.

Viva la Quirks

Instead of labeling personalities within strict categories of dysfunction, mental-health professionals are seeing more gray area between a quirky personality trait and a diagnosable *personality disorder*. For example, we all vary in how comfortable we are in social situations. Some of us have never met a stranger, whereas others consider ourselves shy or reserved. Someone who is shy may feel more uncomfortable meeting new people than you or I, yet genuinely desire to make friends and join the group. In addition, the shy person often succeeds in social situations *in spite of* the discomfort; the desire to connect is strong enough that the anxiety takes a backseat.

On the other hand, someone with an avoidant personality disorder would fall at the extreme end of the "shy" continuum and cross the diagnostic chasm from quirk to clinical quagmire. A personality disorder, as defined in the *Diagnostic and Statistical Manual of the American Psychiatric Association, Fourth Edition (DSM-IV)*, is an enduring pattern of inner experience and behavior that differs markedly from the expectations of the individual's culture, is pervasive and inflexible, has an onset in adolescence or early adulthood, is stable over time, and leads to distress or impairment.

Unlike our shy example, a person suffering from avoidant personality disorder systematically avoids social contacts or any situation that might result in anxiety or embarrassment. For example, s/he may avoid jobs that involve contact with people, may be unwilling to get involved with others unless certain of being liked, and may be unwilling to participate in any new social situation.

From this more flexible perspective, the difference between a personality trait and a personality disorder comes down to where that trait falls on the shyness continuum and what personal consequences it costs that particular individual. Rather than view a trait as pathological or normal, the focus is on how distressed the individual is about

Stress Relief _____

Don't confuse personality with skill. The ability to network effectively or stand up for yourself are communication skills that can be learned by anyone.

the attribute in question and how much it limits his or her life. In other words, we all have kinks in our personalities; when these kinks become extreme, a trait becomes a problem.

Context Is King!

Of course, whether our kinks or quirks cause problems for us doesn't just depend upon how inflexible or severe they are; it also depends upon the context in which they occur. Behaviors rewarded in some contexts can be disruptive in others.

A person with dependent personality traits may be a loyal, cooperative member of a work team, yet falter when forced to lead. Many police officers are discerning, observant, and suspicious, personality traits that allow them to thrive in an environment where caution and wariness are rewarded.

On the flip side of the coin, the conscientious, detail-oriented employee may come unglued when faced with a disruptive corporate transition or sudden change in his work duties. The extrovert may thrive in sales or public relations but suffocate in a marriage to an introvert. Clearly, the "fit" between certain personality traits and our environment can either be a match made in heaven or the source of considerable stress.

If we think of our personality traits as neutral, we can quit seeing parts of ourselves as "good" or "bad." This frees us up to examine how effectively we are expressing them and how often we choose situations that complement our natural attributes. Can we, for example, meet a deadline even though we're obsessively thorough? Can we stand up for ourselves when we're being taken advantage of, even though we're naturally agreeable? If we have a strong need for independence, do we take jobs and pick partners who relish that attribute?

From this perspective, we can analyze and tackle the thoughts, feelings, and behaviors that underlie a troublesome personality trait. "I depend on close relationships for emotional support" is a belief that most of us would find useful. It could serve as a powerful motivator to develop and nurture the kind of social support that research consistently shows buffers us against life stress. "I can't tolerate being alone" or "I can't take care of myself," on the other hand, are beliefs that may lead us to chronic self-doubt and low self-esteem. It may also lead us to make poor relationship choices or stay in interpersonal situations that are abusive or unfair. Rather than rebuild our character, we can simply smooth out the rough edges to become a healthier, happier human being—quirks and idiosyncrasies and all.

The Panic-Prone Personality?

Starting from birth, it seems as if those of us who struggle with anxiety share some common "rough edges." We're all born with certain *temperaments*, innate differences in how reactive we are to our environment and how intensely we express these reactions. These temperaments contain the seeds of certain personality traits; whether or not they grow will often depend upon how often and how extensively they are nurtured by our environment. Research shows, for instance, that babies who are highly reactive to environmental stimuli tend to become children who cry, try to avoid, and show distress in the face of unfamiliar objects, people, and events. Not surprisingly, they are also more likely to develop anxiety disorders as adults.

Of course, between a touchy temperament in infancy and anxiety disorders in adulthood lay two very important things: parents. Babies may be born with a propensity to overexcitability, but parenting practices often determine whether such infants become fearful of unfamiliar people and events later in childhood. In particular, parents who respond to a child's sensitivity with overprotection may unwittingly bring out the child's worst fears by never giving him or her a chance to learn how to handle stress or challenging situations.

As adults, certain personality traits often coexist with anxiety disorders; so much so, in fact, that it's not unusual to see researchers use lingo such as "anxious personality traits." Avoidant personality disorder, dependent personality disorder, and obsessive-compulsive personality disorder are often called the "anxious triad," not because most anxiety disorder sufferers have personality disorders but because we often share similar personality traits, albeit in less-severe form. It's unclear whether these personality traits predispose us to anxiety, exacerbate it, or are part of the same developmental pathway. What is clear is that, taken to excess, they can make our lives miserable.

> ### On the Cutting Edge
>
> A recent Italian study found that panic-disorder patients who were treated with the antidepressants Paxil and Celexa not only showed a reduction in panic symptoms. They also showed a reduction in dependent, paranoid, and avoidant personality traits, suggesting that these may have been part of the panic itself, rather than an enduring part of the patient's psyche.

For example, anxiety sufferers often describe themselves as perfectionistic, emotionally sensitive, and highly performance conscious. Those of us who experience anxiety can be highly sensitive to a wide variety of stimuli, ranging from physical sensations to the feelings of others. I am often amazed at my husband's ability to mentally check out in the midst of our four kids' chaos; to this day, I have to physically remove myself to get some emotional relief. Because of our emotional sensitivity, friends often describe us as highly compassionate and empathetic. On the downside, we may at times feel like emotional tuning forks, picking up on others' distress even when we don't want to.

In addition to emotional sensitivity, many of us acknowledge a strong desire to be in control of ourselves and our surroundings, especially when we are in the company of others. Stoicism may have been a family value; I remember my grandmother proudly telling me of how she didn't cry at her husband's funeral although she grieved terribly following his death. On the plus side, this need to be in control often gives us tremendous self-discipline; on the downside, our ability to conceal our anxiety symptoms (and other emotional pain) may leave us feeling lonely and isolated. Our need for control may also mask our underlying fear of losing control.

Another commonly shared trait is high performance consciousness. Many anxiety sufferers are hyperaware of their performance on any given task, particularly when our performance is being evaluated. We have a strong drive to avoid failure, or at least looking like a failure to others. On the plus side, many of us are highly conscientious; a potential trap is placing excessive pressure on ourselves and giving others undue power over how we view ourselves.

As you can see, traits such as emotional sensitivity, a strong need to control, and high performance consciousness can be both blessings and curses depending upon how much we have them and how we express them. The more extreme these traits are in our own personalities, the more prone we are to experiencing anxiety. In addition, we anxiety sufferers share two personality traits that almost always wreak havoc at some point in our lives. Let's take a look at perfectionism and the need for approval.

Are You Too Sensitive?

At 18, I represented my junior college in the Miss Alabama beauty contest. What I remember most clearly from that experience was how differently it affected me in comparison to the other girls. After the pageant, I was totally and completely exhausted; while most of the other girls were gathering to have fun and socialize, all I wanted to do was go back to my hotel room and get some peace and quiet. It wasn't the first time I'd noticed that I seemed to be more drained after emotion-charged events than most people, but it was the first time I clearly remember thinking, "What's wrong with me?"

"Oh, the *noise!* If there's one thing I can't stand, *it's the noise, noise, noise, noise!*" This line from Dr. Seuss's *How the Grinch Stole Christmas* is a thought any highly sensitive person has either uttered or thought—often simultaneously wondering why other people don't feel the same way or seem as bothered. Ever since research psychologist Dr. Elaine Aron published her research on the "highly sensitive person," there's been increasing recognition that 15 to 20 percent of us Americans are just on a different emotional wavelength than the rest. Just as dogs are able to hear whistles that humans can't hear, the highly sensitive person processes sensory information more deeply and thoroughly than most of the people around her.

This biological sensitivity, which Dr. Aron believes is in-born, brings gifts and causes challenges. On the plus side, our highly developed emotional tuning fork allows us to feel deeply, to have a keen imagination and a rich inner life, and to easily pick up on the moods of the people around us. On the downside, it's not like we can turn our emotional radar off when we want to. As a result, environmental stimulation that wouldn't faze the average person—noises, bright lights, crowds, intense movies—may feel like an assault to the biologically sensitive person.

This biological sensitivity doesn't just apply to the world around us, though; it also applies to our internal world. Highly sensitive persons often have a high sensitivity to pain and can feel overwhelmed when dealing with time pressure, sudden changes or transitions, or multiple demands. "Don't be so sensitive" is a mantra many of us with this biological temperament have heard since childhood, often in response to our distress over other people's moods or comments or because we "overreact" to minor annoyances. It's like we have holes in our psychic armor, the proverbial "thin skin" that leaves us vulnerable to external stimuli.

The highly sensitive person is not anxious by nature but, as you can imagine, is more *at risk for* anxiety. For example, because we pick up so much from the world around us, we are more prone to overstimulation and quicker to feel stress, especially when we can't retreat to a quiet room or place of solitude to get some "downtime." Also recent research suggests that our psyches are more impacted by our life experiences. For instance, recent research found that individuals with this biological sensitivity were three times more likely to suffer from shyness, anxiety, and depression if they had a troubled childhood than persons without this trait. As adults, the highly sensitive person is more likely to be negatively affected by a bad experience; on the plus side, we experience more joy and happiness when good things happen!

So how do we keep the gifts our emotional sensitivity gives us and minimize the intrusions? On a practical level, we can …

> **Myth Buster**
>
> *"People who are 'emotional' make poor decisions."* The truth is, used wisely, our emotions improve decisions because we can better appreciate the importance of something and respond.

♦ Make sure we have plenty of solitude and downtime, especially when we are going through a stressful period.

♦ Quit comparing ourselves to other people who seem less drained or bothered by the world around them.

♦ Take extra steps to guard our physical health; hunger and lack of sleep can make us even more prone to overstimulation and fatigue.

♦ Intentionally put yourself in calming environments when you can, whether it's a quiet room at home or a beach or mountain vacation.

♦ Develop ways to create inner calm, such as through yoga or meditation.

♦ Learn to say "no" even if your emotional side is being tugged on.

Myth Buster

Research shows that highly sensitive persons with a good-enough childhood are no shyer, anxious, or depressed than others.

◆ Break down big goals into small steps and create your own deadlines.

◆ Take new relationships *slowly*. Because of the tendency to feel deeply, we can jump in and get hooked into a relationship before we have the chance to evaluate whether it's good for us.

I Want Everything to Be Perfect

As we've seen, having finely tuned emotional radar can predispose us to both empathy and anxiety. It can work for us, but at times it takes some work to keep it from stressing us out. It's both a blessing and a curse. On the other hand, perfectionism—another personality trait many anxiety sufferers share—rarely does us any good at all. In fact, it can keep us from experiencing joy and pleasure even when we deserve it.

Ever feel like nothing you do is ever good enough? Is it hard to be satisfied with your efforts? If you meet a goal, do you up the ante rather than take the time off to appreciate what you've done? If you answered "yes" to any of the above, welcome to the perfectionist's club. We have high expectations of you, although probably not as high as you have for yourself!

Perfectionism has its roots in childhood when the message "I love who you are" somehow gets confused with "I love what you do." When a child feels that acceptance and love are conditioned upon success, s/he naturally tries to earn it. In adults, perfectionism is often expressed through exceedingly high standards. This, by itself, is not necessarily problematic; if we don't shoot for the stars, we'll never reach them.

What does cause problems is when, no matter how successful we are, we never feel like its good enough. For example, imagine that your daughter comes to you, stressed out because she's convinced that she needs an A+ on a final exam; she believes her chances of getting into the college of her choice will be dramatically reduced if she doesn't get an A in this class. After a week of stress, cramming, and snapping at you, she comes home with her grades. She did it! An A+! However, instead of patting herself on the back, she glumly tells you that she'll never be able to hack college if she has to study so much to ace a stupid high school course. In other words, if she were perfect, she *should be* able to do it more easily.

As you can see, there's a difference between the desire to succeed and excel and the desire to be perfect. It's the combination of high expectations plus dissatisfaction with our performance, no matter how stellar it actually is, that is the pain of perfectionism. The greater the discrepancy between our performance and our satisfaction with it, the more likely it is that we are caught in perfectionism's steel trap.

> **On the Cutting Edge**
>
> Research suggests that first-borns are more likely to be perfectionists than later-born children, perhaps because first-time parents, looking for confirmation of their parenting skills, tend to reward our "eager-beaver" behavior.

The attitudes and beliefs underlying perfectionism fuel anxiety by creating a constant sense of time pressure coupled with a rigid, unforgiving standard of performance. There's no room for mistakes. "I'm a loser unless I reach my ideal. I don't have value unless I'm successful. I should be able to do it better, faster, easier …." In reality, no one can always get everything done on time and perfectly. Stuff happens. Glitches pop up. It's like there's a taskmaster inside us that we just can't escape, one who is never satisfied and waiting to pounce on our slightest setback.

Antidotes for perfectionism often involve an attitude adjustment to catch self-defeating or irrational thoughts, such as the cognitive restructuring strategies discussed in the last two chapters. We can use feelings of anxiety and worry as opportunities to ask ourselves if we have set up impossible expectations in our current situation and explore the fears behind the feelings. In addition, we can intentionally build in some shades of gray in

> **Stress Relief**
>
> Keep a daily journal of everything positive you do to shift the focus from what you haven't done (or why it wasn't good enough) to what you have.

our everyday life that can remind us that few things really are "all or nothing." For example …

◆ Focus on the process of doing an activity, not just on the end result. Evaluate your success not only in terms of what you accomplished but also in terms of how much you enjoyed the task. Recognize that there can be value in the process of pursuing a goal.

◆ Read biographies of famous people who failed often (Thomas Edison, for example) or stories of mistakes that turned into accidental discoveries (penicillin, x-rays).

- When you make a mistake ask, "What can I learn from this experience?" More specifically, think of a recent mistake you have made and list all the things you can learn from it.

- Rank your goals and/or tasks according to how important they are to you. On less important tasks, decide how much is "good enough."

She's Got the Need to Please

We've talked about the kind of perfectionism that drives us to overwork and chronic dissatisfaction with our efforts. But another kind of "perfectionism" can wreak havoc on our relationships and our sense of self-worth. This perfectionism is socially pre-scribed and often takes root in the belief that others will only value us if we are per-fect. This kind of social perfectionism has been linked to both anxiety and depression, not to mention a chronic sense of loneliness and insecurity. This kind of perfectionism can tempt us to put on a mask with others, hide any fears or problems, and focus on pleasing others at the expense of standing up for ourselves.

Now don't get me wrong. There is nothing wrong with wanting to make other people happy; it's an endearing trait. However, when we get stuck in the people-pleasing mode, we may deny, hide, or suppress our own emotional needs because we believe it is the only way to gain the acceptance and approval of others. Normal feelings of anger or irritation can be threatening and, as a result, cause anxiety; after all, how many friends and family members are pleased when we're angry with them?

There's another link between anxiety and people pleasing. New evidence that children who felt unsure of the availability of their primary caretaker, especially those who felt emotionally abandoned during times of distress, are more likely to develop anxiety than children whose attachment was more secure. In addition, these children were more likely to try to hide their emotions and appear neutral, even when experiencing pain and distress, and yet many had greater trouble tolerating separation from the primary caregiver than children more securely attached.

> **Myth Buster**
>
> *"Personalities don't change."* Wrong! In fact, research says that, after age 30, most of us become more consci-entious, agreeable, and emotion-ally stable.

As discussed at the beginning of this chapter, person-ality traits, in and of themselves, are neutral; it's when we become ruled by them that they become problem-atic. Chronic people pleasers tend to have an *excessive* need to seek approval to avoid anticipated rejection, abandonment, or disapproval. We work too hard to keep the peace, do anything to avoid hurting someone's feelings, and often have a problem letting others know how we really think and feel about things. In return, we give too much power to other's opinions about us and, at times, expect others to take care of our feelings.

Give Me Back That Power

Those of us with a strong need for approval work hard at being good in the various roles in our lives—and we are good at them. Unfortunately, though, we may wait for others to give us recognition or credit rather than honor ourselves. This dependence on others to boost our self-worth can create a constant state of tension; after all, we have no control over what others say and think about us. It's like our self-esteem is walking around outside of ourselves, freely buffeted by the ebbs and flows of our relationships.

Inevitably, this takes its toll on our relationships. The people who love us may treat us with kid gloves, trying their best to reassure us and boost our self-esteem. They may become overly protective, not telling us the truth for fear of hurting our feelings or damaging our egos. They may also feel resentful and overwhelmed by the need to "be there" for us. If we have the misfortune to hook up with a power tripper, s/he will gladly take advantage of our need for approval, either using it to manipulate us to carry more than our share in the relationships, or taking delight in wielding power over our self-esteem. Most of us know a friend or acquaintance who stays involved with a critical partner, and are driven batty as we saw a decent human being believe—and tolerate—a bunch of manipulative bull.

Ultimately, no one else can satisfy the deep need to be accepted that approval seekers desperately pursue. We've got to confront our fears head on. We've got to find the security and trust in ourselves. When we start identifying and restructuring our irrational beliefs about rejection, neglect, abandonment, and disapproval and uncover where these fears came from, we can get to the root of the need for approval.

A first step is to ask ourselves what we really gain by trying to please everyone in our lives. What do we give up when we keep our opinions and feelings to ourselves or when we can't make a decision without consulting someone? What are the taboo subjects that limit our intimacy with our

Stress Relief _____

Religious or spiritual beliefs can be a powerful antidote for perfectionists, especially when we find it difficult, if not impossible, to forgive ourselves when we have made a mistake or done wrong.

partner? Taking a small risk—by saying "no," by sharing a problem, or by giving honest feedback—can be a giant step in providing evidence that we can please people by being ourselves. In fact, one of the biggest benefits of an anxiety support group is sharing feelings and thoughts that many attendees have never disclosed to anyone— and never imagined they could.

As discussed in this chapter, personality traits are neither good nor bad; they only become problematic when they don't fit the situation or when they are taken to extreme. This chapter has also explained how certain personality traits and anxiety often go hand in hand; they can push us in the direction of anxiety, exacerbate an existing anxiety disorder, or, in excess, cause anxiety themselves. Reassigning the role perfectionism plays in our lives, or tackling an excessive need for approval, can help us address some of the underlying thoughts and feelings that increase our stress level and create tension and worry.

This section has focused on the mental part of the mind-body connection. However, anxiety takes place in the body and the mind. In Part 4, we will discuss the importance of using our bodies to build up our resilience and reduce our stress. Let's start by addressing one of the best ways to self-medicate stress and anxiety: exercise.

The Least You Need to Know

- Personality traits are neither good nor bad; they may help us or cause trouble depending upon the context and how much they rule our behavior.

- Anxiety sufferers often share certain personality traits such as perfectionism, a high level of emotional sensitivity, and a strong need for approval.

- Highly sensitive persons have built-in emotional radars that pick up data that most other people would miss, ignore, or not care about.

- Tackling perfectionism and the need to please others often involves addressing underlying fears of rejection, abandonment, and disapproval.

Part 4

Boosting the Mind-Body Connection

This section focuses on how we can build a physical foundation that promotes peace of mind. Starting with the myths and realities of what exercise can do for anxiety, we then turn our attention to diet and sleep. Finally, we outline the stress-management tools that can prevent the build up of daily hassles that can eventually lead to clinical distress.

Chapter 11

Let's Get Physical

In This Chapter

- Find out what exercise can—and can't do—for your state of mind
- Develop a strategy for successful workouts
- Uncover your motivation for regular exercise
- See how you can breathe some calm into a stressed psyche
- Explore some at-home breathing strategies

"Mom, why don't you go to the gym?" Out of the mouths of babes—or 10-year-old boys! That suggestion arose one day after my admittedly cranky mood had spilled over into a 60-second lecture surrounding the critical life skill of keeping track of your shoes.

Sure, we all know exercise keeps us strong, builds our endurance, and sheds those holiday pounds. But with our society's emphasis on the physical-health benefits, not to mention physical appearance, it can be easy to lose sight of the mental-health benefits. Can a workout really boost our mood and reduce our stress? And can regular exercise cure depression and anxiety?

In this chapter, we take a look at the mind-body connection as it relates to exercise and mental health. We look at what exercise can do for you and what it can't. And, of course, we focus on the fascinating link between exercise and anxiety; what exercises promote calm, what exercise can stir things up, and how simple breathing and meditation techniques can soothe a troubled psyche.

Work Out and Work It Out

Ann was diagnosed with panic disorder and depression two years ago. She would often isolate herself and stay home, feeling unable to face work or enjoy social outings. She sought help from her general practitioner, who prescribed an antidepressant and recommended psychotherapy. Ann started feeling better; she returned to work and made more of an effort to get together with friends. However, she still felt exhausted by the demands of a stressful job.

At her doctor's insistence, Ann began to exercise, starting out slowly just by walking and gradually increasing her workout routine. She also found a walking buddy, which made her feel less isolated and gave her an extra incentive on the days she felt too tired or stressed to move. Within three weeks, her energy level improved. She also began to appreciate the calm she felt after her workout. When Ann felt ready to discontinue her medication 14 months later, she upped her exercise routine a bit; not only did it rev up those endorphins, she found it helped her with the anxiety she felt over discontinuing her medication.

An increasing number of health professionals are prescribing exercise as an add-on to other treatments when helping an emotionally distressed patient. It's no magic bullet (what is?), but a growing body of literature suggests that increasing physical activity is a positive and active way to help manage anxiety symptoms—*and* boost self-esteem.

On the Cutting Edge
Research has found that levels of phenylethylamine, a feel-good hormone, are lower in people suffering from a mental disorder; exercise seems to boost its production.

But how can physical exercise have any affect upon the mind or mood? Let's take a look at what we know about the mental benefits of physical exercise—and what we don't.

Blood, Sweat, and *No* Tears

We don't fully understand how exercise improves emotional health, but we've got some pretty good ideas. For example, on a physiological level, exercise may positively affect the levels of mood-enhancing neurotransmitters in the brain. The increased body temperature may also have calming effects. In addition, physical activity may boost feel-good endorphins, release tension in the muscles, help you sleep better, and reduce the stress hormone cortisol.

Exercise also seems to have a number of direct and indirect psychological and emotional benefits when you have depression or anxiety. These include the following:

- **Confidence.** Engaging in physical activity offers a sense of accomplishment. Meeting goals or challenges, no matter how small, can boost self-confidence at times when you need it most. Exercise can also make you feel better about your appearance and your self-worth.

- **Distraction.** When you have depression or anxiety, it's easy to dwell on how badly you feel. But dwelling interferes with your ability to problem solve and cope in a healthy way. Dwelling also can make depression more severe and longer lasting. Exercise can provide a good distraction. It shifts the focus away from unpleasant thoughts to something more pleasant, such as your surroundings or the music you enjoy listening to while you exercise.

- **Interactions.** Depression and anxiety can lead to isolation. That, in turn, can worsen your condition. Exercising can create opportunities to interact with others, even if it's just exchanging a friendly smile or greeting as you walk around your neighborhood.

- **Healthy coping.** Doing something beneficial to manage depression or anxiety is a positive coping strategy. Trying to feel better by drinking alcohol excessively, dwelling on how badly you feel, or hoping depression and anxiety will go away on their own aren't helpful coping strategies.

It appears that our bodies—and our minds—will always reward us for taking good care of them.

Myth Buster

"Exercise can cure anxiety or depression." Physical activity cannot cure clinical levels of anxiety or depression, but it can provide psychological and physical benefits that alleviate symptoms and can be an important part of the recovery process.

Anxiety Attack

Check out www.remedy-find.com, an independent site where consumers rate the effectiveness of treatment for various disorders. Aerobic exercise was the top-rated "treatment" for generalized anxiety disorder and second for panic disorder.

Too Much of a Good Thing?

It's great that our bodies have a feel-good system built in. We even have in-house painkillers. As an example, the brain's pituitary gland produces beta-endorphins, which can attach themselves to the same receptors that morphine uses, producing the same delightful feelings. Another chemical, PEA (phenylethylamine), is produced during exercise and is related to amphetamines but without the long-term side effects. So are you ready for a serotonin, beta-endorphin, PEA cocktail? These chemicals can be powerful foot soldiers in the calming-mood battle.

Some studies have shown that these feel-good chemicals are released whenever we take action to get our needs met. Apparently, it's our body's way of saying, "You done good. Do more of this." It's also one of the reasons some people get hooked on exercise, and why athletes often describe the buzz of a workout as a natural high.

> **Anxiety Attack**
>
> It may take at least 30 minutes of exercise a day for at least 3 to 5 days a week to see an improvement in anxiety symptoms. However, even 10 to 15 minutes of exercise can improve mood in the short term.

On Your Mark ...

So you're convinced that exercise might be a good addition to your weekly activities. Now what? On January 1 each year, thousands of Americans make New Year's resolutions that involve exercise—and few of us keep them. To improve the odds that you'll win the exercise game, take some time to plan before you lace up those sneakers. For example ...

- **Get your doctor's advice.** Your therapist or doctor may have some excellent exercise plans and advice. Use their support to talk over your thoughts and concerns

- **Go with your natural flow.** Start with things you like to do, perhaps activities you've enjoyed in the past or new things you'd like to try. If you're a people person, find an exercise buddy. If childcare is a problem, involve your kids. Don't plan to exercise at the crack of dawn if you're a night owl.

- **Do an attitude adjustment.** Keep track of the immediate benefits of exercise, such as a calmer state of mind and better sleep. Give

> **Stress Relief**
>
> Exercise builds up your mental muscles as well as your physical ones. Anxious exercise buffs say that their workout routine serves as a form of predictable stress that supplies a kind of "vaccination" against the uncontrolled stress that leads to depression and anxiety.

yourself credit for every step you take, and use setbacks as an opportunity to learn. Set realistic goals and go at your own pace.

◆ **Reframe your motivation.** Don't let exercise be a burden; instead, think of exercise as your own private therapy session or personal meditation time.

Been a couch potato for so long you can't imagine anything remotely appealing about shuffling your feet? How about:

Indoor	Outdoor
Yoga	Bicycling
Aerobic dance	Skating
Jumping rope	Fitness walking
Stair climbing	Running
Ski machine/steppers	Swimming
Aerobic/water aerobic classes	Gardening
Working around the house	Mowing

There are two types of physical fitness that can help improve mental health: aerobic exercise and anaerobic exercise. Aerobic exercise involves a continuous and intensive exercise of the heart and lungs. These are activities that typically end with "-ing": walking, running, biking, swimming, skiing, and so on. The second type of physical fitness is anaerobic exercise. The goal of this type of exercise is muscular strength and/or flexibility. Examples of anaerobic activity would be weight lifting, Pilates, and yoga. Both forms of exercise can be great stress busters; aerobic activity can "burn off" excess tension while anaerobics can relieve tension-related sore muscles.

Anxiety Attack

Some people worry that exercise might trigger an anxiety or panic attack—sometimes the feeling from working out such as breathlessness and a faster heart rate can feel similar to some of the early signs of a panic attack. It's best to start slowly—take a little walk at first, then build up.

Get Set ...

Here's Gary's story: "At first I found it hard to get excited about any exercise. I used to enjoy mountain biking, so I thought I would try that. I found a route that would give me opportunities to stop—I'm not as fit as I used to be. But once I cleaned up my old bike, I just let the days go by without doing anything, until one day I was talking to my friend. He saw my bike sitting out and offered to go riding with me. We went. It was tough, but it felt great to be out again."

Gary got the push he needed from a friend; luckily, he noticed some benefit from his first outing. What gets us out there, though, may not always keep us going. For example, over time, he may get bored with biking and need to vary his activities. If he's not too confident about biking alone, he may not be able to always rely on his friend to be available. Also biking is seasonal; it may be hard to get through a snowdrift on a mountain bike.

We can all boost our long-term commitment to exercise by …

On the Cutting Edge
Preliminary research suggests that yoga, with its focus on mind-body harmony and breathing techniques, can lower anxiety levels. Regular practitioners report better concentration, improved perception, and an enhanced ability to calm troubled feelings.

- Varying our activities; have two or three alternate exercise options.

- Including a friend.

- Starting off gently and building up slowly.

- Setting a specific time of day to exercise and stick to it.

- Preparing for setbacks.

- Avoiding "lazy" or counterproductive thoughts.

Go!

When Kirsty's therapist suggested exercise, the first thing she thought was, "What has that got to do with anxiety? Between work and family, I'm already stressed enough." She listened to some exercise suggestions, but she couldn't find anything that suited her. She works long hours and doesn't have access to a gym or exercise equipment.

However, don't we have to treat our bodies just as we would any other valuable possession? If our Rolls Royce developed a glitch, we wouldn't just sit there and feel depressed because it's not working. We'd check the engine, the starter, and the gas tank. We might call in a mechanic. In other words, we'd find some way to problem solve out of our dilemma. It's hard to make excuses or feel deflated when we're busy solving a problem.

Take Kirsty. After several stops and starts, she decided to fit it in wherever she could. She took the stairs rather than the elevator. She walked to work twice a week and went for a walk during her lunch hour. By breaking up exercise throughout her day, Kirsty was easily able to achieve her goal of 30 minutes of physical activity per day.

The key is to be flexible and have a backup plan. If your last workout was too much, scale it down. If you're bored, try something else. See obstacles as hurdles rather than defeat.

In addiction to tackling our exercise routine stumbling blocks, focus on the opportunity. What *will* happen if you exercise regularly? So you're only able to fit in 10 minutes of jogging; you *will* feel better than if you did nothing.

Play games with yourself. For example, keep track of the number of steps you take or try to walk a little faster than you did yesterday. Use humor; keep track of all the creative excuses your mind comes up with and post them somewhere it your house. And, finally, watch a few Nike commercials and just do it.

> **Myth Buster**
>
> *"Isn't yoga a religion?"* No! Some simple yoga techniques include breathing exercises and simple stretches. In fact, the first principle is learning how to relax your body and mind.

The Breath of Life

Our breath is an amazing barometer of our mental and physical state. For instance, when we're stressed, our breathing tends to become shallow and rapid as our bodies sense danger and shift our oxygen from our brains to our muscles. This is why extreme stress can cause us to feel light-headed and give us tingling sensations in our limbs.

Our breathing also sends feedback to the rest of our bodies, not to mention our psyches. Don't believe me? Try feeling calm and relaxed when you're hyperventilating. It's impossible. Noticing the feedback loop between our breathing, our feelings, and our physical sensations, mental-health practitioners began teaching effective breathing as a way to control arousal and reduce anxiety. And it works!

It may sound silly to think we need to learn how to breathe, but it's amazing how learning can wreak havoc on our natural instincts. Many of us, for example, breathe using our chest muscles. We expand our chest or raise our shoulders when we breathe in. This is excellent for getting ourselves energized for a sporting activity, or to prepare for a fight, but lousy for relaxation.

Instead, for relaxation, we need to shift our breathing down into our diaphragm. This fills our lungs from the bottom up. Here's a quick lesson:

> Lie down on your back, place your hands on your stomach and loosely interlock your fingers. As you breathe in, your stomach should rise and your fingers become separated. Breathe in through your nose and out through your mouth. When you've gotten the breathing down, capitalize on your physical calm by using your mind. You might try mentally repeating "My toes are relaxed; I can feel my toes relax. My calves are relaxed; I can feel my calves relax" and working your way up through the rest of your body.

Anxiety Attack

Want to give yoga a quick try? Check out this anxiety-busting yoga technique at abc-of-yoga.com/yoga-and-health/yoga-for-anxiety.asp.

The more you practice deep breathing when you're already relaxed, the easier it will be to achieve when you're under pressure. Advanced students are able to do it wherever they are—even when they're about to give a speech or face a scary medical procedure. Just as it's hard to relax when you're hyperventilating, it's hard to feel terror when you're breathing slowly and calmly.

After you've gotten the basic breathing technique down, you can add extra impact to your deep breathing by doing some of the following:

◆ Control your exhale—a longer "out" breath activates the parasympathetic nervous system, your built-in relaxation mechanism.

◆ Address anxious feelings by mentally repeating, "I feel scared/anxious/vulnerable," while breathing in, and welcoming relaxation by thinking, "I'm letting these feelings go," as you breathe out.

◆ Occasionally add meditative qualities to your breathing by fasting (no food or drink) for a couple of hours, but time this around your workouts so you're not depleting yourself of needed water or energy.

◆ Don't give up! Many people find it difficult to get the hang of it at first (or stop because they think it's stupid). In reality, the ability to control our breathing can help us reduce the physical effects of stress and regain a sense of control when anxiety overwhelms us.

Isn't the mind-body connection amazing? It's incredible that two physical activities —exercise and proper breathing—can play such a powerful role in boosting a bad mood and calming a psyche. In the next chapter, we further explore the mind-body connection by looking at how taking care of our bodies—through good nutrition and the right amount of sleep—can improve our mental well-being and lower anxiety.

The Least You Need to Know

◆ Aerobic exercise can be a great add-on in the arsenal against anxiety by stimulating natural painkillers, boosting our confidence, and distracting us from worrying thoughts.

◆ Regular exercise provides immediate benefits (a mood boost) and long-term rewards (a sense of calm).

◆ To get the best bang for your exercise buck requires 30 minutes of aerobic exercise a day.

◆ A regular exercise routine requires motivation, flexibility, and a willingness to overcome external and internal roadblocks.

◆ Learning to control our breathing can be a powerful step in soothing troubling physical symptoms and taming fear and anxiety.

Chapter 12

Mom Was Right: Eat Well and Get Some Sleep

In This Chapter

- ◆ Find out how your food affects your mood
- ◆ Discover and eliminate agitating foods
- ◆ Learn which foods promote calm
- ◆ Investigate the relationship between anxiety and insomnia
- ◆ Get surefire strategies for better Z's

In the preceding section, we discussed how exercise can boost our mood, improve our health, and help us relax. But we won't get the peak benefits from our exercise routine if other areas of our life are working against us. For example, it will be harder for me to remain peaceful after my yoga session if I slam a double shot of espresso on my way home. And imagine the impact of that Starbucks-induced jolt of adrenaline on top of a sleepless night!

From the ancient East to Hollywood's latest food fads, nutrition has always been a focus for those looking for better physical and mental health. More recently, the role sleep plays in the quality of our waking state is gaining attention, perhaps because most of us are suffering from the lack of it.

In this chapter, we examine the roles nutrition and sleep play in mental well-being and how what we eat and how much we sleep can either prime our bodies for panic or prep our bodies for peace.

Recipes for Disaster

We've all heard it; you are what you eat. Every day, we take in fuel to keep our body functioning and rebuild worn-out cells and tissue. An increasing body of evidence tells us that the grade of that fuel—the quantity and quality of our nutrition—can impact our mood and our ability to manage our emotions. Think about how irritable many of us get when we're hungry; it's easy to see the link between mood and food. The stress we feel when we need food is our body's way of telling us that our nutritional needs are not being met.

> **On the Cutting Edge**
>
> Research shows that mood, motivation, and mental performance can all be influenced by our diet. For example, three 2005 studies found that a diet rich in vitamins and Omega-3 fatty acids (found in foods such as nuts, salmon, spinach) significantly reduced violence in prison inmates.

> **Anxiety Attack**
>
> A magnesium deficiency can cause anxious feelings, so make sure you're eating enough magnesium-rich foods such as nuts, cereals, and certain fish such as halibut. You can also take it as a supplement.

But the key isn't just eating *enough* food; it's eating the *right* foods and avoiding the wrong ones. The chemical properties in some foods tend to trigger calming chemicals in our brain, whereas others tend to stir things up.

Let's take a look at two different menus—one anxiety promoting, the other anxiety busting. See which menu most closely resembles your daily intake. Here are some of the specials on the menu at the Heart-Race Hotel:

- Caffeine
- Nicotine
- Stimulant drugs
- Salt
- Sugar
- Alcohol

Caffeine stimulates our adrenal response system, and, in excess, can trigger feelings of anxiety and nervousness in all of us. It can also extend the time necessary to pass through the early stages of slumber into deep sleep. Not surprisingly, individuals with agoraphobia and panic disorder reported significantly more anxiety, nervousness, fear, nausea, heart palpitations, and restlessness depending on their caffeine intake, sometimes after as little as one cup of coffee.

Smokers often reach for a cigarette when under stress and believe that nicotine helps them calm down. In reality, though, nicotine can act as both a stimulant and a sedative. Nicotine delivers an immediate "kick" caused by stimulation of the adrenal gland, which results in the sudden release of glucose and an increase in heart rate, breathing, and blood pressure. Recent research suggests that cigarette smoking may increase the risk of anxiety disorders during late adolescence and early adulthood; in other words, the smoking came before the anxiety, not the other way around.

Some over-the-counter and prescription drugs contain caffeine and/or amphetamines. Recreational drugs such as cannabis and cocaine also raise anxiety levels.

Excessive intake of salt not only raises blood pressure, which in itself makes us feel more stressed and anxious, but it also robs us of potassium, a much-needed fuel for the nervous system.

Consuming large amounts of sugar and sweets can put your body on a roller coaster between feeling weak and feeling high-strung and jittery—your body's response to low blood sugar at one extreme, and elevated sugar levels at the other.

 **Stress Relief**

Healthy 19- to 50-year-old adults should consume no more than 3.8 grams of salt a day. However, 95 percent of American men and 75 percent of American women exceed this amount.

Alcohol is a sneaky little devil when it comes to anxiety. In the short run, it provides relief for those of us who are anxiety sensitive, which is one reason why highly anxious people are at risk for alcohol abuse. In the long run, though, alcohol use can stress the nervous system, worsen anxiety symptoms, and significantly disrupt sleep cycles.

The Good-Mood Foods

Now that we've seen what's likely to rev us up, let's take a look at the vitamins that buffer our physical and mental selves from stress, how they do it, and what foods have them.

Nutrient	What It Does	Where to Get It
Magnesium	Regulates blood-sugar levels, normalizes blood pressure, keeps heart rhythm steady, supports immune system	Green vegetables, beans, peas, nuts. Unrefined whole-grain foods
Vitamin B_{12}	Maintains healthy nerve cells and red blood cells	Fish, meat, poultry, eggs, milk, and milk products
Niacin (Vitamin B_3)	Maintains normal nervous system function, blood pressure, mental alertness	Liver, chicken, tuna, eggs, milk, broccoli, tomatoes, sweet potatoes
Glycine	Reduces the release of anxiety hormones	Gelatin, fish, meat, beans, dairy products
Omega-3	Boosts levels of a mood-balancing neurotransmitter	Mackerel, salmon, Serotonin, anchovies, herring, sardines, walnuts, lingonberries
Folic Acid (Vitamin B_9)	Helps proper nervous system function	Leafy vegetables, citrus fruits, dried beans and peas
Thiamin (Vitamin B_6)	Supports nervous system function	Pork, soybeans, peas, liver

On the Cutting Edge

Preliminary studies suggest that low blood sugar can increase and/or mimic anxiety symptoms.

So a feel-good grocery shopping excursion would have us buying healthful foods such as lean meat, fish, whole grains, vegetables, and fruit. Food Mom (and our bathroom scales) would be proud of!

Making the Most of Every Mouthful

Now let's talk a little bit about *how* we eat. After a few years of eating in the company of 3 kids under 5, I can personally attest to how stressful it is to eat standing up or to gobble my food so quickly that I barely recognized what was on my plate.

Taking the time to focus on our food (whenever possible) can not only ease our digestion, it's also a chance to slow down and refocus on our breathing. For instance:

- Don't eat standing up.

- Don't do anything else (read, watch TV, drive) while you eat.

- Chew at least 15 times per mouthful.

- Take periodic breaks to give your stomach time to tell you whether it's full, satisfied, or still hungry.

- Eat regularly (at least every five hours) to keep your blood sugar at a normal level.

> **On the Cutting Edge**
>
> According to the International Food Council, the FDA has listed the following herbal supplements as "risky": chapparel, comfrey, DHEA, dieter's tea with senna, aloe, rhubarb root, buckthorn, cascara, castor oil, penny royal, and sassafras.

The Truth About Supplements and Herbal Remedies

Much has been written about the pros and cons of taking herbal and other dietary supplements; so much, in fact, that it's hard to separate the wheat from the chaff. On the one hand, many experts say that the best way to make sure your body gets the right nutrients is through a balanced, healthful diet. My pediatrician "poo poos" the idea of vitamin supplements in healthy—and healthful-eating—children.

On the other hand, if a food source isn't particularly appealing, supplements can be a good way to ensure that vital nutrients find their way into our bodies. Personally, I'd much rather swallow an Omega-3 supplement than take a bite of fish.

Some people adapt a "double insurance" approach to vitamins and nutrients, either taking more than the recommended amount or taking vitamins when they are getting everything they need through their meals. If vitamins and nutrients are good for you, aren't more even better?

No. Vitamin toxicity is becoming increasingly common in developed countries because of the popularity of vitamin supplements. Taking too much of any vitamin can have a toxic effect. In fact, megadoses of vitamin D, vitamin A, and vitamin B$_6$ can be

> **Anxiety Attack**
>
> Our bodies use tryptophan to make serotonin and melatonin, two feel-good brain chemicals that aid sleep. Tryptophan is plentiful in oats, bananas, dried dates, milk, cottage cheese, meat, fish, turkey, chicken, and peanuts! These foods, eaten a couple of hours before bed, may just get you feeling sleepy.

fatal. For that reason, discuss with your physician whether to take a supplement, just to be sure that your body receives the right levels of nutrients and doesn't get overwhelmed.

The Power of Plants

Many herbal supplements are available for anxiety and stress. Each has its loyal supporters, but the jury is still out for many of these remedies.

Remedy	What It Does	Side Affects?
Passion flower	Acts as a mild tranquilizer	No known side effects
Skullcap	Calms nerves	No known side effects
Kava kava	Mild sedative	Some side effects reported
Chamomile	Calms nerves	No known side effects
Mugwort	Assists nervous system	No known side effects
Valerian	Mild sedative	Some side effects reported, health problems reported if abruptly stopped

Myth Buster

A recent clinical trial of herbal remedies discovered that kava kava and valerian were no more effective than an inactive placebo.

Just because herbs are promoted as all-natural alternatives doesn't mean they aren't potent; many of them are as powerful as their pharmaceutical cousins. For instance, *never* mix St. John's wort with a prescription medication without consulting your doctor first. Otherwise, you're likely to run into serious drug interactions.

What's more, herbal medications do not have to meet the same federal regulations as other drugs do, meaning the potency, purity, and safety can vary from brand to brand. The bottom line: do your homework, check carefully for interactions with other medications—and, when in doubt, ask your doctor.

I've Just Got to Get Some Sleep

What do Courtney Cox, Madonna, Britney Spears, and Eminem have in common? They've all suffered from bouts of insomnia. Apparently, fame and fortune are no guarantees of a good night's sleep; in fact, after enough sleepless nights, we'd probably trade both for some regular Z's.

Sleep problems are amazingly common. At any given time, 1 out of every 8 Americans is struggling with insomnia and, in one survey, 60 percent of the respondents said they had some trouble getting to sleep the previous week. Life events such as moving, the birth of a child, or the loss of a loved one can be particularly difficult times.

Anxiety and fear can really wreak havoc on our sleep cycle. Research has consistently shown that even mild worries tend to delay the onset of sleep. Even worse, the fatigue from lack of sleep—or the worry about another sleepless night—can increase our anxieties during waking hours *and* make it still more difficult to get to sleep. It's a vicious cycle! Let's take a look at what happens when we sleep and how we can get more of it.

Stress Relief _____

Studies have shown that a cooler body temperature can help you get to sleep. Allow at least three hours between exercise and bedtime, and keep your bedroom cool and dark.

It's Just a Stage

The first phase of sleep is a light slumber, during which our minds begin to free themselves of waking concerns. It is possible to dream during this phase, but the dreams are easily broken by sudden jolts of mental activity, known as a spike. The next phase is a deeper sleep where our brain activity slows down. Dreams are rare during this phase, as the aim of the sleep stage is to rest.

After we're refreshed with slow-wave sleep, the REM stage begins. This is where the mind gets to dream. REM sleep, named for the rapid eye movement sleep researchers noticed during this phase, lasts for about two hours for individuals without disrupting the sleep cycle. Research suggests that depression may extend active REM at the expense of slow-wave sleep; and anxiety may delay REM, make it harder to fall asleep, and make a person sleep less deeply. As a result, even if they're able to get eight hours

Anxiety Attack

Spend no more than 20 minutes lying in bed trying to fall asleep. If you haven't drifted off, get up and do a relaxing activity until you feel sleepy again. Repeat this process until you fall asleep.

of sleep, anxiety or depression sufferers may have a very real physical reason for feeling tired upon awakening.

If you're waking up feeling tired and unmotivated, chances are you've been having far more REM sleep than non-REM sleep. Your mind has been very active, not allowing you the deep rest you need. One solution is to lower worry levels during the day—this will make your mind more able to relax as you drift off.

Signposts to Slumber

In general, most healthy adults are built for 16 hours of wakefulness and need an average of 7 to 8 hours of sleep a night. Grandma may be raring to go after sleeping only 5 hours, but Junior can still feel groggy after getting 10 hours of snooze time.

Our ability to get that sleep, though, can be a challenge. Sometimes it seems that the more we need our Z's, the harder it is to get them; stress is the number one cause of short-term sleeping difficulties.

Usually, sleep problems pass when a stressful situation gets resolved. However, if short-term sleep problems aren't handled properly from the beginning, they can persist long after the original stress has passed. Worrying about lack of sleep, for example, can make it even harder to relax at night, actually exacerbating the insomnia.

Myth Buster

Think TV helps you unwind? Think again! Bursts of light and sound from a TV or video game signal the brain's orientation response, the attention focusing part of the brain usually reserved for activities such as crossing a busy road or hunting woolly mammoths. Real life routinely triggers this a couple of times an hour; TV can do it a few times each minute.

The first step in getting the best snooze is to develop some consistently good sleep habits. For example, here are some basic bedtime rules:

♦ Lower caffeine intake during the day and avoid it altogether for four to six hours before bedtime.

♦ Avoid alcohol, nicotine, and heavy meals before bedtime.

♦ Go to bed and get up at the same time every day and avoid daytime naps.

♦ Try to wake up without an alarm clock when possible. And no snooze button!

- Minimize non-sleep-related activities such as TV watching or computer use in the bedroom.

- Remove or minimize distractions. Use eye shades or ear plugs if needed.

- Don't do anything too mentally or physically stimulating in the few hours before bedtime.

Sleep's Biggest Enemy

Our basic bedtime rules help us get ready for sleep. However, despite our best efforts, most of us will have the occasional bout of sleeplessness. During these times, the trick is to take some additional steps to promote sleep without panicking in the process:

- If you've had trouble falling asleep, don't let yourself sleep later or spend excessive time in bed. These strategies usually backfire.

- Check those catastrophic thoughts such as "I'll get sick if I don't get enough sleep" or "I won't be able to function."

- Incorporate relaxation techniques into your bedtime routine. Listen to a relaxation tape an hour before bedtime or learn self-hypnosis.

- Keep a sleep diary for a week, keeping track of what time you go to bed, what time you wake up, how often and how long you wake up after falling asleep, how long you slept, and how good it was.

As you can see, our relationship with sleep, or lack of it, can be pretty tricky. On the one hand, we are constantly hearing about the dangers of sleep deprivation: drowsy driving, less motivation, more irritability. On the other hand, just because we need seven or eight hours of sleep doesn't mean we can always make our bodies get them. And stressing about our lack of sleep—when it's stress that's causing our sleeplessness in the first place—can add caffeine to our mental coffee pot!

In this chapter we've explored the relationship between mood and food. We've seen how what we feed our bodies can impact our emotional well-being. We've also explored the importance of sleep, how to develop sleep habits, and what to do when sleep eludes us.

Stress Relief _____

Research shows that just *believing* you slept badly will effect you negatively the next day. One or two nights of bad sleep won't hurt the work performance of the average person on the average day.

We've seen yet another example of the circular nature of the mind-body connection; lack of sleep and poor nutrition can make anxiety worse, and stress can make it harder to get enough sleep or make the right food choices. We've spent the last two chapters looking at how we can address the first part of this feedback loop; that is, how we can strengthen the "body" part of the mind-body connection through exercise, relaxation, healthful eating, and adequate sleep.

In the next chapter, we shift our focus to the mind, exploring how life stressors create stress, how to evaluate our own stress levels, and what coping strategies can restore our mental equilibrium.

The Least You Need to Know

◆ Our diet can impact our mood by stimulating brain chemicals that either promote calm or rev us up.

◆ Most of us get adequate nutrition through our meals and don't need vitamin supplements.

◆ Vitamin supplements and herbal remedies should be investigated carefully before use; they can be as powerful as prescription drugs.

◆ Developing good sleep habits can up the odds that we'll get our hours of needed sleep.

◆ Stress is the number one cause of short-term insomnia. The way we handle our restless nights can either minimize their impact or contribute to a bigger problem.

Chapter 3

Undoing Perpetual Stress

In This Chapter

- ◆ Get the real scoop on defining stress
- ◆ Recognize the smoke signals of stress
- ◆ Take an inventory of your arsenal against stress
- ◆ Buffer yourself from the boomerangs of stress
- ◆ Find out how normal stress becomes a disorder

Monday—I'm stuck in traffic on my way to work. I'm running 15 minutes late. I can feel my heartbeat speeding up and my chest tightening. The minute I get to work, the boss dumps a ton of work on my desk and—oh great, my computer has crashed!

I try taking some deep breaths, and it helps a little. I have to keep taking breaks during the day because it's hard to concentrate.

Home isn't much better. My kids are unusually demanding, making a seemingly endless number of requests on me. My chest is very tight; I feel like screaming. I'd love to go for a long walk to calm down, but I can't leave the kids. I settle for a handful of cookies instead.

I know all this stress isn't good for me. I've read that it can put a strain on your heart and lower your immune system. But how do I manage my stress when I don't even have time to breathe?

Most of us have experienced some version of the above. We all feel stressed at times; the daily hassles pile up, we suffer a major life event, or we just run out of the emotional resources to cope. Of course, some of us work best "under pressure," thriving on the "buzz" of energy we get from life's curveballs. One person shines when her back is up against the wall; another says stress destroyed his marriage and sabotaged his career.

How much stress is too much? In this chapter, we look at what stress is and isn't, what is most likely to cause an unhealthy level of stress, and how to keep stress from getting the better of us.

What Is Stress?

"I'm so stressed out." Most of us have said this at some point. But what exactly *is* stress? Is it having a really bad day? Having too much to do? Dealing with a difficult person?

Actually, these pressures can build up and cause stress, but they're not "stress" in and of themselves. Stress is what we experience when we start feeling like the demands life is placing on us are greater than our resources for coping with them. A pending layoff might cause most of us to worry (and polish up our resume); however, our level of stress will probably vary depending upon how easily we think we can get another job, how much of our self-esteem is tied up in our profession, and how much savings we have in the bank.

> **On the Cutting Edge**
>
> New research suggests that people who respond poorly to stressful situations are likely to have higher-than-normal levels of cholesterol, leading to later heart problems.

Your stress level isn't just impacted by the immediate resources you have at your disposal. Positive habits you develop to take care of yourself—humor, self-awareness, relaxation, creating pleasurable experiences, exercise—are like money in your mental bank account. These daily uplifts can build up your mental muscles, making it easier to marshal your coping mechanisms when faced with a tough life circumstance.

All Stressed Out and Nowhere to Go

As we've seen, stress is what we experience when we feel overwhelmed by what we have on our plate. Not surprisingly, the belief that we don't have the resources to cope with life's demands is likely to trigger an internal alarm that "rings" through our stress symptoms. Some of the most common stress symptoms include the following.

Physical Symptoms	Psychological Symptoms	Behavioral Symptoms
Muscle tension (clenched jaw, grinding teeth, tight shoulders)	Sensitivity to criticism/ critical of others	Insomnia
Increased blood pressure	Moodiness (tense, irritable)	Appetite changes
Restlessness, fidgeting	Concentration problems	Withdrawing from others
Headaches, stomachaches, indigestion	Indecision	Less self-control (smoking, drinking, overeating)
Shallow breathing	Rigid thinking, no sense of humor	Verbal outbursts

As you look through these, perhaps you noticed that, although unpleasant, these signals serve a useful purpose. Essentially, they narrow our focus and energy to the threat at hand. However, it's the side effects that we have to watch out for. For example, because it's so all-consuming, stress can adversely impact our ability to communicate clearly, control our behavior, or to be sensitive to others. In addition, our mental attention gets locked on our problems, and we can become rigid in our decisions, despite the facts.

Myth Buster

"No symptoms, no stress, right?" Well, perhaps. Some medications can mask the symptoms commonly associated with stress. Be sure any prescription medication isn't covering up stress symptoms. And remember, stress affects us all differently—your symptoms won't exactly match someone else's.

Give Me a U!

We all know that sometimes a little stress helps us get things done. Deadlines can provide the adrenaline boost we need to finish a daunting task. In moderation, stress is a motivator; it can rally our resources, wake us up, and get us moving. The trick is finding the balance between too little stress and too much. No one ever made it to the Olympics without performance stress; on the other hand, too much pressure leads to mistakes, not medals.

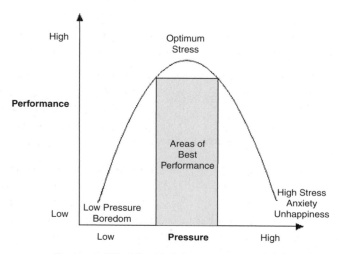

The inverted-U relationship between pressure and performance

Researchers have found that the relationship between pressure and performance is like an inverted *U*: too little pressure and we can't muster the energy; too much and we can't focus. Think of it as the Goldilocks rule! If you feel motivated *and* able to concentrate; focused on the task at hand but able to retain a sense of composure; open to broader thinking and different ways of accomplishing the task—then you're in the peak performance zone.

On the Cutting Edge

Stressful situations can interfere with mental agility. Studies at Ohio State University have found that stressed-out research subjects were less capable of solving problems and word puzzles than those who were at ease and calm.

But if we cross over the stress threshold, our performance deteriorates. A bank robber was once caught red-handed simply because he couldn't open the door. Loot in hand, he repeatedly tried to push the door—even though the sign "Pull" was clearly visible. His brain closed down and he kept pushing the door and pushing the door—until the police arrived.

Stress Inventory: Lifestyles of the Famously Stressed

Celebrities are known to suffer from more than their fair share of stress. Busy work schedules, little privacy, and an industry governed by critics and the unpredictable tastes of the public mean that Hollywood therapists have become experts in helping their clients cope with stress. Climb into the therapist's chair and ask yourself the following questions to see how stressful your lifestyle really is:

- **How would you summarize your friendships?** A supportive network of friends and acquaintances is one of the most powerful buffers against stress. It's not just the number of friends, though; it's how available they are, how often you see them, and how much you can trust and confide in them.

- **How do you use your free time?** Having hobbies and outside interests is a great way to keep active and emotionally fit. However, if they leave you with no "downtime," it can be too much of a good thing. In addition, consider leisure activities that balance your life: a little bungee jumping might liven up a boring work routine; a reading group might be a relaxing break from a high-stress job.

- **Have you experienced significant changes in your life over the past year?** Any significant life event will stir the emotional pot. Don't overlook the stress of even positive changes. A wedding, for instance, can cause tremendous stress. And be especially tuned in to the stress of loss, which seems to be an emotional Achilles heel for most of us. Acknowledge the normal emotional wear and tear following a loss and give yourself time to recover.

- **How are things at your job?** Too much responsibility (work overload, unrealistic expectations) in combination with too little control (demanding boss, conflicting or unclear communication) is double trouble when it comes to work-related stress. And work stress can be particularly hazardous because most of us spend more time there than anywhere else.

- **How do you feel at the end of the day?** Do you obsess about what's happened? Can you unwind, or do you feel tense yet exhausted? Your ability to unwind at the end of the day is a powerful indicator of how your coping mechanisms are working.

> **On the Cutting Edge**
>
> Recent research has produced the first-ever visualization of psychological stress in the brain. During a "stress test," MRI scans showed increased blood flow in the prefrontal cortex, an area long associated both with anxiety and depression as well as working memory and goal-oriented behavior. Interestingly, the blood flow continued even after the test was completed.

Samurai Swords Against Stress: Choose Your Weapon

After five years working nights with a demanding boss and trying to raise a family, Sarah decided enough was enough. She quit. Within three weeks, she found a new job with better hours, a better boss, and closer to home. Her lower stress more than made up for the slight reduction in pay.

When Bill's father was diagnosed with cancer and had to move in with him, it brought their longstanding relationship problems to the fore. Bill struggled with often feeling angry and short-tempered with his father—and then feeling guilty about it. When a friend commented one day that Bill was lucky to have this special time with his father, it gave him some food for thought. He made more of an effort to get to know his father and better understand the choices and actions he had made. It didn't change his father's personality or make up for past tensions, but Bill was surprised that it did take away his resentment and give him a sense of peace.

Greg's world exploded when his daughter died. He felt anger over his loss and resentful toward his friends who had healthy, happy children. Only when his marriage began to deteriorate did he agree to attend a support group for grieving parents. As he listened to parents who had gone through similar experiences, he felt less alone. Three years later, Greg's marriage is great and he's started a research foundation to find a cure for the illness that took his daughter's life.

> **Myth Buster**
>
> *"Stress is a sign of spiritual weakness."* Although faith can be a source of great strength, it does not make us immune to stress. Stress is a natural motivator designed to help us improve and move us to do better.

Sarah, Bill, and Greg each found ways to channel their stress into positive action. In Sarah's case, she was able to remove the stressor. Bill and Greg had to first deal with the emotions around their stressful life event before they could decide what to do. We can deal with stress lots of ways, and the most effective strategy often depends upon how much control we have over it and how intense our feelings are about it.

Lights, Camera, Action?

When Sarah couldn't renegotiate her work hours or get transferred to a better boss, she decided to change her situation. This decision didn't come lightly; she had to first look at the risks versus the rewards, deal with the fear and uncertainty of potential unemployment, and initially exert more effort (preparing a resumé, conducting a job search) when she felt exhausted already.

When experiencing stress, one of the most useful questions to ask ourselves is "What do I have control over and what can't I change?" For instance, you may not be able to change the uncomfortable physical sensations that accompany panic, but you can change how you interpret them (unpleasant but not dangerous). You can keep them from controlling your life by refusing to avoid situations where you have felt panicked before. Similarly, you can't change a power-hungry manager, but you can "watch your back" by putting everything in writing and figuring out how to defuse his tactics.

Nothing More Than Feelings ...

On the other hand, perhaps—like Bill or Greg—the stressor in your life isn't something you can control. Unfortunately, we can't make a life-threatening illness, the loss of a loved one, or a company merger disappear. During times like these, it's easy to feel helpless and out of control. But even in these situations, there are things you can *do.* You can change the story you tell yourself about what's happened; you can develop the skills to more effectively manage your feelings; you can surround yourself with caring people; and you can use your grief or fear to get more information or help others.

For instance, imagine how your stress would differ if you interpreted a company merger with a neutral, "let's wait and see" attitude versus a career-threatened panic. It doesn't mean you shouldn't go ahead and polish up that resumé (prepare for the worst) or do some research on the success rate of similar mergers; but you're staying with the facts versus embellishing them with catastrophic interpretations.

Emotion-focused coping, as opposed to active problem solving, is a way to manage the negative feelings toward your stressor. On the positive side, emotion-focused coping strategies such as relaxation and distraction can help you pay more attention to what your emotional signals are telling you and free you from obsessive worrying. On the other hand, you don't want to use them as a replacement for dealing directly with aspects of your stressor that you can control: crying on a girlfriend's shoulder may make you feel better, but it does nothing to get you out of an abusive relationship.

Even in situations that seem unavoidably stressful, there are often ways to cope. For

> **Anxiety Attack**
>
> Yet another reason to tackle stress: research has found the link between dieting, stress, and overeating. A combination of deprivation (such as dieting) plus stress causes a "hedonic deprivation state," a craving for something pleasurable. "Comfort foods" high in fat and sugar were found to mimic the brain's natural pleasure chemicals, opioids.

instance, the book *Full Catastrophe Living* by Jon Kabat-Zinn is highly recommended for people experiencing the stress of chronic pain or illness.

Stockpile Those Resources

You've just found out your life depends on completing a marathon that will take place in four weeks. With that kind of motivation, most of us could muster our way through. But think what an advantage we'd start with if we were already working out.

Stress Relief

Use a mental picture as a calming anchor. For example, develop a mental picture of your perfect place (beach, mountain scene) and practice conjuring it up at the same time you focus on slowing your breathing; the more detail you can insert, the better. Pair this scene with relaxation often enough and you can take it anywhere you go.

It's the same way with stress management. Situational stressors often require tailor-made responses; but living a healthful lifestyle, knowing yourself, and developing an arsenal of coping skills gives you a head start when life gets tougher. Studies confirm that people who are clear about who they are and where they want to go are better able to handle stress. In particular, those who take preparation time seriously are less stressed. UCLA researchers, for example, found lower levels of the stress hormone cortisol in people who had been asked to think about their values and priorities before being submitted to a stressful experience.

Create Your Secret Stress Journal

In a life filled with daily hassles, it can be hard to keep track of the sources of our stress, the emotional reactions we have to them, and what we do when we encounter them. Keeping a stress diary for a couple of weeks can help us connect the dots between our external reality and internal stress, and provide insight into what we're doing right and what's not working. This helps you to separate the common, routine stresses from those that only occur occasionally.

To get started, buy a notebook and record your stress statistics for 14 days. Make a note every hour or so, particularly when you pick up on your stress signals.

Here's a typical stress diary entry:

Monday, 10 A.M.

Happiness level: (Scale of –10 to +10) *+4*

Mood: *I feel relieved that I wasn't late for work!*

Work efficiency: (0–10) *6*

Stress level: (0–10) *3*

Most recent stressful event: *Thinking about the presentation I need to give next week*

Stress symptom felt: *Butterflies, sweaty palms*

Cause of stress: *Worrying I'll look stupid*

My chosen reaction: *At first I panicked, but then I relaxed my breathing and thought about how to prepare for the presentation. The stress dropped.*

After you've collected your 14 days' worth of data, sort it into the following lists:

◆ **Stress frequency.** What are the recurring stressors in your life? List the most frequent source of stress at the top, progressing to the occasional or infrequent stressor.

◆ **Stress level.** The stressors that occur most often aren't always the most stressful. Rate the most unpleasant stress you've experienced over the past two weeks at the top, the least stressful at the bottom.

◆ **Stress trigger.** What daily hassles and life events are wreaking havoc on your physical and mental health? List all the stressors you've experienced.

◆ **Stress response.** What did you do when you felt stressed? Did you overeat, lose your cool, or make a plan? Did your coping strategy work for you or not? What would you do differently; what *will* you do differently?

Stress Relief

Believe it or not, for most of us, the daily hassles (work overload, a chronically procrastinating child, an unreliable car) cause more stress than big life events. Don't let these pile up just because they aren't crises!

By the end of this exercise, you'll have a pretty good handle on recurring stress triggers, how they impact you, and how you try to manage them. You'll also get a sense of the effectiveness of your current coping strategies and can begin to think about alternatives that might work better.

Damage Control: Relating Under Stress

When I'm stressed, my husband calls me a firecracker. And although I defend myself vehemently against this nickname, secretly I know that it's true. Given enough pressure, my normally expressive, assertive communication style turns into quick-tempered explosiveness. Of course, he's no angel; when he's stressed, his normally efficient, bottom-line communication style transforms into a flat-out dictatorial style.

Our communication style changes under stress. There's a good reason for this; we stop responding to external cues and start listening to internal ones that tell us we're in a crisis and we've got to fight to survive. We stop responding to what the interpersonal situation calls for and start trying to reduce our stress, regardless of its effectiveness or the feelings of others. In essence, we resort to fallback mode. Our typical communication style may become exaggerated and inflexible:

- The emotionally responsive, assertive person attacks.

- The bottom-line leader becomes controlling.

- The reserved, cooperative person becomes ingratiating.

- The quiet, analytical person goes into avoidance mode.

This fallback mode is an extreme manifestation of our normal communication style. If our communication is a ladder, the lowest rung is the most primitive. As we grow and develop, our interpersonal skills (we hope) move up the ladder; we have wisdom and more strategies to choose from and we're able to respond to the cues of the interpersonal situation we're in. When we experience enough stress, though, we get knocked back down the ladder and often wind up clinging to old, outdated communication strategies that are ineffective but make us feel safe. This is our fallback communication mode.

As such, although our fallback mode can disrupt relationships, it serves a good purpose by helping to reduce our stress. Which is why telling someone to "snap out of it" or pointing out how ineffective the communication is *when someone is in it* never works. What *does* work is learning to recognize the signs and symptoms of a fallback communication mode and developing strategies for minimizing its impact on our relationships.

Keeping Cool Under Pressure

One reason my husband and I have been happily married for 15 years is that we've learned to recognize the stress signals in each other and adjust accordingly. When you see a work colleague or a loved one losing his or her cool, to avoid becoming equally stressed (and unintentionally responding with your own fallback behavior), use the following:

- **Don't take it personally.** Remind yourself that a fallback communication mode is a survival strategy rather than a personal attack or a plot against you.

- **Avoid analysis paralysis.** If you're drowning, the last thing you need to do is puzzle over how you fell in the ocean. You need a lifeboat. Avoid theoretical discussions or explanations for how the current situation was created; instead, engage in crisis management by focusing on realistic, short-term goals.

- **Sidestep the fallback position.** Don't waste your breath trying to get someone to stop operating from fallback. If they could, they would. Instead, the trick is to minimize the damage this crisis communication style can have on interpersonal relationships. For instance, if you're a manager, teach your employees to recognize their own fallback communication signals and encourage them to find ways to vent their stress without passing it to someone else.

Odds are that you, too, will occasionally find yourself in fallback communication. When this happens, here are things you can do to relieve the pressure in the short-run without increasing stress over time:

- **Postpone what you can.** When we're operating under extreme stress, we're much more likely to say or do things we later regret. This is the time to reschedule meetings or postpone appointments if possible and avoid making major life decisions.

- **Get feedback from others.** It's hard to see ourselves clearly, especially when we're clouded with emotion. Getting a view of ourselves from the eyes of the people around us can provide powerful clues for further personal and professional development stress.

Stress and Trauma: From Order to Disorder

If upsetting life events and daily hassles can take such a toll on our mental health, imagine what a catastrophe can do. An extreme emotional reaction to trauma is normal; even the most resilient among us will feel devastated or frightened after a life-threatening or life-altering event. Depending upon the nature of the trauma, our exposure to previous trauma, our pre-event mental health, and our internal and external resources, these natural emotions may or may not lead to a clinical disorder.

Within the first month of surviving a serious accident, violent assault, or natural disaster, the survivor experiences intense fear, helplessness, emotional numbing, and a sense that both he and the world around him are unreal. Anxiety symptoms can include irritability, sleep problems, and being easily startled. This cluster of symptoms is often diagnosed as *acute stress disorder.*

If the symptoms persist longer than four weeks and are severe enough to interfere with the person's life, the diagnosis will be changed to *post-traumatic stress disorder.* PTSD is a condition in which a person continues to be affected by trauma even though it may have happened years ago.

Symptoms include the following:

◆ Reexperiencing the trauma, sometimes known as flashbacks, which can happen while awake or asleep

◆ Avoiding people, places, and things that remind the person of the initial trauma

◆ Loss of normal feelings—numbness, losing interest in important life activities, and feeling isolated

◆ Hyperarousal—feeling on guard, overreacting to noise or other environmental cues, often leading to lack of sleep and concentration

The majority of serious trauma survivors do not develop post-traumatic stress disorder or acute stress disorder. In fact, we can see how these disorders are yet another example of how stress is an interaction between what happens to us (the nature and severity of the stressor) and the resources (genetic, social, and so forth) we have to cope with it.

Pop artist Andy Warhol summed it up well: "They always say time changes things, but you actually have to change them yourself."

Each of us experiences stressors, whether they come as minor hassles, moderate life events, or extreme trauma. How well and how easily we cope with them is a combination of both skill and luck, how resilient our genetic make-up is, how stressful our life experience is, and how skillfully we've built up our resources. In the next chapter, we take a look at a stressor that requires superpowers to survive and thrive against—panic disorder—and learn how we can learn to mentally surf the tsunami.

The Least You Need to Know

- Recognize your own stress levels by being conscious of how narrow your focus is becoming.

- Keep a stress diary to understand your sources of stress, and how it affects you.

- Use three stress-busting tools—taking action, taking charge of emotions, and acceptance.

- Translate language, for calming stressed-out relationships.

- Understand that trauma can trigger an anxiety disorder, but even survivors of serious trauma handle stress differently

Part 5

Survive-and-Thrive Strategies for Diagnosed Distress

Now that we've strengthened our mental resilience and physical well-being, we turn our attention to the "big guns"—the clinically diagnosed anxiety disorders. From panic disorder to social anxiety, we look at the most effective strategies for coping with physical symptoms, disrupting irrational or obsessive thoughts, and reentering fearful situations. We then consider the evidence on the most effective treatment for anxiety and how we can ensure that our treatment team is up to the challenge.

14

Surfing the Panic Tsunami: Self-Help for Panic Disorder

In This Chapter

◆ Determine whether or not you've been emotionally hijacked

◆ Discover the difference between a panic attack and panic disorder

◆ Find out why panic attacks aren't the real problem

◆ Develop panic attack survival skills

Drs. Jack Loehr and Jack Groppel, founders of LGE Performance Systems, use this corporate training exercise as part of their training: a group of NFL superstars is given a mission. They must follow a wilderness trail for 1 mile, touch a white fence, and return to the training center in less than 18 minutes. For such elite runners, this should be easy. However, before the run begins, the runners are warned to look out for water moccasins, alligators, and wild boars in the area. "If you see a wild boar," says the instructor, "take appropriate action, but complete the mission!"

The run begins. A staff member is planted in the bushes at the half-mile mark; when a runner reaches this point, the hidden instructor makes the sound of a wild boar. Inevitably, in spite of their instructions and with no visible evidence of a wild animal bearing down on them, the runners panic and sprint back to the starting point. The only explanation offered for the failed mission? "We heard something."

This same "wild boar" exercise, when given to elite law-enforcement units or military units, yields dramatically different results. Trained to respond to threats, these individuals stop, turn in the direction of the threat, and assume a crouched position. As a result, they quickly determine that there is no wild boar and are able to complete the mission.

For panic sufferers, this story makes some powerful points. First, fear can overpower *anyone's* rational thought. Second, there's a difference between being "tough" and being prepared; law-enforcement personnel felt the same rush of adrenalin and fear that the other trainees did. Their training didn't prevent them from *feeling* fear; it just prevented them from *giving in* to it.

For the three million Americans who have panic attacks, "wild boars" can show up anywhere at any time—at the grocery store, in the pediatrician's office, or at work. Suddenly, we experience the terror people feel when faced with life-threatening danger—and the same urge to escape. This chapter is all about training ourselves to respond like Green Berets when we face our own "wild boars."

The Emotional Hijacking

"Help! I've been hijacked!" No, don't call the FBI; the culprit isn't a terrorist. Panic attack sufferers get ambushed by our *amygdala*, the danger-response center in our brain's limbic system. And although it's not the smartest group of cells in our gray matter, it has a very important job—to ensure our survival.

> **Myth Buster**
>
> *"I'm having a heart attack!"*
> A rapid heartbeat might make you think so, but the heart can beat rapidly for a long time without causing any damage. In a real heart attack, people are only aware of crushing pain.

In fact, our amygdala is sometimes a real hero. It has the ability to respond directly to input from your senses before the brain's master strategist—the neocortex—even begins to register it. Our amygdala spurs us to rescue that baby from the burning building or turn the wheel in response to an oncoming car before we have time to think about it. Perhaps this is why the limbic system is one of the oldest parts of our brain; what it lacks in analytical thinking it makes up for in speed and action.

Dan Goleman, the author of *Emotional Intelligence*, used the term *emotional hijacking* to refer to situations in which our rational mind is taken over by our emotional response. The problem with emotional hijacking is that it doesn't always result in heroics; emotional hijacking can lead to road rage, domestic violence, and countless other harmful our counterproductive acts. And with panic attacks, the alarm signals go off needlessly; there is no real danger we need to protect ourselves from.

> ⟩**Myth Buster** _____
>
> *"I'm going to lose my mind!"* No one with panic attacks has ever become psychotic during one. The very fact that the panic attack sufferer is aware of how irrational the symptoms are and is concerned about his or her mental health strongly indicates sanity!

So It's All in My Head?

Well, yes and no. Our inappropriately aroused amygdala is in our head, but the physical symptoms that occur during a panic attack are very real. Common symptoms include the following:

◆ Racing or pounding heart

◆ Dizziness or lightheadedness

◆ Nausea

◆ Terror or sense of impending doom

◆ Sense of unreality

◆ Fear of dying, losing control, or doing something embarrassing

◆ Flushes or chills

◆ Chest pains

◆ Tingling or numbness in the hands

◆ Difficulty breathing

Not everyone experiences *all* of these symptoms, but all panic attack sufferers experience some of them. Not only are the symptoms themselves terrifying, they're unpredictable. First panic attacks, in particular, tend to show up "out of the blue" when we're doing something ordinary like driving to work, having dinner with friends, even sleeping. A testament to their sheer terror is the number of people who drive themselves to the emergency room after having their first panic attack.

Not everyone who has a panic attack develops a panic disorder. A fortunate few experience one panic attack and never have another; for example, the night before college graduation or walking down the altar might create such anxiety that it triggers a panic attack. Others—up to 10 percent of otherwise healthy Americans—have them occasionally but continue to lead unrestricted lives. In fact, it's not the number of panic attacks that determines whether or not a person develops panic disorder; *it's the response we have to them.*

For one in 75 U.S. citizens, though, the first panic attack sets in motion a vicious cycle. The fear of another panic attack—of having to go through those distressing symptoms again—causes the panic attack sufferer to worry about having another one. S/he may avoid things/situations in which the person has experienced panic attacks in the past. As a result, even when we panic-attack sufferers are not in the grip of the actual attack, we're consumed with the desire to avoid one.

With Friends Like These ...

Unfortunately, the people we rely on to help or support us can unintentionally make things worse. Physicians, for example, frequently fail to recognize panic disorder. Many panic attack sufferers see as many as 10 doctors before meeting one who makes the right diagnosis. In the meantime, we've undergone all sorts of unnecessary, expensive, and anxiety-provoking tests!

Then when we finally meet a medical professional who identifies panic disorder, the explanation often sounds as if there is nothing *really* wrong. *"There's nothing to worry about, you're just having a panic attack"* or *"It's just nerves."* Although meant to be reassuring, such words can be dispiriting to the frantic person whose terrifying symptoms keep recurring.

The same can be true of well-meaning friends and family members. People who've never had a panic attack sometimes assume that it's just a matter of feeling nervous or anxious—the sort of feelings that everyone is familiar with. *I was so nervous about that test I almost had a panic attack! I just panicked at the thought of my boss realizing I hadn't quite finished that project.*

A friend and fellow panic attack sufferer once told me that, during the worst period of her life, she had disclosed her experience of panic attacks to a work colleague, who responded with something like, "You know, I get pretty uptight about things some-times. I wonder if I have panic attacks." My friend comically asked her coworker if she knew of any new mothers who *wondered* whether or not they had experienced labor pains. If you've had them, you know it. If you haven't, there's no way anyone can adequately describe them to you.

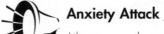

Anxiety Attack _____

Like many other anxiety disorders, the development of panic disorder seems to be caused by a combination of bio-logical vulnerability and life expe-riences; they often start during a stressful period in a person's life.

And Then It Gets Really Complicated

We've already outlined the vicious-cycle characteristic of panic disorder: a panic attack that triggers intense fears of having another one and a strong motivation to avoid any situation that is associated with it. If you have a panic attack while walking your dog, you may avoid the area where your symptoms appeared. If you have two or three while dog walking, you may avoid taking the dog out at all. Even if we know that the situation did not cause the panic attack, the very fact that the two are associated with each other can make us fearful that revisiting the same situation will bring on another one. Avoid the situation long enough and we develop a panic-induced phobia.

Of course, the reverse is also true. People who suffer from phobias can have such strong situational anxiety that it triggers a panic attack. Social-anxiety sufferers, for example, might only have panic attacks in distressing social situations. A person who has a driving phobia may be so afraid of getting behind the wheel that just opening the car door triggers a panic attack. In theses cases, the panic attack did not cause the phobia; it does, however, give the phobia additional ammunition and make it harder to tackle. We discuss self-help strategies for phobias in Chapters 15 and 16.

When panic attacks occur randomly and frequently, we can come to fear any situa-tion in which we can't easily escape. This is called *agoraphobia*, and it affects about one third of us with panic disorder. Here are other physical and mental conditions that can coexist with panic disorder:

- **Depression.** Affects about half of all panic disorder sufferers.

- **Obsessive-compulsive disorder** (OCD). Characterized by repetitive, distress-ing behaviors.

- **Alcohol and drug abuse.** About 30 percent of panic disorder patients abuse alcohol; 17 percent abuse drugs.

◆ **Irritable bowel syndrome.** When someone has IBS, panic disorder is often overlooked.

◆ **Mitral valve prolapse.** This is a heart defect that can cause chest pain, rapid heartbeat, breathing difficulties, and headache. Some experts think that people with this defect are more likely to develop panic disorder.

Because panic attacks are so disturbing, they can quickly take over our lives. Not only can they impact day-to-day activities, our attempts to survive or avoid them can create additional problems. The good news is that you can deal with panic attacks. They don't have to lead to panic disorder, depression, or social isolation.

Preparing for Boot Camp

Here's another piece of good news: whether or not you get professional help, you can do a lot to take control of your panic attacks. It might be hard to imagine right now, but you can prepare for panic ahead of time, building up your coping skills so that you are able to cope with your symptoms and, over time, reduce the number of attacks you have. Think of it as your panic attack boot camp, the psychological equivalent to the elite military training that enabled the soldiers and law-enforcement professionals to succeed in the story at the beginning of this chapter.

Anxiety Attack _____

To jump-start your self-help program, visit www.panic-attacks.co.uk for a free online course.

Unlike military or police training, though, you will be in control of your own curriculum; only you know what will work for you. You will also be in charge of how hard you work and how quickly you progress. Before we get to specifics, though, make sure you have the right attitude.

Evaluate your progress in terms of what you *do*, not how you *feel*. The more you are able to remain in an uncomfortable situation *despite* anxiety or panic, the more progress you will make in taking away the grip your distress currently holds on you.

Expect the beginning to be the hardest. Why is it that the first 10 minutes of an exercise routine are the hardest? It's a bummer, but it's true for new exercisers as well as seasoned athletes. The difference between those who stick with it and those who don't is commitment coupled with frequent self-reminders that the initial discomfort will pass and the end result will be worth it. This applies to self-help, too.

Make deals with yourself. It takes a leap of faith to stop running from panic attacks and turn around to face them. You may find a part of yourself shouting at you to get out of there, while another part is struggling to stay put; when this happens, strike a bargain. If your anxiety is a "9," try to stay in the situation until it subsides to a "5." If you have to leave, go back in when the panic subsides. Feel good about each step forward, no matter how small.

In addition to these empowering attitudes, examine your beliefs about asking for help. We may hide our panic symptoms from friends and family, or feel tremendous guilt because our panic attacks are disrupting our home life. As a result, many of us lack the social support that can help us get through the stress and help us stretch our mental muscles. While we're helping ourselves, why not let our families in on our self-help plans? They can be valuable cheerleaders, especially when they see us playing so hard to win.

Therapists, support group members, and online communities can also be resources, especially if you have permission to call them when you're in the middle of a panic attack. Some panic sufferers carry a telephone list of phone numbers they can call any time day or night—even though they've never used it. Having other resources always makes us feel stronger; in fact, just knowing we have the option of calling someone at the peak of our anxiety can give us the courage to stay in a frightening situation until the symptoms resolve.

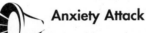 **Anxiety Attack**

An additional resource for panic attack sufferers is the National Institute of Mental Health's Anxiety Hotline— 1-888-826-9438.

Survival Skill 1: Reclaim Your Body

Given that panic attacks make us feel so mentally and physically out of control, it makes sense that skills that help us control our bodies will be useful. For instance, the hyperventilation that often accompanies a panic attack can be countered—or even prevented—by diaphragmatic breathing.

The middle of a panic attack is no time to learn new breathing techniques; but if you practice breathing control techniques for five minutes twice a day for a few weeks, you can perform them more easily when you feel the onset of panic symptoms. The kind of steady, persistent breathing practice outlined here will get your body in the habit of always breathing deeply and slowly. This will decrease and hopefully eliminate any anxiety attacks while at the same time relieving your anxiety.

1. Begin by lying flat on your back or standing up straight. You may also sit up straight in a chair, if that is more comfortable.

2. Place your hand on your stomach area.

3. Breathe as you normally would and notice whether your hand rises or your chest rises. To breathe properly, your stomach area must rise as your diaphragm expands.

4. Begin by slowly breathing in through your nose to the count of five while gently pushing your hand up with your stomach.

5. Hold the breath for a count of five.

6. Slowly exhale through your mouth for a count of five while gently pushing down on your stomach.

7. Repeat this process for five minutes.

Again, similar relaxation exercises can help train your muscles to relax, a response incompatible with the tense muscles you have during a frightening situation. Any activity (biofeedback, progressive relaxation, meditation) that helps you become familiar with how your body feels when you are under stress can help you consciously relax. You can find some sample relaxation exercises in Chapter 16; in addition, numerous meditation and relaxation exercises are available on CD or video.

Don't get frustrated or impatient with yourself and give up if you cannot do these exercises correctly right away—or if you feel yourself panicking when you try them. They take practice. In the beginning, only do them as long as you are able. Remember that you are in control and can stop at any time. Take it as slowly as needed.

Anxiety Attack

Because the physical sensations (rapid heartbeat, shallow breathing) created during aerobic exercise so closely match those generated during panic attacks, some panic suffers cannot tolerate one without generating the other. You can still engage in health-boosting activity such as leisurely walking or swimming.

If you continue to practice your breathing techniques or relaxation exercises, you will soon be more naturally relaxed throughout the day. As you gain more awareness and control over your body, you will be able to tolerate daily hassles and minor stressors with a sense of calm and peace. However, if everyday stressors create little waves on our surface of calm, gaining control over our body is like becoming a better swimmer. Panic symptoms, though, are like tsunamis; we've also got to prepare for emergencies.

Survival Skill 2: Stock the Life Raft

Our first survival skill focused on managing the uncomfortable physical sensations during a panic attack. In addition to the bodily discomfort, though, is the spiral of fear that sets in when panic attacks start. Our thoughts begin to race, filling us with dire predictions that we are going to pass out, die, make a fool of ourselves, or lose control. The faster we can interrupt this spiral, the more we can allow our uncomfortable anxiety symptoms to pass through us without taking control over us.

The best way to control catastrophic thoughts is to focus your attention on something else, something simple enough that you can do it while you're afraid. This is not the time, for example, to try to rationally combat irrational thoughts. On the other hand, it must be complex enough that it requires some mental effort. Turning your breathing exercise into a mental activity is one idea; you might count each inhale and each exhale. You could perform simple arithmetic (counting backward or reciting the multiplication tables), repeat the words to a favorite song or poem, focus on memorizing the details of your environment, or play simple words games. It doesn't matter what it is as long as it keeps you from "what ifs" and grounds you in the present.

An especially useful distraction can be to repeatedly recite a list of rational reassurances that you have memorized or written down. *These symptoms are unpleasant but they're not dangerous. This is just my alarm system going off. These feelings have passed before and they'll pass again. What doesn't kill me makes me stronger.*

You'll probably find clues to the most effective reassurances by examining the self-talk that typically surfaces during a panic attack. Think back to the automatic thoughts you had during your last panic attack and write out a rational reassurance in response. For example, if one of your thoughts was *"I can't stand this!"* consider something like *"I've been through this before. It's not fun, but I can stand it."* Keep this list with you at all times; it can be a great security blanket the next time your emotions are hijacked.

Speaking of security blankets, are there certain items that you own that calm you down? A journal? A portable CD player with a favorite CD? A rosary? A cell phone? Anything you can carry with you that will help you feel more secure is fair game. One woman I know still carried antianxiety medication in her purse for five years after she and her mental-health team decided she was ready to discontinue it.

> **Myth Buster**
>
> *"I'm going to pass out!"* You may fear this because of temporary dizziness, but it can't happen. A sudden drop in blood pressure is what causes fainting. Your blood pressure actually rises during anxiety, because your heart beats faster.

She never took a pill, but knowing she *could* gave her the extra courage and confidence she needed to keep moving forward.

Survival Skill 3: Renegotiate Your Relationship with Panic

When I was at the mercy of my panic symptoms, the relationship seemed to be one of master/slave. My panic attacks would come out of nowhere and "tell" me how to feel and what to think. All I could do was react; all I could focus on was survival.

However, as I learned ways to prepare for panic, the relationship began to change. Instead of feeling powerless, I began to feel an increasing sense of control over what I could do when panic showed up. I and many other panic sufferers have discovered a paradox: the less I feared panic attacks, the less frequent and less intense they were. When I tried to avoid them, they hung on tighter; when I quit fighting, they loosened their grip.

Just knowing this, however, doesn't make it easy. To handle panic paradoxically is to go against our basic instincts. Logic tells us that in a threatening situation we should flip on our emergency response, tense the body, and get ready to fight or run like the devil before we get hurt. What we need to do, though, is flip on our controlled breathing, relax the muscles of the body, don't fight your physical sensations, and stay in the situation. Martial artists know these tricks well. Someone who doesn't know how to fight will let his or her anger take over, will wildly attack someone, and will likely end up getting hurt. A trained martial arts expert will stay calm, controlled, and focused—and will be much more likely to win a fight.

With anxiety, the very act of choosing to take control in response to panic keeps our neocortex (remember the master strategist?) in charge rather than the alarmist amygdala.

Refusing to be subservient to our panic symptoms allows us to renegotiate our role to one of curious inquiry. Instead of doing all we can to avoid those feelings, let's take an interest in them. In fact, let's get downright scientific about them. Develop your own symptom severity scale; 1 signals complete relaxation, and 10 indicates outright panic. Practice doing this when you have symptoms and when you don't. Notice which thoughts and actions raise or lower the rating. Notice that, even at their worst, panic symptoms actually have a very short life. They can't stay at a very high intensity for more than a few seconds.

Investigating your symptoms gives your thinking a focus, and so it's not as susceptible to emotional hijacking. If you're busy observing your symptoms, you're not as caught up fighting or escaping from them. In fact, when you learn to observe your panic symptoms without resisting them, you may consider purposefully *increasing* them.

Advanced Training for Special Forces

When we're having trouble tolerating our panic symptoms, it can seem impossible to ever consider *inviting* them. And yet, when we consider how much the unpredictability of our panic attacks contributes to the havoc they wreak, we can see how empowering it would be to consciously seek them out. When we know that, we can begin to control our reactions.

Cognitive behavior therapists often do this in therapy sessions to desensitize their clients to the terror that these harmless (but seemingly life-threatening) symptoms create. For example, a client who hyperventilates during a panic attack might be instructed to breathe rapidly; a client who gets dizzy might be encouraged to spin around and around. A client may be asked to respond to mild symptoms by consciously attempting to make them worse. All of these exercises allow the panic attack sufferer to take voluntary control over symptoms.

Panic disorder develops when we repeatedly try to control or avoid our anxiety—and fail. By taking charge of our anxiety, we don't set ourselves up for failure. As we get better at tolerating our symptoms, we can stay put long enough for our mind to register that there's no real danger in the situation.

Think about any new activity that you felt nervous about. Maybe you sang in church or gave a school presentation. Maybe it was asking your girlfriend out for a date or going on your first job interview. It was nerve-wracking at first, but you became more comfortable as you got used to it; your brain recognized you weren't in danger and called off the "red alert." As a result, your butterflies subsided and your heart quit beating so fast.

> **Myth Buster**
>
> *"I might lose control during a panic attack."* Some people with panic disorder are afraid they'll either become totally paralyzed or run around wildly, yelling obscenities and hurting other people. But the body's response during anxiety is the result of a desire to escape rather than paralysis or harm toward others.

Here's another analogy. Let's suppose that new security system you installed in your house has a bug in it. As a result, it occasionally triggers a false alarm. Imagine the police showed up in response—and you tried to keep them out of the house, shouting, "There's no danger!" through the door. Without question, they would insist on coming in to make sure you're safe. The tighter you held the door shut, the more insistent they'd become. On the other hand, if you sheepishly invited them in and assured them you have no emergency, they'd look around the house and leave. If this happened often enough, they wouldn't come out in the first place.

Practice, Not Perfect

Initially, as we learn to stay put in panic situations, our goal is to keep our discomfort zone from spreading. Make a pact with yourself that you *will not* leave a situation until your anxiety subsides. If the anxiety is intense, give yourself a small but manageable goal: "I will leave in 20 seconds" or "I will go down one more aisle and then leave." The idea is to delay your exit long enough for the panic to subside—and it *will* subside; the most frightening part of a panic attack rarely lasts longer than 10 to 20 seconds.

When your goal is met, leave if you have to. But go back to the situation as soon as possible. The longer you delay returning, the harder it will be. Spend as much time as possible in the anxiety-producing situation; the more time you spend, the easier it will become. Be prepared to backslide occasionally; don't beat yourself up if you fail once in a while.

But what about the panic-induced phobias you've already developed? If you've had panic attacks for any length of time, you've probably already had some strong mental links between your panic attacks and certain situations. A couple of panic attacks on the road can trigger a driving phobia, or a panic attack at the mall can lead to a fear of your favorite shopping venue or crowded places in general. In Chapters 16 and 17, we examine self-help strategies for phobias—panic induced or not.

For now, focus on setting up small goals that force you to stay in current situations. Every time you attempt to master your response to panic symptoms is a step in the right direction. Hold yourself accountable, but give yourself a mental break. Replace any harsh self-talk or discouragement with this truth; "I am working to rewire a complex system. I don't have to do it perfectly. As long as I keep practicing, I'm going to get where I want to go." And give yourself permission to bring in the reinforcements—professional help—if the going gets too hard.

In this chapter, we've explored the tsunami of anxiety—panic attacks. We've seen how our brain's misfiring results in a terrifying cascade of symptoms that traps us in an endless cycle of anxiety and avoidance. We've also seen how the best way to deal with them is *exactly the opposite* of what every fiber of our being tells us to do. By accepting (rather than fighting) our symptoms and staying (rather than fleeing) the situation, we ultimately regain our sense of control and power. In the next chapter, we investigate obsessive-compulsive disorder and see how to break free of the obsessions and compulsions that fuel this painful condition.

The Least You Need to Know

- Panic disorder starts in the brain, but it's not all in your head. The physical symptoms are very real and are caused by the misfiring of our brain's emergency responder, the amygdala.

- Left untreated, panic disorder can become complicated by phobias, depression, and other disabling conditions.

- The fears that are typical during panic attacks, such as fears of dying or losing control, have no basis in reality.

- Panic disorder can be successfully treated with cognitive-behavioral therapy, medication, or an intensive self-help program. Most often, it is through a combination of some or all of these.

- Tried-and-true self-strategies center on breathing/relaxation techniques, distraction strategies to stop fearful thoughts, and practice sessions that require staying in an anxious situation until the symptoms subside.

Snapping the Chains of Compulsive Behavior

In This Chapter

◆ Discover why obsessions are so hard to shake

◆ Understand how obsessions and compulsions feed on each other

◆ Investigate the daily impact of your obsessions and compulsions.

◆ Explore what OCD recovery looks like

◆ Boost your motivation to stick with an OCD self-help program

"If I don't do my rituals, what will I do to feel safe? My rituals are necessary to ward off the dangers I fear. I'm afraid my anxiety will get out of control."

These were some of the thoughts that kept swirling through Laura's head as she practiced her self-help strategies. But she wanted to get better. She knew it would take work. So she plugged along.

"Climbing out of the hole was almost as weird as falling in it to begin with. I can't really remember every detail of the climb; I just kept moving at first, like a machine. I learned to accept the setbacks and just kept going through the motions no matter how weird I felt. I just kept telling myself, 'When I'm over this, life will be even better than it was before.'

"You know what? I didn't really believe it when I was telling myself that, but it's true. Looking back, I'm amazed at what I managed to get done in spite of how I was feeling. And now, life is better than before because I'm the person I wanted to be."

Laura was able to get her OCD under control, and you can, too. Whether it's as an adjunct to medication and psychotherapy or whether you've decided to try self-help first, some powerful techniques can help break the obsessive-compulsive cycle. In Chapter 3, we looked at the symptoms of various anxiety disorders, including OCD, and how they are diagnosed. This chapter looks at the emotional costs associated with OCD and the steps we can take to regain control of our lives.

Cognitive Itches: Thoughts That Won't Stop

Everyone has odd or distressing thoughts or images occasionally run through their minds. Most of us are able to shrug them off. Obsessions are thoughts and ideas that we *cannot* stop thinking about; these distracting or distressing thoughts get stuck, and we can't get them out. It's like our brain replays the same song over and over no matter how much we don't want to hear it.

> **On the Cutting Edge**
>
> On average, OCD sufferers spend more than nine years seeking treatment before they receive a correct diagnosis, according to the Obsessive-Compulsive Foundation.

Obsessions are not the same as the negative replaying of painful memories, nor are they negative self-statements. A depressed person, for instance, might ruminate about how he cheated on his first wife 20 years ago or focus on what a bad person he is. A person with OCD, on the other hand, might have thoughts like "I'm going to get deathly sick if I don't keep the house completely free of germs" or "What if I forget to turn off the stove and the house burns down?" The person knows these thoughts are nonsensical but just can't keep them out of her head.

In fact, the problem is that, although we *know* that our thoughts are irrational, we *feel* like they're true. Not surprisingly, these feelings are disturbing and paralyzing. Those who feel most guilty, distressed, or disturbed by these thoughts may unwittingly bring these thoughts back into their minds *because* of their distress. The more we try to get rid of an upsetting thought, the more it intrudes. If I told you, "For the next five minutes, *do not* think about the first person you ever kissed," images of that very encounter would immediately pop into your head. There's truth in the saying, "What we resist, persists."

From this perspective, the problem isn't so much the obsessive thoughts (we all have them), but the emotional significance we attach to them. For example, the internal response to an obsessive thought around hurting a child is, "My God! What kind of person would have this thought! I am a horrible, disgusting person. What if I actually do it?" You can imagine how fearful and worried you might become. You can envision actively working hard to *avoid* those thoughts, to put them right out of your mind.

On the other hand, viewing our *response* to obsessive thoughts, rather than the thoughts themselves, as the root of the problem also sheds light on how we might find light at the end of the obsessive tunnel; we discuss this a little later on. But first, let's look at the second half of the obsessive-compulsive equation—the compulsions.

> **On the Cutting Edge**
>
> Most people have experienced some form of repetitive thinking. For example, getting a song stuck in your head isn't unhealthy or uncommon. Researchers sometimes refer to this as a "cognitive itch" and report that 97 percent to 99 percent of the population has this happen to them.

> **Stress Relief**
>
> OCD has nothing to do with intelligence; it is an illness that can affect anyone. For instance, Hans Christian Andersen and Charles Dickens both suffered from it.

Sweet Relief Through Rituals and Restraint

Compulsions are our attempts to regain control over our runaway thoughts and painful feelings. They are useless, repetitive, but calming behaviors; a woman with obsessive thoughts around germs might wash her hands 200 times a day or launder her clothes over and over. A husband preoccupied with thoughts of his family dying in a fire may constantly check and recheck the stove and electrical appliances. Unfortunately, the tension relief is only temporary and ultimately prevents us from dealing directly with our irrational thoughts. In fact, the rituals give the obsessions more power by seeming to control our behavior.

We may also resist doing certain things because we associate them with our fears. Someone preoccupied by thoughts of running someone over with a car may avoid driving near schools or any place with pedestrians, and may avoid driving altogether. A person obsessed with fears of germs may avoid telephones, shaking hands, library books, and other potential germ zones.

The first self-help strategy in dealing with OCD is to get a sense of the big picture, to connect the dots between obsessions and rituals; the latter should include both the things we do and the things we avoid to get some temporary emotional relief.

OCD Symptoms: Up Close and Personal

Although each OCD sufferer is unique, obsessive thoughts and compulsive rituals often share common themes, and certain thoughts and behaviors often go together. Here are some examples:

Obsessive Thoughts

- Fearful thoughts or images about germs or contamination with an illness

- Frightening thoughts/images that some serious or harmful event will occur because of your carelessness

- Pictures or words in your head that suggest you will harm others, especially those you care for and would never want to harm

- Pictures come into your mind of your loved ones dead

- Things in your life are not in the correct order or not symmetrical enough or in the right place

- Blasphemous or unpleasant thoughts/pictures and doubts about your faith come into your head

- Fearful thoughts around the irretrievable loss of possessions

Compulsive Rituals

- Wash/disinfect frequently

- Check body for signs of contaminations

- Check feared situations/appliances or journey route many times

- Seek reassurance regularly from another person that everything is all right

- Think something to yourself to "put right" the frightening thoughts

- Think neutralizing thoughts to counteract the frightening images

- Carry out some task that will neutralize the thought (for example, counting panes in windows or billboards on highways, or saying a special word or prayer a certain number of times)

- Put things right or make them symmetrical many times until they "feel" right

- Frequently pray or seek forgiveness

- Consult minister/religious leader to seek reassurance

- Excessive collecting and saving of things that you believe might be of future use

Avoidance of Situations/Objects

- Avoid going to places or touching objects that you fear may contaminate you

- Avoid being the last person to leave the house

- Avoid responsibility

- Avoid situations that you feel put you at risk of harming (for example, hide kitchen knives)

- Avoid or minimize contact with the person you're afraid of harming (for example, a father avoids hugging or changing an infant after having obsessive molestation thoughts)

- Avoid contact with things that make you feel like this

- Avoid church if these thoughts appear in religious surroundings

- Avoid decisions, particularly about discarding objects

To determine how much OCD is affecting your life, make a list of your obsessions and compulsions, including the situations or objects you avoid because of them. On a scale of 1 to 10, rate how frightening each symptom is for you. Don't let shame stand in the way of honesty; OCD is not a condition that anyone chooses. In fact, the feelings around our OCD—the anxiety around the obsessions and the guilt/shame about the compulsions—give OCD its power and sets in motion a vicious cycle.

Anxiety Attack

When starting a self-help program, it can be hard to know where to get started. Ask yourself which symptom would make the most difference in your life if it went away; attack this one first.

The Vicious Cycle

Many people with OCD are anxious when experiencing the obsession and then relieved when they have acted on the obsession. This turns into a vicious cycle that becomes stronger with each obsessive-compulsive repetition. Those who suffer from OCD often feel guilty, which in turn makes the thoughts more likely to come back because they have been given such negative importance.

This vicious cycle might look something like this.

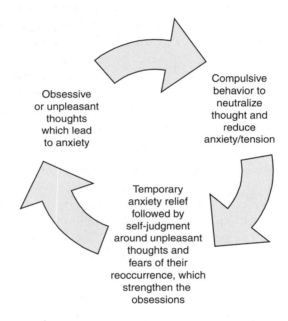

Obsessive or unpleasant thoughts which lead to anxiety

Compulsive behavior to neutralize thought and reduce anxiety/tension

Temporary anxiety relief followed by self-judgment around unpleasant thoughts and fears of their reoccurrence, which strengthen the obsessions

Anxiety Attack

Self-help for OCD is not an "all or nothing " proposition. It is often best used in conjunction with medication/psychotherapy.

What does your vicious cycle look like? How do your obsessions and compulsions feed upon themselves? Now that you've seen the connections between OCD thoughts, feelings, and behaviors, let's take a look at how we can break the links between the chains that binds us.

Working from the Outside In

Think of all the things we humans do to cope with our feelings; we overeat, we buy clothes we don't need, we drink alcohol. We perform rituals. Personal growth would be so much easier if we could feel better *before* we gave up our security blanket. Alas, that's not the case. Recovery from OCD involves learning to tolerate the emotional discomfort associated with not performing the ritual. Self-help starts with *doing* things differently through a combination of *exposure and response prevention*.

Exposure and ritual or response prevention are cognitive behavior techniques that work in tandem with each other. Over time, we gradually expose ourselves to the very things or situations we're afraid of, and simultaneously prevent ourselves from following through with our customary rituals. By gradually but diligently approaching our fears, we become less afraid with each passing exposure and learn that we will not come to harm if we stop our compulsive responses. (In Chapter 16, we explore exposure therapy, also known as systematic desensitization, in more detail.) The longer and more often we stay in an uncomfortable situation, the sooner our anxiety will ease; as we become more accustomed to the situation, our anxiety will subside.

In many ways, the cognitive behavioral strategies for OCD are similar to the systematic desensitization for simple phobia in Chapter 16. Just as someone with a fear of flying associates a number of lesser (entering an airport) or greater (sudden turbulence) fears associated with his phobia, we OCD sufferers develop a hierarchy of fears associated with our particular thoughts. Breaking down our bigger goal into manageable thoughts or situations is a great way to begin chipping away at the little ways our compulsions rule our lives.

For example, Heidi is afraid of being contaminated by illness, especially AIDS and HIV. She has taken numerous HIV tests, and she routinely checks herself and her children for lumps or other symptoms of the virus. She also obsesses about infecting others with genital herpes through nonsexual contact; she washes her hands numerous times a day and is constantly cleaning objects she touches. Here are some items from her anxiety hierarchy, from most feared to least threatening:

- Receiving a blood transfusion or giving blood
- Walking into a hospital known to treat AIDS patients
- Being visited by someone who went to visit someone in the hospital
- Shaking hands with a "sickly looking" person
- Using a public toilet

Anxiety Attack

Identify a supportive person in your environment who would be willing to "coach" you through your self-help efforts. This person should be knowledgeable and accepting of OCD, have a sincere interest in helping you, and be willing to engage in a little "tough love" when needed.

- Touching buttons on a public elevator
- Using a public phone
- Using the bathroom at work
- Passing a homeless person on the street
- Parking her car next to a recently ill neighbor

Heidi's exposure practice could start with her fears of transmitting genital herpes through nonsexual contact (for example, by allowing someone to hold her purse), or it could focus on her fear of AIDS contamination, starting with her least frightening fear and moving her way up. Regardless of the situations she chooses to tackle, she must also refrain from engaging in the compulsion that typically follows.

Taking the First Step

It's all well and good to give examples of how exposure and response prevention might work. But how can you put this in to practice in your real life. Here are some examples:

- If you're obsessed with germs, touch a "contaminated" object, person, or place. Then, do not wash.

- If you're a compulsive "checker," turn off lights, stoves, and appliances. Allow yourself to check once.

- If you like to "order" your surroundings or environment, leave household items "imperfect." Don't straighten them.

I know; if it were this easy, you would have already done it. You *can* do it, though; if you've failed before, don't give up. Now is the time to take a step back and finesse your approach. Try these tips:

- Review systematic desensitization in Chapter 16. It may be that your anxiety hierarchy is too hard or needs to be broken down into smaller steps.

- List all of the fears you have about facing the situations in your anxiety hierarchy. Identify the beliefs that are perpetuating these fears; for example, "I won't be able to stand the anxiety." "Someone I love will get sick." "I might really hurt my child." Revisit Chapters 8 and 9 and apply the irrational thought stopping techniques to these beliefs.

◆ Keep a diary during your exposure practice so that you can observe how your anxiety gradually lessens the longer you stay in a situation.

◆ Reward yourself when you avoid a ritual. Don't, however, replace old compulsions with new ones, such as rubbing your hands instead of washing them.

◆ Create a neutral zone. Find a place in your home where you can go to sit, relax, and distract yourself until the urge subsides. It can be a secluded den or office, bedroom, backyard patio … any place where the urge to ritualize can be allowed to subside. After about 30 to 60 minutes in this neutral zone, you may find it possible to return to your normal activities.

> **Stress Relief** _____
>
> Obsessions and compulsions may have been occupying most of your thinking for some time. Physical activities, crafts, or hobbies can help to take the place of the OCD thoughts in your mind.

If you can't stop the compulsive behaviors altogether, try to lessen the amount of time you spend on the behavior or the number of times you do it. Check only once, for example, that the lights are turned off.

It's All in My Head

Whereas 90 percent of us who struggle with OCD have both obsessions and compulsions, 10 percent suffer from obsessions only. In addition, sometimes the compulsions that follow our obsessive thoughts are mental behaviors (that is, additional thoughts). For example, Harold responds to his sacrilegious thoughts by repeating the same scripture verses over and over in his head. Jean counters thoughts of harming her daughter by obsessively repeating "I don't want to do this" over and over in her head. Although these mental rituals provide immediate relief, they can begin to consume more and more of a person's day.

If you have a similar pattern of having a disturbing thought and then trying to get rid of it with another, less-disturbing, thought, here are some ways to break this cycle:

◆ Give your obsessive thoughts a nickname or label. Just as this strategy can teach children to get some distance from obsessive thoughts (oops, Mr. Clean is here again), it can help remind us that we are not our obsessive thoughts.

◆ Write your thoughts down, including what triggers them and what you do in response. Putting these down on paper can help identify stressors in your life, thoughts that come up in response to stress, and what mental behaviors you use to cope with them. In addition, some OCD sufferers who've forced themselves to write down every obsessive thought that popped up found the fatigue that came from writing actually loosened the thought's grip.

◆ Use empowering self-talk. We can tolerate a lot of things we don't like, including our obsessive thoughts. Give yourself permission to have them and remind yourself that the reason they are so upsetting is because they are the *exact opposite* of your true character. Praise yourself whenever you make progress in controlling a compulsive behavior.

◆ Postpone your rituals. Take control over when you have your obsessions; put them off for a few minutes or hours or consider scheduling a daily "worry" time. The more time that passes between the initial thought and your impulse to act on it, the more chance you have that your anxiety will subside.

Anxiety Attack

It can be hard to tell the difference between an obsessive thought and a mental compulsion. In general, if the repetitive thought causes anxiety, it is an obsession; if it temporarily releases anxiety, it is a compulsion.

Boost That Motivation and Prepare for Stumbling Blocks

Conquering OCD is doable, but like overcoming any challenge in life, it can be difficult. It is hard to stay motivated, especially when there are bound to be times when the "cure" seems worse than the "illness." It's also frustrating when two steps forward is followed by one step back—or worse, when it seems like the other way around!

So how do we psych ourselves up and stay with it when the going gets tough? First, we have to be clear about the "up" side of getting better. Think about how your OCD impacts you on a daily basis: how much time it consumes, how it affects your options and choices, how it limits your relationships. Now imagine how your life will improve as you get your OCD under control. What will you be able to do then that you can't now? How will you feel differently? How will it positively impact the way you view yourself or the way you interact with the people you love?

Write down all the payoffs you will receive by taking control of your OCD and read them three times a day *every single day*. The only way to stay motivated over the long haul is to renew our desire to move forward each and every day.

Second, work hard enough to see some results. Set specific, measurable goals for the next four to six weeks and commit to a minimum of two hours of daily work. For example, perhaps you spend the first week simply recording your obsessive thoughts and compulsive behaviors as well as the impact they have on your daily life. Spend week two creating your anxiety hierarchy or practicing thought stopping.

In Appendix B, you'll find several self-help books specifically devoted to obsessive-compulsive disorder; these can provide worksheets, structured recovery steps, and so forth. What matters most is that you make your recovery from OCD a priority in your life and give your work on it as much time and attention as your OCD has taken.

Third, create a conducive environment. Social psychologists are constantly reminding us that we humans are greatly influenced by the things and people around us; why not use them to our benefit? Research, for example, shows that social support is a great aid in boosting our motivation and commitment to change. A loving family member or friend can provide words of encouragement when our courage is failing, remind us of the progress we've made, and help provide an atmosphere of acceptance and security. Warning—relying on a family member for reassurance or asking him or her to participate in your rituals can foster dependency and impede your progress.

And finally, approach your recovery from OCD with a flexible attitude. It doesn't matter if you start with medication and then move to self-help or vice versa. Experiment with various self-help techniques; one strategy may work better for you than another, and some may not work at all. For example, a person who finds that writing out obsessions doesn't work may find great relief in singing her worried thoughts.

There *will* be ups and downs and times when the effort may not seem worth it. As long as you see all of this as part of the process, and keep your eyes on the prize, you'll get to where you want to go.

Anxiety Attack

Self-help for OCD may not be the best road to take if you also suffer from depression or substance abuse. In addition, major life stressors are also likely to interfere with self-help efforts. A mental-health professional, especially one who specializes in OCD, can evaluate your situation and offer help with your own self-initiated efforts.

Don't Forget the Mind-Body Connection

For obvious reasons, we've spent this chapter talking about the mind. However, it's equally important to take care of our bodies. On a basic level, this involves being careful about what we put into our bodies. For instance, no matter how much our anxiety increases, we shouldn't up our antianxiety or antidepressant medication without our doctor's input; nor should we abruptly discontinue medication no matter how good we feel. This also means paying attention to our alcohol use; having a few drinks to "calm down" during an exposure exercise prevents us from experiencing what we need to feel in order to get better.

> **On the Cutting Edge**
>
> Researchers are now studying the possible use of deep brain stimulation as a treatment for severe obsessive-compulsive disorder. Often referred to as the "brain pacemaker," preliminary results suggest it may help the 20 percent of OCD sufferers who don't respond to traditional treatment.

Living with OCD is stressful, and although stress-relieving practices aren't a proven treatment for OCD, they can help us cope with our symptoms and reduce the odds that they will get worse during stressful times. The strategies we covered in Chapters 11 through 13 apply to all anxiety sufferers; in particular, OCD sufferers can benefit from the following:

- Breathing and relaxation techniques

- Regular exercise

- Listening to soothing music

- Yoga/meditation

The Least You Need to Know

- Obsessions are unwanted, distressing thoughts that seem out of our control.

- Compulsions are our responses to these obsessions. They are thoughts or behaviors we use to temporarily reduce our anxiety and neutralize the power of the obsessions.

- Obsessions and compulsions feed off each other. As a result, we can get trapped in a vicious cycle that consumes hours each day.

- Learning to face frightening situations and tolerate upsetting thoughts without relying on our compulsions is the key to recovery from OCD.

- Self-help can be used as an adjunct to medication, psychotherapy, or as a first attempt to get better. Stress-management techniques can also help us cope better with OCD and reduce the odds that our symptoms will escalate during stressful times.

Chapter 16

Expose Yourself! Self-Help for Phobias

In This Chapter

♦ Learn to recognize phobias and their interference

♦ The development of simple and complex phobias

♦ The role of body and mind in maintaining phobias

♦ Using systematic desensitization to cure phobias

Howard Hughes grew up during a time when mothers didn't let their kids play in rain puddles out of fear of the polio germs they thought might lurk there. His mother was especially cautious; she constantly worried about Howard's germ exposure, was extremely careful about what he ate, and checked him daily for symptoms of disease.

Howard's fear of germs grew throughout his life. As an adult, he once wrote a manual on how to open a can of peaches. The manual included instructions for removing the label, scrubbing the can down to its metal, washing it again and pouring its contents into a bowl without letting the outside of the can touch the bowl.

Howard Hughes was creative and brilliant. He grew up to be an acclaimed airplane pilot, a movie producer, and a billionaire business tycoon. And yet, as anyone who has seen the movie *The Aviator* can attest, Howard Hughes is often remembered as the fear-controlled recluse who spent the end of his life in darkened hotel rooms.

Howard Hughes's problems were complex; he had an addiction to codeine as well as obsessive-compulsive symptoms around his efforts to protect himself from germs. Yet his fear of a single thing—germs—powerfully illustrates how strongly a phobia can grip us. In this chapter, we explore phobias: how they develop and what we can do to overcome them.

Not That Unusual

Most of us with phobias aren't famous billionaires who can afford to pay people to cater to our fears. Yet we often cater to them ourselves. A simple phobia is an irrational fear of a situation, event, or object coupled with a strong need to avoid whatever it is.

Most of us know someone who is deathly afraid of spiders or who can't stand high places; one of my family members avoided escalators her entire life. Some of the most common simple phobias are of closed spaces (claustrophobia), heights (acrophobia), water (aquaphobia), snakes (ophidiphobia), or lightning (astraphobia). Howard Hughes's fear of germs or contamination is known as mysophobia.

Stress Relief

Fear of beautiful women? A parents-in-law phobia? Check out the A–Z list of phobias at theamt.com/modules.php?name =News&file=article&sid=204.

A phobia is different from panic disorder (discussed in Chapter 14), even though we may experience panic when faced with the thing we fear. With panic disorder, the fear is of *the anxiety symptoms themselves* or of losing control. In phobia, it's the actual object or situation that we judge to be dangerous, *even when we know it's irrational or out of proportion.*

Faced with a "danger," it makes sense that we'd want to avoid that which we fear might harm us. Unfortunately, this avoidance only strengthens the connection between our fear and the object of it, and, depending upon how often we need to encounter it, can significantly disrupt our lives. Think of the person who lives on the twentieth floor who suddenly develops a fear of heights, or the bus driver who suddenly develops a driving phobia!

Specific or simple phobias such as these may develop rapidly or build up over time. A car accident can suddenly trigger a driving phobia, particularly in a victim who was genetically or environmentally predisposed to anxiety. It's probably no surprise that flight attendants are more likely to develop a fear of flying than someone who rarely flies; fly often enough and you're bound to encounter some scary (although usually not dangerous) turbulence. Phobias may also develop gradually from learning and observation, as in Howard Hughes's mother's fanatical focus on the avoidance of germs.

When Fear Gets More Complicated

Whereas a simple phobia has just one object—insects, dentists, heights—complex phobias are made up of multiple fears. For example, agoraphobia involves a whole network of anxieties. There is the fear of entering shops, crowds, and public places. There may be fear of traveling alone in trains, buses, or planes. On top of all this is the fear of what might happen if we are unable to get ourselves to safety (home) right away. The more this phobia develops, the easier it seems to just stay home.

Social phobia is another complex phobia, marked by fear of performance or social situations. However, this might include any number of situations and fears. We might be afraid of embarrassing ourselves or of someone else humiliating us. We might worry that we'll forget how to talk or behave. Some people with social anxiety have trouble eating in front of others; others shy away from parties and public speaking. So even though there is the general fear of social situations, what this means for each social anxiety sufferer can differ. In extreme cases, we can end up in almost complete social isolation.

Even seemingly straightforward phobias are often complex. The fear of flying, for instance, almost certainly involves the fear of crashing. However, it can also involve a fear of closed spaces (you can't exactly walk off an airplane when you feel closed in) or be part of a more general fear of heights. Part of the treatment for complex phobias involves peeling away the onion: uncovering and addressing all the underlying fears that make up the "social phobia."

> **Myth Buster**
>
> *"My phobia will just go away on its own."* Whereas childhood phobias often disappear over time, only 20 percent of adult phobias fade without any direct steps to tackle them.

What Primes the Phobia Pump?

We don't know exactly why some people develop phobias and others don't. Because phobias run in families, though, it seems likely that some of us are genetically predisposed to intense, irrational fears.

For those of us who have this built-in sensitivity, certain circumstances are likely to light the kindling that starts the fire. Most phobia sufferers can identify at least one of following:

You had a frightening experience. Maybe you got bit by a spider and were sick for a few days. Maybe you suddenly felt dizzy while looking at the view from the Sears Tower. Maybe your childhood pediatrician didn't realize that a 12-year-old girl would be humiliated for her father to see the rash on her chest. People who can identify a specific incident that either triggered or made worse their phobia consistently describe it as personally threatening (although not necessarily dangerous) and as feeling out of their control.

You learned by observation. Elizabeth was 6 when her 3-year-old brother was hospitalized for suspected leukemia. To keep him from walking on his stiff leg, nurses placed him in a playpen with a net on it. She vividly remembers seeing her beloved brother screaming to get out and clawing at the top of the net; while her fear of doctors did not peak until she went through a period of stress as an adolescent, she traces the seeds back to this memory.

For Howard Hughes, his mother's fears and the impact this had on her parenting caused him to develop a full-blown germ phobia. Our brains often can't tell much difference between what we experience and what we *imagine* experiencing, a blessing when we start curing our phobias but a curse when we imagine the worst.

> **Anxiety Attack**
>
> Phobia sufferers often pay attention to information that reinforces their fears and overlooks contrary data. The antidote is to study accurate information about your fear: How often do elevators really fail? What are their safety standards and emergency procedures?

Other problems are linked to the feared object/ event. It wouldn't take many panic attacks while driving to become afraid of getting behind the wheel. Individuals with panic attacks often develop fears of the situations in which they happen even though they know there is no real relationship.

You've gone through several months of stress. A fearful thought or event packs a bigger wallop if it occurs during a stressful time. Not only do traumatic events often trigger the development of specific phobias (specific locations, objects, situations), but stress can make it harder to address or make it worse.

Your Body Chips In

So what tips the scale from a normal level of distress to a full-blown phobia? First of all, with a genuine phobia, the fear we feel is far out of proportion to the reality. For example, it's normal to feel some anxiety when driving late at night on a foggy, unfamiliar road. On the other hand, if I'm so afraid of driving through a tunnel or over a bridge that I would drive miles out of the way to avoid one, the fear is out of proportion to the risk.

Another difference between normal fear and a phobia is the way the body reacts to what we're afraid of. Many of us with phobias experience the same "fight-or-flight" response we would if we were in a life-threatening situation. Our adrenaline rushes, our heart pounds, and we wind up in a full-blown panic attack.

In response to the unpleasant physical and emotional symptoms, we then find ourselves obsessing and worrying about any possible encounter with the feared object—or anything associated with it. For example, a person with a fear of dogs may become anxious about going for a walk because he or she may see a dog along the way.

Unfortunately, this becomes a vicious feedback loop. When we remember the bad experience we had with that mean dog, our body triggers the same emergency signal as when we were running from it. Our alarm goes off when we worry about it happening again. In fact, any kind of stimulus like this can trigger our negative memory because our mind will retrieve the past relevant event that has the strongest emotion; even if we're taking a leisurely bath in the comfort of our own home, if we start "seeing" ourselves around dogs, our body will have anxiety symptoms. In other words, our bodies respond to that imagery almost as if the event were happening again. We, in turn, get even more anxious.

> **Anxiety Attack** _____
>
> If the slightest phobia-related thought sends you into a panic, or if your phobia is causing significant impairment in your life, it may be time to seek professional help.

Reversing the Vicious Cycle

So how do we turn this energy-draining cycle around? Through a process called *systematic desensitization*. Systematic desensitization was developed in the 1940s by a clinician named Joseph Wolpe, who found that he could use relaxation techniques to recondition his patients' responses so that they no longer experienced irrational fear when faced with certain situations. Although initially used with the help of a therapist, Wolpe's method has proven to be a very effective self-help strategy for phobia sufferers.

On the Cutting Edge
New research suggests that phobias can be successfully treated with Internet-guided self-help. Successful help most often includes guided exposure exercises with backup telephone assistance from a clinician.

Systematic desensitization is a process whereby we *gradually* expose ourselves to the things/situations/ events we fear the most. The thinking behind it goes like this: a phobia is basically an irrational fear we have developed because we have *learned* to associate something bad (pain, fear) with the object of our phobia. Why not unlearn it by pairing a different response (relaxation) with the phobia?

On a practical level, this involves three steps. First, we become relaxation gurus, practicing various breathing techniques until we feel confident that we know how to calm our bodies down. Second, we create an anxiety hierarchy, making a list of scary situations related to the phobia, ranking them in order of their fear factor. Finally, we gradually progress up our anxiety ladder, starting with the least frightening and, over time, making our way to the top.

With sufficient repetition through practice, the imagined event loses its anxiety-provoking power. At the end of training, when you actually face the real event, you will find that it too, just like the imagined event, has lost its power to make you anxious.

Sound easy? Heck, no! There are three reasons why we stayed away from our feared object in the first place—danger, danger, danger! Remember us talking so much about motivation as we explored the journey from anxiety to peace in Chapter 4? The hardest step in overcoming a phobia is the first one: developing the commitment to see it through. To develop that kind of commitment, our determination must be voiced in terms of the positives.

It's not as helpful to say "I don't want to be afraid of heights anymore." There's a lot more power in focusing on what you do want. If you have a phobia of flying, think about what you have to gain by overcoming this fear. If flying is a necessity in your profession, there are financial and career incentives. You can take faster, more exotic vacations if you travel by air. You can even focus on the increased safety of flying over other forms of transportation; it's the safest way to travel. Steadily focusing on the positives—and developing a concrete reward as we succeed—can help us take the first step up the desensitization ladder.

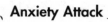

Anxiety Attack

Regaining a sense of control is critical in dealing with many phobias. If you have a dental phobia, for example, select a dentist who will go slowly, offer treatment options, and allow you to call for a break at any time.

Experiment with Your Emotions

What we resist persists. Our internal alarm system goes up to help us; struggling against it only increases the very symptoms we want to get rid of. Instead, welcome them as you might welcome a well-meaning but clumsy friend. "Oh, look, here's my emergency response, trying to save me when I don't need to be saved. I expected that, and it came right on time." Then you just let those feelings in the door and get ready to make them feel at home and comfortable in this situation.

If you can't manage quite that much playfulness, just tell yourself, "It's okay I'm feeling this way. In fact, I expect to be nervous right now. I can handle this." The point is not to talk yourself out of your feelings, but rather just to let them be there. Don't hold them at bay, and don't obey them, either. Just notice them and remind yourself that it's okay to feel nervous. Feeling nervous is uncomfortable, but it won't actually harm you.

Myth Buster

"Systematic desensitization works equally well for any phobia." In fact, Systematic desensitization is more effective for simple phobias than "free-floating anxiety" disorders such as social phobia or agoraphobia.

Then while you allow your feelings just to be as they are, you move on to the next step. You breathe.

Allow Yourself to Relax

"I was in the dentist's chair for three hours. If I hadn't had the tools to do my breathing exercises … I would have jumped out of that chair and would have had a panic attack at any moment. I did not have a panic attack and I was so much more comfortable when I had something else to think about."

We all have a tendency to hold our breath when we're frightened. In fact, most of us are in the habit of breathing more shallowly than our bodies would like. The problem is that shallow or erratic breathing can feed anxiety. On the other hand, learning to breathe properly can be a valuable tool, especially as we work up our nerve and begin to approach our fears.

Learning to breathe properly, and practicing various relaxation methods, is like the training before a marathon. It's what gives many of us the courage to sign up for the "big race," it helps us stay in tough situations during the process, and it helps us regroup after a practice session.

There are a ton of relaxation and breathing exercises; it doesn't matter which ones you choose as long as you stick with them. Here are a couple to get you started.

> **Anxiety Attack**
>
> Learning to control your breathing is one of the best ways to relax. For a selection of exercises, visit www.pe2000.com/anx-breathe.htm.

Calming Counts

This breathing technique takes about 90 seconds to complete, during which time you focus on counting. In addition to giving your mind a break, your body has more time to relax.

1. Sit comfortably.

2. Take a slow, deep breath and exhale slowly while saying the word *relax* silently.

3. Close your eyes.

4. Allow your body to take 10 easy breaths. Count down with each exhalation, starting with 10 after the first breath, 9 after the second, and so on.

5. While doing this comfortable breathing, become aware of any tension in your body and imagine it loosening.

6. When you say "1" on the last long, deep breath, open your eyes.

The Ten-Second Grip

This is a relaxation technique that helps you let go of tension in your muscles. Remember that "what you resist persists"? This technique also works on that principle. When you tense your muscles on purpose, it's easier to let all that tension go.

1. While seated in a chair with arms, grab the arm rests and squeeze them as hard as you can to tighten your lower and upper arms. Tense your stomach and leg muscles, too.

2. Hold that contraction for about 10 seconds, still breathing.

3. Let go with a long, gentle calming breath.

4. Repeat Steps 1 through 3 twice.

5. Now loosen by moving around in your seat. Shake out your arms, shoulders, and legs; and gently roll your head around.

6. Close your eyes and breathe gently for 30 seconds. Enjoy letting your body feel warm, relaxed, and heavy.

These skills work to the degree that you concentrate on them. The trick is to stay in the present moment, concentrating on the breathing exercise, and replacing any negative thoughts with thoughts of counting and loosening.

Arrange Your Fears in Order

You're motivated, accepting, and able to relax. Now it's time to begin dissecting your phobia by developing a "hierarchy of anxiety." Start out with 15 to 20 items on the list, ordering them from 1 (relaxed) to 100 (terrified) in terms of how scary they are.

These situations will most often be those that you have actually experienced. However, they can also be situations that you're afraid of even though they have never actually happened to you. For example, you may want to include "Having to wear the oxygen mask during flight" even though this has never actually happened to you. The important point is that items included in an anxiety hierarchy describe situations that produce varying levels of anxiety, some more worrisome than others; this is what hierarchy means, and the details of this will be presented.

Describe the items on your anxiety hierarchy in sufficient detail to enable you to vividly imagine each one. It might be sufficient to say, "Standing in line at the ticket counter," but it might be more graphic to say, "Standing in a long line at the crowded ticket counter, with nothing to do but wait to get my luggage checked." Remember that items are most effective if they can help you experience the event in your imagination, not just describe it.

The following is a sample hierarchy to help you develop your own hierarchy. Your items should, of course, be more fully detailed. Also note that any item's relative anxiety level does not necessarily relate to the order in which it would happen during flight; for example, landing might come before takeoff on your anxiety hierarchy.

Anxiety Hierarchy (1 = least anxiety-arousing; 25 = most anxiety arousing)

__1__ Thinking about/deciding to travel by plane
__3__ Making the phone call to book a flight
__2__ Packing
__4__ Traveling to the airport
__5__ Arriving at the airport
__6__ Checking in
__8__ Going through security
__7__ Going to your gate
__9__ Boarding the plane
__11__ Seeing/hearing the doors close
__10__ The safety drill
__12__ The plane taxis on the runway
__20__ Takeoff
__16__ Climbing/gaining altitude
__17__ Changes in plane speed
__21__ Changes in engine noise
__13__ The plane's maneuvering
__18__ Beginning descent
__22__ Final approach
__23__ Touchdown
__19__ Decelerating
__14__ Doors open

_15_ Getting off the plane
_24_ Experience turbulence
_25_ Emergency landing

As you start listing your feared situations, it's normal to feel some unease. Just remember that you can let these feelings be what they are and practice your new breathing skills, even as you move forward in this next step.

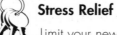

Stress Relief _____

Limit your news watching and newspaper reading. Media coverage of airline crashes and catastrophic car collisions can skew our sense of the relative danger involved in these modes of transportation.

The Three R's: Reintroduce, Refocus, and Repetition

Self-administered systematic desensitization consists of seven steps. These steps should be repeated—in order—for each item of your anxiety hierarchy:

1. Use your favorite relaxation technique to create a state of calm.

2. Read the appropriate item from your hierarchy. (In the first session, this is the first item in the hierarchy. In all other sessions, this is the last item from the previous session.)

3. Imagine yourself in the situation for a tolerable time. (Start out slowly and work your way up until you can tolerate at least 30 seconds of exposure. This might take more than one practice session.)

4. Stop imagining the situation and determine the level of anxiety that you are experiencing (on a 0–100 scale). Reestablish your relaxation again and relax for about 30 seconds.

5. Reread the description of the situation. Imagine yourself in the scene for a tolerable time.

6. Stop and again determine your level of anxiety. If you are still experiencing anxiety, return to Step 2. If you feel no anxiety, go on to Step 7.

7. Move on to the next item of your hierarchy. Repeat the above procedure for this next item, beginning with Step 1.

Anxiety Attack _____

As a general rule, systematic desensitization practice sessions should last no more than 30 minutes and should tackle no more than 3 items on your list.

Experiment with your hierarchy, fine-tuning the level of anxiety each item generates to make it challenging enough but not overwhelming. If your first few items don't cause any anxiety at all, perhaps you're not imagining the situation vividly enough or for a long enough time period. If an item is still terrifying after several cycles, maybe this item should come later in the hierarchy or you should decrease the amount of time you spend imaging the scene.

It may be tempting to rush up that list, but stick with each item until you're comfortable with it. End each session with several minutes of relaxation. This process is not complicated, but it requires persistence. When you become bored or discouraged, it's okay to take a break, but aim for a minimum of two practice sessions a week.

Anxiety Attack

Be practical. Lower your odds of having an accident by driving the #1 car for safety; keep an emergency or poison control phone number handy if there's any reality to your concerns about snakebites, rabies, or other concerns.

In this chapter, we've looked at the best phobia self-help has to offer. Developing strong relaxation skills and slowly pairing them with the feared object or event can help us reacquaint ourselves with long-avoided situations. But what if the object of our fears isn't so simple? In the next chapter, we explore the most common complex problem, social phobia, and how we can use what we've learned in this chapter to get a leg-up in reducing our social anxiety.

The Least You Need to Know

◆ A phobia is an intense, irrational fear coupled with a strong desire to avoid the object or situation that triggers it.

◆ Phobias can develop suddenly, often after a bad experience with the feared object or situation, or they can be learned gradually.

◆ Simple phobias involve only one fear, whereas complex phobias involve a collection of related fears.

◆ We are more likely to develop a phobia during periods of prolonged stress, especially if we already have a built-in sensitivity to fear.

◆ Systematic desensitization involves relearning to associate a relaxation response with the object of our phobia.

Chapter 17

Moving Confidently Through Social Anxiety

In This Chapter

- ◆ Discover the difference between social anxiety and social butterflies
- ◆ Understand the complexity of social anxiety symptoms
- ◆ Learn how to get out of the spotlight
- ◆ Identify your self-help plan of attack
- ◆ See how the Internet can help—or hinder—social anxiety relief

Jack used to feel self-conscious walking down the street, dreading the possibility of running into someone he knew and being forced to say hello. Nancy hated to stand in line at the grocery store; although she knew it wasn't actually true, she couldn't shake the feeling that everyone was staring at her. Every time she had to deal with the grocery store checker, she started sweating and her mouth felt like it was full of cotton. "I'm making a total fool of myself," she thought.

Jennifer once agonized over returning a phone call from a new work acquaintance inviting her to an informal get-together. Maybe she'd call at the wrong time—the other person would be busy and wouldn't want to talk to her. It was unbearable to feel rejected, even over the phone, even from someone she barely knew. After the call was made, Jennifer didn't feel any better. She endlessly analyzed what she said, how she said it, and what the other person likely thought about it. And the party she was invited do? Forget it; as lonely as Jennifer felt, she couldn't imagine walking into a room full of people.

Granted, meeting someone new, giving a speech, or going on a job interview are nerve-wracking experiences for all of us. However, what Jack, Nancy, and Jennifer experience far surpasses the social butterflies or performance jitters that afflict all of us now and then. Nancy, Jack, and Jennifer have social anxiety, a disorder in which the sufferer is plagued by such an excessive fear of embarrassment in social situations that it impacts his or her life.

Here's a list of just a few things I've seen people do who were once completely controlled by their social anxiety: give a presentation, join a drama club, go out to a nightclub, make good friends, and be the center of attention at a birthday party. Some of these courageous individuals did it with the help of medication or therapy; others did it by themselves. In this chapter, we take a look at the best self-help weapons against social anxiety—and how to use them.

Under the Microscope

Ever walked up to a group of people who suddenly stopped talking? Or made a late entrance to a party and found yourself confronted by a roomful of strangers? All of us have been under the social microscope at some point, and it's darned uncomfortable.

We might have put on a brave face, but underneath the alarm bells were ringing. *Why did they shut up? Were they talking about me? Who are all these people and why are they staring? They must think I'm an idiot!*

Social anxiety sufferers feel this way much of the time when we're around others. Some of us may be anxious in one or two situations, such as when we have to give a speech or consider asking someone on a date. This is often referred to as a *specific*, or *discrete*, social phobia. Those who are afraid of and avoid many or even most social situations suffer from generalized social anxiety disorder.

> **On the Cutting Edge**
>
> Research has shown that people suffering from generalized social phobia have more active brain activity when confronted with threatening faces or frightening social situations. We may ultimately be able to use this finding to help assess the severity of a person's social anxiety and evaluate the effectiveness of treatment.

Regardless of the number of situations that trigger it, the symptoms—racing heart, trembling voice, shaky hands, and rapid breathing—are similar. Many of them are shared by panic-attack sufferers; we discussed ways to handle these symptoms in Chapter 14.

As if these physical sensations weren't bad enough, they are magnified by our fear that others will notice and judge our emotional distress. As a result, some anxiety sufferers become so afraid that they literally feel paralyzed—as if they are unable to move. Not surprisingly, it doesn't take too many negative experiences to try to find ways to avoid stressful situations and, when that's not possible, to worry long before the event, suffer through it, and obsess about it afterward.

Throughout this section of the book, we've seen how each anxiety disorder sets up its own vicious cycle; for example, the obsession in obsessive-compulsive disorder leads to anxiety, which leads to responses that temporarily reduce tension but ultimately create more anxiety. Social anxiety sufferers, too, get stuck in their own fear of ridicule or humiliation. We worry about the possibility of doing something embarrassing, which makes us anxious. The more anxious we become, the more likely we are to tremble, blush, or make abrupt, clumsy movements. Our fear of disapproval, more than their fear of the actual situation itself, is what's responsible for our anxiety.

But why are we afraid of *social situations?* Why does our anxiety center on fears of embarrassment or humiliation instead of snakes or spiders? Let's take a look at the unique factors that can lead us down this particular anxiety path.

The Perfect Storm of Social Anxiety

In the movie *The Perfect Storm,* George Clooney and his cast of characters encounter a merging of weather conditions that collide together to form the perfect storm. Had even one of them been missing, the result might have been vastly different. A similar conclusion might be drawn for the development of social anxiety disorder; an accumulation of risk factors add up to tip the scale from shyness to social phobia.

Risk factors for social anxiety disorder include the following:

- **Gender.** About twice as many women as men have social anxiety disorder.

- **Family history.** Some research indicates that you're more likely to develop social anxiety disorder if your biological parents or siblings have the condition.

- **Environment.** Your environment may influence the development of social anxiety disorder in a number of ways. Some experts theorize, for instance, that social anxiety disorder is a learned behavior. That is, you may develop the condition after witnessing others with symptoms. In essence, you may be learning social anxiety disorder by example. In addition, there may be an association between social anxiety disorder and parents who are more controlling or protective of their children.

♦ **Negative experience.** Children who experience high levels of teasing, bullying, rejection, ridicule, or humiliation may go on to develop social anxiety disorder. In addition, other negative events in life, such as family conflict or sexual abuse, may be associated with social anxiety disorder.

♦ **Temperament.** Children who are shy, timid, withdrawn, or restrained when facing new situations or people may be at greater risk of social anxiety disorder.

♦ **New social or work demands.** Meeting new people, giving a speech in public, or making an important work presentation may trigger the signs and symptoms of social anxiety disorder. These signs and symptoms usually have their roots in adolescence, however.

As we can see, a number of things can contribute to the development of social anxiety. And, like a perfect storm, it's often a matter of certain risk factors converging: biology (anxiety runs in families); temperament (some people are just more inhibited in social situations than others); and life experiences (a humiliating event, the parenting style you grew up with, and other situational experiences). For instance, a shy third grader "freezes" when called upon in class and, as a result, is reprimanded by her teacher and teased by her peers.

> **Anxiety Attack**
>
> Many people think that having a drink before an experience that makes them nervous is a good way to calm down. However, there's a strong link between social anxiety and alcohol abuse; self-medicating with alcohol or drugs (recreational or prescription) can easily become a crutch.

When we begin to feel socially anxious—often as a result of a stressful event or period in your life—it usually doesn't go away on its own. The good news though is that social anxiety, like other forms of anxiety, is treatable.

What Are You Afraid Of?

Social anxiety is complex; not everyone is afraid of the same situations. I may be petrified about speaking in public. You may be nervous about eating in a restaurant. Underlying each situation are fears of scrutiny (criticism or ridicule arising from attention or evaluation from others), humiliation (being rejected), or embarrassment (from making a mistake or appearing foolish). Here are some common anxiety-provoking situations; check the ones that consistently make you nervous:

- ❑ Acting, performing, or giving a talk in front of an audience
- ❑ Talking to people in authority
- ❑ Expressing your opinion
- ❑ Interviewing for a job
- ❑ Voicing your disagreement
- ❑ Speaking at a meeting
- ❑ Responding to criticism
- ❑ Giving a report to a group
- ❑ Giving and receiving compliments
- ❑ Eating out in public
- ❑ Asking for a date
- ❑ Drinking in public places
- ❑ Answering personal questions
- ❑ Urinating in a public bathroom
- ❑ Meeting strangers
- ❑ Being the center of attention
- ❑ Getting onto a crowded elevator
- ❑ Calling someone unfamiliar
- ❑ Entering a room when others are already seated
- ❑ Returning items to a store
- ❑ Going to a party
- ❑ Making eye contact
- ❑ Giving a party
- ❑ Resisting a high-pressure salesperson
- ❑ Joining a conversation already in progress

❏ Making mistakes in front of others

❏ Participating in small groups

❏ Taking a test

❏ Bumping into someone you know

❏ Writing while being observed

❏ Talking with people you do not know very well

❏ Working while being observed

❏ Initiating conversation with someone you're attracted to

> **On the Cutting Edge**
>
> New research indicates that one of the most stressful situations for those of us with social anxiety is meeting people we consider "authority figures," whether that's a boss at work or your future in-laws.

Many of the these activities are things most of us typically do every day. Many of them are also vital to our career success and personal relationships. As such, untreated social anxiety can wreak havoc on virtually every aspect of our lives. On the positive side, when we decide to face our fears, we have a lot of opportunities to practice. And practice we must if we're going to take control over our social fears. This practice involves changing our mental behaviors as well as our outward ones.

"Do You Really Care What People Think?" *Yes!*

Most people consider the term *performance* to mean some type of formal presentation or event. Those of us with social anxiety can feel performance pressure in the simplest social interaction; shaking someone's hand or greeting a stranger can feel like a test. In fact, one of the hallmarks of social anxiety sufferers is the tendency to misinterpret

> **Anxiety Attack**
>
> If your social anxiety causes severe physical symptoms, use the panic-attack survival strategies we discussed in Chapter 14.

neutral social cues as evidence that others are negatively evaluating us. People who suffer from shyness or social anxiety often believe that other people will think badly of them or that people will be judging them. Because of our vulnerability to rejection and disapproval, we also tend to be overly concerned with making a positive impression on people.

In Chapters 8 and 9, we examined the link between our negative automatic thoughts, irrational beliefs, and feelings of anxiety. For instance, we discussed how negative thinking (*"What if I lose it?"*) in response to an uncomfortable feeling (fear) or unpleasant physical sensation (dizziness, rapid heartbeat) can add fuel to our emotional fire. With social anxiety, our automatic thoughts and irrational beliefs center on social situations, the opinions of others, and our sense of our own competence/lovability as influenced by interpersonal interactions. In other words, our fear about what others are thinking is often a reflection of what we believe about ourselves. It's these thoughts and beliefs that we have to change.

We start by catching our automatic thoughts and slowly beginning to replace them with realistic, rational ones. We can easily get so caught up in the anxiety and dread around stressful situations that we don't pay attention to the negative conversation we're having with ourselves. To get used to this process, think back over three or four actual occasions that you found difficult over the past month and try to re-create your thoughts before, during, and after this situation. Create something like this:

Situation: *Giving a presentation.*

Thoughts beforehand: *Man, I dread that talk next week. I don't know what to say. Maybe I'll go blank; I'm going to make a total fool of myself.*

Thoughts during: *Oh, god. I'm sweating. I know the boss can see how nervous I am. She must think there's something wrong with me.*

Thoughts afterward: *Well, I blew it again. How could I have missed that statistic?! John does these kinds of things like they're a piece of cake.*

Conclusions: *I can't handle things the way other people can. Some people have and some people don't; I don't.*

Now, keep a social anxiety diary over the next two weeks. Write down what situations you felt anxious in as well as the thoughts, feelings, and physical sensations you experience before, during, and after. As you journal, begin using the strategies we discussed in Chapters 8 and 9 to counter your social-anxiety-specific thoughts and beliefs. Remember, the trick is to recognize the thinking errors that are common in social anxiety—catastrophizing that a minor faux pas is a major disaster, personalizing reactions from others without any concrete evidence, focusing only on what you did wrong and ignoring situations you handled with ease—and begin to make them rationally neutral. The more we consciously practice and repeat this process, the more automatic it will become.

Anxiety Attack

Volunteer work naturally focuses on helping someone else and, as such, can be a great way to practice letting go of the "spotlight" effect.

In addition, as we become well acquainted with the negative thoughts that plague us, we often discover dysfunctional beliefs that form the core of our social anxiety. *"I just can't handle rejection. If someone criticizes me, it means that I am a bad person. I just can't fit in with other people. No one loves people who are weak or make mistakes. My self-worth depends upon the opinions of other people."* These are the kinds of beliefs that have often been around for a while and take more time to correct. By paying attention to and correcting the conclusions we draw about our social anxiety, we can begin to chip away at these core beliefs. *"I can't tolerate rejection"* gradually turns into *"I don't like to be rejected, but I can handle it. And it doesn't say anything about my value as a person."*

Getting Out of the Spotlight

One of the most common cognitive distortions we social anxiety sufferers tend to share is often referred to as the "spotlight effect," the excruciating sensation that all eyes are on us and that we are being judged. We tend to *consistently* overestimate the degree to which other people's attention is focused on us, how much they remember about what we said or did, and how much importance they attached to it. It's not that we're self-centered; it's just that we're so negatively self-conscious in social situations that we can't help but think others see—and judge—what we're doing. In fact, research shows the root of the "spotlight effect" lies in our excessive self-processing in anxiety-ridden social situations. This means that we …

◆ Zoom in on what is happening inside our bodies, especially anxiety symptoms like shaking, sweating, red face, difficulties in speaking.

◆ Focus on the negative images and thoughts that are swirling around in our heads.

◆ Are less able to pay attention to, and evaluate, the reactions of others.

◆ Easily interpret ambiguous responses (body language, unclear comments) as confirmation that we are being rejected/ridiculed.

In other words, we are likely to see what we already believe. However, understanding the reason for the spotlight effect doesn't make it go away. What can help, though, is to *plan out* ways to shift the focus from ourselves to others. In fact, a good strategy is to find ways to engage in competing activities.

For example, at a small gathering, we might make a goal of helping another person feel more comfortable. We might decide to find out three things about another person in the room and prepare questions that another person would enjoy answering. We can practice being a good listener, making a point of reflecting back what we are hearing to ensure that the other person feels heard.

We can look around the room and see if anyone else seems nervous. Social phobia affects between 3 and 5 percent of the U.S. population; the odds are, someone else in the room has some degree of it. Can you spot who it might be? If you can't, then the odds are that *no one can spot you, either*. But what if you do spy someone who seems unsure or anxious; how would you feel toward that person? Would you instantly dislike him or her and direct the rest of your time and attention to negatively critiquing him or her? *No?* Then why would anyone do that to you?

When we shift our focus in social situations, we begin to see that we are not, in reality, the center of anyone else's attention. In social situations where we're feeling especially vulnerable, we can be skeptical of what our thoughts are telling us.

> **Stress Relief** _____
>
> As part of an experiment, students wearing what they believed to be embarrassing T-shirts were sent into a room of their peers. Although the students were convinced (and mortified) that most everyone would notice the T-shirts, fewer than 50 percent actually remembered them.

> **On the Cutting Edge**
>
> Although social anxiety is highly treatable, 80 percent of the people who have it never seek professional help.

Behave Yourself

It's possible, though, that I'm putting the cart before the horse; maybe you don't go into social situations. At all. Many people who have suffered from social anxiety for years have become exceptional escape artists, learning to either avoid a threatening situation altogether or use enough "tricks" while in one so that they never truly engage. Unfortunately, learning to think new thoughts isn't going to get us very far if we don't get in the saddle and ride.

Changing our behavior is just as important in conquering social anxiety as changing our thoughts. In fact, in the long run, changing what we *do* is probably the most helpful way to overcome social anxiety. Many of the strategies we discussed in the preceding chapter are extremely relevant to social anxiety; we need to develop an anxiety hierarchy where we list our feared social situations, ranking them from most frightening to least. We start at the shallow end of the swimming pool and work our way to the deep.

Because social anxiety is so complex, it may be useful to develop different hierarchies for different situations. For example, a fear of speaking in front of a group can be broken down into various steps, starting with an easy one and moving up to a challenging item. The same can be done for going to a party or interviewing for a job. A social anxiety hierarchy for fear of talking in front of a group of people might look something like this:

Most Stressful

Giving a formal presentation

Leading a team discussion in front of a boss

Asking a question or giving input during a staff meeting

Joining a group of coworkers already sitting at the lunch table

Engaging in casual conversation with strangers in the elevator

Going with a friend to a party where I don't know many people

Bumping into a couple I don't know very well

Least Stressful

As we discussed in the preceding chapter, the goal is to gradually tackle each item on our anxiety hierarchy. However, unlike simple phobias that we can avoid altogether, many of us find that we actually have to do a few of the items on this list. As such, we need to also take an honest look at ways we mentally escape while we are in an uncomfortable situation and gradually eliminate these, too.

For instance, we may make it to the party but sit in the corner, say little or let someone else do the talking, or stick closely to a safe person. These "safe" behaviors allowed us to stay in a stressful situation, but now we need to move beyond merely surviving our social anxiety. We want to take charge of it!

On the bright side, in between practice sessions when we focus specifically on the items in our hierarchy and on restructuring our negative thoughts, countless opportunities exist for us to boost our social confidence. Some of these need last only a few seconds or a few minutes at most. For example:

- Return a greeting from a neighbor or coworker

- Say hello to a neighbor or coworker without waiting to be greeted first

- Ask a clerk where to find something in a store

- Ask a stranger for directions

- Accept an invitation to lunch with a small group where other people will do most of the talking

- Accept a compliment with a simple thank you

- Give someone else a compliment

- Respond to a simple question with a brief answer if you have one

- Respond to a question you honestly can't answer with a simple admission that you don't know

You will gradually learn that you can cope and feel comfortable in social situations. It is worth remembering that many other people feel anxious in social situations too, it just doesn't show. You are not the only one.

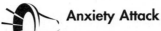 **Anxiety Attack**

Medication by itself does not seem to be effective in alleviating social anxiety, although it can be an effective adjunct for severe social anxiety sufferers. Eighty percent of social anxiety sufferers report significant improvement from cognitive-behavioral psychotherapy.

Work It, Girl!

To manage your recovery from social anxiety, you need to consistently and repeatedly practice your newfound skills. There are several issues to keep in mind as you do this:

- **Divide and conquer.** It can be daunting to think of all the skills you need to work on to conquer social anxiety—dealing with the uncomfortable physical sensations that occur, challenging negative thought patterns, and socializing with other people at the same time. Instead, look at your recovery as a three-pronged approach and, in the beginning, work on them individually.

- **Schedule practice sessions.** Don't wait for situations on your hierarchy to appear before you start working on them. If nothing's coming up on your schedule, create situations that will force you to practice; go to the grocery store, ask a friend to look over your shoulder while you're writing, or go out to eat in a public restaurant.

Stress Relief _____

The first few minutes of a presentation are usually the most anxiety provoking. You can plan ahead for this by memorizing the first few minutes of your talk, getting to the room early and meeting everyone there, and asking the audience several questions to shift your mental focus from yourself to others.

◆ **Expand your social skills.** No one is born with the gift of gab. We learn how to join in, listen, make memorable presentations and communicate effectively. Build your social confidence by acquiring knowledge in which you feel lacking; this could be anything such as reading _Miss Manners_ to _How to Win Friends and Influence People._

◆ **Don't set yourself up.** Studies suggest that as many as 70 percent of social anxiety sufferers also suffer from other challenges such as agoraphobia, panic disorder, or depression. And approximately 20 percent of those with social anxieties use alcohol to ease their fears. If you are experiencing other difficulties in addition to social anxiety, consider seeking professional help.

Virtual Help or Alternative Reality?

In other chapters, we've discussed how virtual reality is being used to help people overcome debilitating fear; for example, people who are too terrified of flying to make the leap between visiting an airport and actually taking a flight can benefit tremendously from therapy that includes a simulated airplane ride. Could the Internet provide a "virtual" social setting, a safe place where a severe social anxiety sufferer could jump-start his or her recovery?

The answer appears to be a qualified "yes." There are wonderful online support groups for all anxiety disorders, including social anxiety. Some of these are filled with lots of good tips, warm support and encouragement, and touching personal experiences. Chat rooms or discussion boards can be a great way to put one's toe in the water and try out social contacts with which we're less comfortable in the real world.

On the downside, we can't allow online relationships to substitute for "real-world" ones. Chatting on the Internet is no substitute for face-to-face interaction. Allowing the Internet to become one's entire social network is not a therapeutic use of virtual reality; that's more like creating an alternative reality. When it comes to the social anxiety, the Internet best serves as a stepping stone; we try out our new skills with our online contacts and then take them out into the real world.

In the past four chapters, we've looked at the best self-help has to offer in helping us get a grip on our crippling anxiety. In this chapter, we've reviewed strategies for recognizing, and slowly tackling, the distressing thoughts, feelings, and physical symptoms that plague anxiety sufferers. We've also reviewed systematic desensitization, a way we can gradually train ourselves to face social situations that we have either avoided or sabotaged through minimal participation.

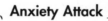 **Anxiety Attack**

Not sure if your Internet use is too much? Ask yourself whether your relationships have improved or deteriorated since you went online and whether you spend more or less time interacting with others.

These self-help techniques work as long as our psyches are ready and able to use them. The reality is that many of us anxiety sufferers have struggled for years with our fears and have developed some pretty ingrained habits of survival. Or we find ourselves battling more than one problem; perhaps an additional anxiety disorder, a secondary depression, or excessive drinking.

Getting control of an anxiety disorder should not be an "all-or-nothing" proposition; instead, you should take the attitude of "whatever works." In the next chapter, we explore state-of-the-art anxiety disorder treatments and how "self-help" can include finding the right assistance.

The Least You Need to Know

- People suffering from social anxiety disorder fear ridicule, rejection, or embarrassment to such an extent that they avoid the social activities that are essential to professional success and personal satisfaction.

- Social anxiety is often a result of a biological vulnerability (shy temperament, family history of anxiety) colliding with certain life experiences (critical parenting, humiliating social experiences).

- Social anxiety is a complex phobia. The fear of public humiliation and scrutiny can generalize to many different situations.

- The most effective self-help for social anxiety incorporates strategies for managing the physical symptoms, reprogramming dysfunctional thoughts and beliefs, and gradually reintroducing socially anxious situations. Boning up on our social skills can also increase our interpersonal confidence.

Chapter 18

Need Some Help? Consider the Evidence

In This Chapter

- Learn what's "state-of-the-art" in anxiety treatments
- Discover what the best anxiety treaters do with their clients
- Do a "background check" on a prospective therapist
- Know when it's time to seek a new treatment angle
- Evaluate the risks and rewards of medication for anxiety

Not only should we bring motivation and openness to our professional's office, we should also come armed with knowledge; accurate information about our symptoms and also an awareness of what treatment is likely to work best and what kind of therapist we're looking for. In this chapter, we take a look at how we can get the most benefit from anxiety treatment.

Sarah's Story

"I first started having anxiety symptoms in 1993. After several trips to the ER and numerous visits to my general practitioner, I decided perhaps it was time to find a specialist. My health insurance company hooked me up with a psychiatrist, who put me on antidepressants. It took a while to get the right dose, but I finally started feeling better.

"After a while though, my anxiety got worse again. When I called my doctor, he upped my meds and offered to give me a note so I could take a few weeks off work. Okay, I thought, I can sure use the time off. The problem was, this 'treatment' continued for seven years. I would feel better for a little while, my anxiety would come back or get worse, and my doctor would increase my medication and tell me to take some time off. Not only did I start feeling like a zombie from all the drugs, I felt increasingly depressed and hopeless.

"The last straw came for me when my doctor told me he thought I needed to go on disability. I'm 32 years old, for God's sake. I guess that was a wake-up call that my doctor had given up on me; he didn't think I would ever get better."

Anxiety Attack

Research has shown that anxiety patients whose spouses or parents express hostility toward them were almost six times more likely to stop treatment than those whose families were not hostile. On the flip side, families who are too involved, or "hovering," can impede progress. Having a therapist willing to involve family members in treatment—as needed—can increase the effectiveness of treatment.

Sarah found a new doctor, who put her on a different—and much lower—dose of antidepressant and got her into therapy. Three years later, Sarah has gone from daily panic attacks to an average of one every six months. And she hasn't missed a day of work because of her anxiety in two years.

Why did it take Sarah so long to change doctors? Why *wouldn't* it? It takes a tremendous amount of courage to admit that our best self-help strategies haven't worked and to seek help from a professional. When we do, it's natural to place our trust in our treater; after all, s/he is the "expert."

However, blind faith in a person just because s/he has some fancy initials after his or her name isn't always warranted.

The Sherlock Holmes's Guide to Anxiety Treatment

Anxiety disorders can compromise your quality of life, to be sure. That's the bad news. The good news is that they are highly treatable: 80 percent of anxiety sufferers get better with medication, therapy, or a combination of both. But what kind of therapy? What kind of medication, how much, and for how long?

One strategy that is increasingly being adopted by anxiety experts—and by savvy consumers—is to examine the evidence. The philosophy behind *evidence-based treatment* is simply that clinical decisions should be based on sound research; by looking at studies comparing treatment outcomes with different strategies, we can tease out how to get the most bang for our treatment buck. It's like going to the horse track and betting on the horse with the best odds; it doesn't mean another horse won't win, but the favored horse is the one with the proven track record.

Because the anxiety disorders share certain features, it's not that surprising that the same family of medications and psycho-therapy frameworks tend to work well with all of them. For instance, cognitive-behavioral therapy (CBT) is the psycho-therapy of choice for obsessive-compulsive disorder, panic disorder, social anxiety, generalized anxiety disorder, and simple phobia. CBT is a combination or a "pulling together" of various strategies, tools, and techniques to help anxiety sufferers change the way they think and what they do in response to their fear.

> **Anxiety Attack**
>
> If you're looking for online help, check out *The Online Counseling Consumer's Guide* at www.CounselingPros.com.

> **Anxiety Attack**
>
> Because many people have more than one anxiety disorder or may also suffer from depression or substance abuse, each person needs an individual treatment plan tailored specifically to his or her condition. Your therapist will choose one—or a combination of several—that will work best for you.

Give Me a C

The cognitive part of CBT targets the way we think. The idea is that our thoughts exert a strong influence on how we feel and what we do. A major focus of therapy, then, is helping the client learn how to recognize and dispute irrational thoughts and beliefs—and replace them with more rational ones.

The therapist might use dozens of techniques and strategies to meet this goal. The therapist might encourage the client to pay attention to the negative thoughts that pop up automatically during the day, or pop up in response to anxiety symptoms. Perhaps the focus will be on identifying the possible triggers (thought, situation, physical sensations) that lead to a panic attack and learning to attach less importance to them.

A person suffering from obsessive thoughts might be taught a thought-stopping technique; someone with a specific phobia might slowly visualize increasingly close encounters with the feared object or situation until s/he is ready to take actual steps to directly face those fears. Another common cognitive strategy is playing out the "What if?" worry to give it less power. What if I panic in the store? I can always leave. What if I feel faint? Someone will help me.

As you can see, no matter what anxiety problem the person suffers from, the philosophy behind cognitive therapy is the same: to harness the power of our minds to positively influence our feelings and actions. The specific techniques and methods used to achieve this goal should be tailored to the particular problem at hand. One thing we can expect, though, is homework; the "learning" part of cognitive therapy takes place in the therapist's office, but the real work happens during the rest of the week.

Give Me a B

The *B* in cognitive behavioral therapy stands for behavior. If we're really going to conquer our anxiety, we've got to go into the lion's den. We've got to face head on the very thing we're most afraid of. We've got to touch the germy object we're afraid will make us sick, we've got to go to that party, we've got to get back behind the wheel of our car.

This is where a good therapist can be critical, helping us move forward in a gradual, step-by-step process, assigning us real-world experiments that are challenging but not terrifying. She can help us mentally prepare for these experiences, teach us distraction and relaxation techniques to cope with the uncomfortable physical sensations, and guide us through any glitches or setbacks.

Stress Relief

Use your natural strengths to jump-start your treatment. If you're a "thinker," focus initially on ways of restructuring your thoughts and feelings. If you're a "feeler," start with relaxation techniques and calming music. And if you're a "doer," focus on small behavioral goals that will get you to where you want to be.

All Together Now: Cognitive Behavior Therapy (CBT)

A combination of cognitive and behavior strategies seems to be the most effective treatment for anxiety disorders. The important elements of CBT include cognitive restructuring (changing negative and self-defeating thoughts) and exposure (gradually facing our fears). These strategies are often used side by side; for example, mental techniques can help me approach a scary situation.

Our cognitive behavior therapy journey will take different twists and turns depending upon our diagnosis and our personal goals/challenges. Here's a chart to give you a rough idea of how CBT might tackle different anxiety disorders.

 **Anxiety Attack**

One aspect of cognitive behavioral therapy focuses on learning effective relaxation techniques, such as deep breathing and guided imagery, because this helps most people move more easily through uncomfortable anxiety symptoms.

Problem	Irrational Belief	Restructuring	Problem Behavior	Gradual Exposure
Panic disorder	I'll be trapped if I have a panic attack in the grocery store.	I can leave the store at any time. I'll check and see where the exits are.	No grocery shopping	Visualize going into the store, walk up to it, walk in and leave, buy one item, etc.
Phobia	The plane will crash.	The odds of a plane crashing on any given day are astronomically small.	Refusal to fly	Visualization, gradual exposure to airport, virtual reality to simulate flight, take real flight.
OCD	The house is going to burn down while I'm away.	I have made the house as safe as I can.	Repeated checking of stove, doors, etc.	Go through prepared safety list, stop after complete.
Social anxiety	No one will talk to me at the party. I'll look like an idiot.	There will be other quiet people at the party, too. I can help someone else feel more comfortable.	Turn down social invitations.	Role-play social situations, plan conversation starters, accept invitation.

Better Living Through Chemistry?

Medication is often part of the clinical treatment of anxiety disorders. The way meds are used often varies with the treatment philosophy of the practitioner or the personal philosophy of the client. For instance, it can be a "take-as-needed" strategy for extremely stressful events, it can be a complement to psychotherapy, or it can be used on its own. It can be viewed as a critical part of treatment or as a stop-gap measure until the person's anxiety symptoms are in control enough for him or her to concentrate in psychotherapy.

In analyses of short-term studies, a combination of antidepressants with some form of cognitive behavioral therapy has proven more effective than antidepressants used alone.

Many medications that were originally developed and approved for the treatment of depression are also effective in treating anxiety disorders. The newest antidepressants are in a category of drugs called *selective serotonin reuptake inhibitors* (SSRIs), brand names include Lexapro, Zoloft, Paxil, and Prozac. Members of this class are usually among the first choice for physicians because they generally have fewer side effects than earlier generations of drugs; if these fail, a physician may fall back on older antidepressants such as the tricyclics (Tofranil, Anafranil) or MAO inhibitors (Nardil, Parnate, Marplan).

On the Cutting Edge

An older category of antidepressants known as tricyclics (TCAs) have been widely studied for their use in treating anxiety disorders. With the exception of OCD, tricyclics are as effective as SSRIs, but tend to have additional side effects, including dizziness, drowsiness, dry mouth, and weight gain.

Your doctor may also prescribe anti-anxiety medications instead of, or in addition to, an antidepressant. A category of drugs known as benzodiazepines (benzos for short) ease symptoms quickly and have few side effects, other than drowsiness. You can develop a tolerance to them, however, which would call for increased dosages, so they are usually only prescribed for short periods of time.

People suffering from panic disorder, though, may be prescribed benzodiazepines for six months to a year. If you have problems with drugs or alcohol, you probably will not be a good candidate for these drugs because you may become dependent on them. Some people do experience withdrawal symptoms when they stop taking benzos, although gradually reducing the dosage will usually alleviate that. In some cases, symptoms may come back after the medications are stopped.

Buspirone (brand name BuSpar) belongs to a class of drugs called *azipirones*, and is also used to treat general anxiety disorder. Dizziness, headaches, and nausea are possible side effects, and like antidepressants, Buspirone must be taken on a regular basis for at least two weeks before it reduces symptoms of anxiety.

Before taking any medication, ask your doctor about the desired outcome of the drug and also the side effects. Tell your doctor about any alternative therapies or over-the-counter medications you are using. Ask your doctor when and how the medication will be stopped, and whether there are any dangers in stopping the medication abruptly. (Some medications must be gradually decreased under a doctor's care.)

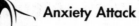

Anxiety Attack

If you're seeing a new mental-health professional, be specific about what you've tried: medication, dosage, side effects, and length of treatment. If you had psychotherapy, what kind, how often, and for how long? People often believe they have "failed" at treatment, or that the treatment failed them, when in fact it was never given an adequate trial.

Condition	Drug	Dose
Panic disorder	Benzodiazepines	
	Xanax	.5 mg 3/day
	Klonopin	.5 mg 3/day
	SSRIs	
	Celexa	40 mg/day
	Prozac	40 mg/day
	Luvox	150 mg/day
	Paxil	40 mg/day
	Zoloft	50–200 mg/day
	TCAs	
	Anafranil	75–150 mg/bed
	Tofranil-PM	150 mg/bedtime
Generalized anxiety disorder	Benzodiazepines	
	Xanax	.5 mg 3/day
	Klonopin	.5 mg 3/day

continues

continued

Condition	Drug	Dose
Generalized anxiety disorder	SSRIs	
	Celexa	40 mg/day
	Prozac	40–80 mg/day
	Luvox	150 mg/day
	Paxil	40 mg/day
	Zoloft	50-250 mg
	Lexapro	10-20 mg/day
	Azapirones	
	BuSpar	Up to 60 mg/day
Obsessive-compulsive disorder	TCAs	
	Anafranil	Up to 250 mg/day
	SSRIs	
	Luvox	Up to 300 mg/day
	Paxil	40–60 mg/day
	Prozac	40–80 mg/day
	Zoloft	Up to 200 mg/day
	Celexa	Up to 60 mg/day
Social anxiety disorder	SSRIs	
	Zoloft	up to 200 mg/day
	Paxil	up to 40 mg/day
	Effexor	up to 225 mg/day
	Beta Blockers	
	Inderal	10 to 40 mg/usually 20-60 minutes before event
	Innopran	10 to 40 mg/usually 20-60 minutes before event
	Benzodiazepines	
	Klonopin	.25 to 1 mg/day
	Xanax	.25 to .5 mg before exposure to stressful event

The previous list is not comprehensive; new medications are being added all the time as are new ways to use existing ones. In fact, because the FDA approval process is lengthy and time-consuming, some of the above medications are prescribed off-label; in other words, they haven't yet been formally approved by the FDA although research supports their effectiveness. As of June 2006, 39 psychotropic drugs were in development to treat anxiety.

Anxiety Attack

Support groups are often an invaluable part of treatment. These groups provide a forum for mutual acceptance, understanding, and self-discovery.

Inside the Matrix

Whether they're a new twist on a solidly established treatment or at the edge of the treatment frontier, treatment options for anxiety disorders continue to expand. One of the most exciting is the use of virtual reality as an adjunct to cognitive behavior therapy. For example, unlike elevators or bridges, it's impossible to *gradually* fly in an airplane; you're either in your passenger seat or you're not. And, what about the practice necessary to lock in that new found courage? Bill Gates aside, few of us have the money to spend hours making practice flights.

That's where virtual reality comes in. Virtual reality uses computer technology to stimulate the real experience right there in the safety of the doctor's office. Dozens of studies in the past 10 years have demonstrated that virtual reality is effective in helping people overcome their fears of spiders, heights, storms, flying, and even public speaking (usually cited as most people's number one fear).

Consider the Alternatives

Since 1958, the American Medical Association has recognized *hypnosis* as a legitimate treatment for a number of mind-body conditions. Research suggests that it can be a good relaxation tool and can keep us calm when faced with being overwhelmed by the symptoms of a panic or anxiety attack.

How about *laughter therapy?* Humor visualization is another alternative therapy that can be a great compliment to traditional treatment. Psychologists who incorporate humor into their work with clients suffering from generalized anxiety disorder may offer laughter to help their clients get some distance from their worries; for example, by having the client imagine how a sitcom producer would handle the situation producing the anxiety.

Some therapeutic humor specialists (yes, there is such a thing!) use humor visualization with their panic attack clients, suggesting that they picture themselves at a time when they have laughed uncontrollably. When anxiety symptoms first surface, the panic sufferer focuses on that delightful memory. The theory is that the strong positive image replaces the disturbing fears that surface during a panic attack; furthermore, the laughter will change the physiological symptoms, too. Anxiety increases levels of serum cortisol, the stress hormone, and laughter is thought to reduce the cortisol levels.

Eye movement systematic desensitization (EMDR) is an additional alternative that combines several therapeutic methods—psychodynamic, cognitive, behavioral, and so on—with eye movements or other forms of rhythmical stimulation, such as hand taps or sounds. The theory behind EMDR is that strong emotions at the time of a traumatic event interfere with our ability to process it; as a result, we may intellectually understand what happened but emotionally get trapped into reexperiencing it. EMDR integrates the intellectual and emotional aspects of the trauma. It has been most successfully used to treat trauma-induced anxiety, such as post-traumatic stress disorder (PTSD) or severe panic attacks triggered by a life-threatening event.

Energy therapies, such as thought field therapy (TFT) and emotional freedom techniques (EFT), are new kids on the block. They allegedly utilize "energy healing." The theory behind thought field therapy, for instance, is that each thought we have triggers a chemical change in our body, which can produce changes in behavior and bodily sensations, including racing heart, sweaty palms, dizziness, and shortness of breath. A trained professional teaches the client how to "tap" acupressure points, theoretically disrupting the "chi" or energy associated with the unpleasant anxiety symptom. While there is anecdotal evidence of successful treatment using these techniques, the American Psychological Association has adopted the position that there is little scientific evidence to support the use of energy therapies for treatment of anxiety disorders.

Finding Dr. Right

A good client-therapist relationship is worth its weight in gold, but like a marriage, not all clients and therapists are made for each other. And it's usually not the title that determines whether or not the person will help; effective anxiety treatment can be administered by a psychologist, psychiatrist, social worker, psychotherapist, and so on. The best anxiety professional is likely to be the one with specific experience and expertise treating your specific disorder *plus* a personality and communication style that you can relate to.

Here are a few questions you may want to ask a prospective therapist, either on the phone or in person, before signing up for therapy:

1. (If you are from a different cultural or ethnic background) how much experience do you have treating clients who are _____?

2. What is your treatment approach?

3. Are you able to prescribe medication or can you refer me to someone who can if we agree that it would be helpful?

4. How long do you think I'll need to see you?

5. How do you measure progress?

6. How often would I come and how long does each session last?

7. Would you want to see members of my family as well?

8. Do you provide in-home treatment if a client is unable to come to your office?

9. How much do you charge, and do you have a sliding scale if I can't afford your regular fees?

10. Do you accept health insurance, and if so, which ones?

Think of the initial interview just as you would if you were interviewing job candidates. There are a lot of good "applicants" out there. If you are uncomfortable with any of the therapist's answers (or if s/he refuses to answer your questions), see someone else.

> **Myth Buster**
>
> "I'll have to stay on medication forever." Not true; six months often provides the full benefits and is long enough to prevent relapse.

When to Say Enough Is Enough

Woody Allen notwithstanding, therapy is usually not a lifelong proposition. The objective of therapy is to make the therapist expendable—at least for you. But how long does that take?

Because cognitive behavioral therapy has specific goals, it is, by its nature, time-limited. Treatment goals are generally established during the first session, as is a preliminary, agreed-upon number of sessions (perhaps 10 to 20). This range takes into account the very personal nature of every mental-health challenge (no matter how "standard" the diagnosis) as well as any setbacks/additional issues that may arise. The end of therapy is mutually agreed upon; when your goals are met, the therapist takes a hike.

Occasionally, though, a client gets frustrated or wants to quit therapy before the therapist thinks the client is "ready." Before you cancel that appointment, do a little soul searching. Why? Are you not making progress? Are you going too fast? Has your therapist said or done something you don't like? Discuss your concerns with your therapist, but trust your own instincts, too.

If you think you still need additional help, but you're no longer comfortable with your therapist or feel that that particular therapy isn't working for you, don't leave in a snit. Tell your therapist what's bothering you. The two of you may be able to work it out, but if not, you've taken a mature, sensible approach—which may just mean that you're further along in your progress than you thought.

> **Anxiety Attack**
>
> If you've seen a therapist 10 to 15 times and you feel that you are making no progress, it may be time to consider firing your therapist. At the very least, it's time to tell him that you're dissatisfied and ask whether there are different approaches you can try.

> **Anxiety Attack**
>
> Leaving therapy can be uncomfortable. Don't quit cold turkey; if you've been seeing your therapist once a week, start going every other week, then perhaps once a month.

In this chapter, we've looked at the state-of-the-art in terms of anxiety disorder treatment. We've seen how cognitive behavior therapy and medication, used together or separately, work effectively for 70 percent to 80 percent of the clients who use them.

But what about times when medication isn't the right choice? What do we do when all our hard therapy work takes a sudden back seat to a challenging life event? In the next chapter, we take a look at anxiety and pregnancy; how we can handle our fears while our body is growing a baby and how postpartum adjustment doesn't have to mean anxiety.

The Least You Need to Know

- Anxiety disorders are highly treatable, and a good body of research shows what treatments work best.

- Evidence-based anxiety treatment usually includes cognitive behavioral therapy, medication, or a combination of the two.

- Cognitive behavioral therapy works by eliminating negative or self-defeating thoughts and helping the client gradually face his or her fears.

- Medication can be used by itself but seems to work best in combination with psychotherapy.

- The treatment relationship should be a partnership; you are the "expert" on your illness, and the mental-health professional is the expert on treatment. If it's not working, discuss it with your professional.

- Don't be afraid to investigate alternative therapies such as hypnosis or acupuncture, but let all your health-care providers know what you are doing.

Part 6

Not All in the Family: Keeping Anxiety from the Next Generation

An anxiety disorder does not have to be passed down from one generation to the next. In this section, we explore how new mothers—with or without a preexisting anxiety disorder—can get off to the right start with their newborns by taking active steps to manage their anxiety during pregnancy and after birth. We then turn to the relationship between parenting and anxiety and examine how our interactions with our children can either promote resilience or magnify vulnerability. Finally, we highlight the influence parents have in helping our children work through normal fears and by gathering the best professional guidance when they need more than we can give.

Chapter 19

The Right Start: Anxiety During and After Pregnancy

In This Chapter

- Find out what's normal worry during pregnancy and what's not
- Discover the best-kept secret of postpartum adjustment
- Shed light on the predictors of postpartum anxiety
- Develop your panic-free pregnancy plan
- Explore the pros and cons of medication during pregnancy

"I had a few panic attacks back when I was in college but I could still function. I got some therapy at the university counseling center, still hung out with my friends and made it to my classes. In fact, I graduated with honors and got a great job in the Bay area.

"Nothing prepared me for the panic attacks that hit me six years later, after my daughter was born. I got them more often. They lasted longer. I had a hard time breathing; my heart pounded so I hard I thought it would burst. It was even worse when I nursed. I got tingling sensations and numbness in my hands. I'd pound my hands together or on my leg, but it was kind of out of control, like I couldn't help *it. It got to the point where I didn't want to go out by myself. Even at home, I felt uncomfort-able by myself. My husband tried to help but he didn't know what to do; I'd gone from this independent spirit to this terrified, clingy person, and he'd wind up getting impatient with me.*

"Lucky for me, though, my mom was supportive because she's suffered from panic attacks her whole life. She helped me get back in therapy and gave me some 'time out' from our new baby. It's been two years now, and I feel like I'm pretty much back to normal. But I'll never forget it. We want to add more children to our family, and it scares me. At least I now know what might happen so I can prepare for it. My doctor says there are a lot of things we can do to keep it from being so bad."

By publicly sharing their painful experiences with postpartum depression, celebrities such as Brooke Shields and Marie Osmond have helped the one out of every eight new mothers who suffer through it feel less alone and ashamed. Physicians, too, are slowly making strides in telling the difference between the baby blues and clinical depression.

However, who will shed some light on postpartum anxiety, a condition that touches 4 to 6 percent of new mothers? How does an already established anxiety disorder impact pregnancy? What do we do about medication? What can we expect after the baby's born? We answer these questions in this chapter as we explore how to create a panic-free pregnancy and postpartum plan.

The Anxious Pregnancy Syndrome

Talk to any expectant mother and the conversation will likely include some concern, fear, or worry about her pregnancy. What about the drinks we had before we found out we were pregnant? How much morning sickness is normal, and what if we don't have *any?* What if we decide on natural childbirth and then can't stand the pain? How in the world are we going to juggle motherhood with our careers—as stressful as our jobs already are? With natural concerns such as these buzzing around in our heads, what moms-to-be *don't* worry these days?

Even the information age has been both a blessing and a curse to pregnant women. On the plus side, we can make informed decisions about our medical care. We can carefully weigh the pros and cons of amniocentesis or an at-home delivery rather than automatically take our health provider's recommendation. From conception, we can "parent" our embryo, making sure our developing baby boy or girl is getting the best in utero environment possible by taking care of our physical and mental health during pregnancy.

On the dark side, all information is not created equally. Pregnancy magazines and literature are rife with cautionary tales, sensational warnings, and information about seemingly innocent dangers that could lead to a negative pregnancy outcome. We hear terms such as *ectopic pregnancy*, *blighted ovum*, and *gestational diabetes*, often without understanding the true risks or likelihood. We read warnings about everything from changing kitty litter boxes to eating canned tuna to pumping gas to taking aspirin. Well-meaning friends and family members offer unsolicited advice on everything from traveling while pregnant to avoiding miscarriage.

The result? Obstetricians report a dramatic increase in anxiety-related phone calls from expecting mothers. In fact, some physicians spend up to half their patient-contact time addressing unrealistic concerns and reassuring their clients. And an anxiety-riddled pregnancy can set the stage for a difficult postpartum experience, particularly among women who are already at risk.

Stress Relief

Two of the most common pregnancy anxieties—miscarriage and irreversible weight gain—are largely unfounded. When a woman hears the fetal heartbeat, her chances of miscarrying drop to 2 percent. And the majority of women, without killing themselves with exercise or crash dieting, are back to their pre-pregnancy weight by their children's first birthdays.

The Best-Kept Postpartum Secret

"I was driving to the grocery store with the baby for the first time. Six blocks from home, my heart started pounding. I was sweating. I thought I was going to faint. I went back home. I didn't tell anyone because I didn't want to worry them and I felt so ashamed; why couldn't I do something as simple as go to the grocery store?

"I thought maybe I was still tired from the delivery or was anemic. But it kept happening when I drove, so I made up excuses not to drive. I refused to go out of the house for four months. Finally, my husband got impatient with me and made me go to see a counselor. I found out I was having panic attacks. I never knew other people had the same thing; I mean, I've heard of postpartum depression, but panic attacks?"

As Angela's story above illustrates, new mothers often don't recognize symptoms such as the racing heart and sweating of panic; obsessions about cleanliness, safety, or germs; or an inability to get past the birth experience are surprisingly common symptoms of postpartum emotional complications.

One reason is that *postpartum depression* is often used as an umbrella term for what are really six disorders—simple baby blues, serious postpartum depression, postpartum anxiety disorder, postpartum obsessive-compulsive disorder, postpartum psychosis, and post-traumatic stress disorder due to childbirth. As a result, new moms expect postpartum depression to look just like any other clinical depression—pervasive sadness, frequent crying, lack of energy, and so on. When a new mom feels so anxious she can't sleep, or finds herself haunted by irrational fears of hurting her child, she is more likely to blame herself than look for help.

Anxiety Attack

An important rule of thumb for getting help is that if you are so anxious that you can't sleep when your baby does, it may be time to seek professional help.

Even if she does confide in her physician, the odds are she won't get much help. All new mothers are somewhat anxious; it's tough to be in a new role and responsible for another person. The sleep deprivation alone is enough to make new parents jumpy and irritable. Pediatricians, obstetricians, and nurses are *used to* worries, concerns, and fears and can easily chalk up clinical symptoms to normal new mother worries. In addition, physicians are no different from regular folks in associating postpartum emotional problems with depression.

However, although it's normal for new mothers to worry about their babies, women affected by a postpartum anxiety and/or panic disorder experience excessive worries and fears regarding their child as well as their own actions. A new mother suffering from a postpartum anxiety disorder finds her daily life disrupted by her symptoms and her thoughts consumed by fear much as she would if an anxiety disorder surfaced at any point during her life.

A postpartum anxiety disorder is triggered by and occurs during a time already rife with physical and psychological stress. The dramatic hormonal shifts that occur after birth can make postpartum anxiety symptoms especially intense and unpredictable. In addition, the typical stressors of new parenting—the disrupted sleep, the social isolation, the ongoing role negotiations between husband and wife—can be so overwhelming that we can't get enough distance to realize that our anxiety has gone way beyond worry.

Women who have experienced an anxiety disorder in the past may have an edge when it comes to recognizing their symptoms but can fall prey to another postpartum trap: the bad mother complex. Few roles carry as much psychological significance as that of "mother." As a result, new moms can feel overwhelming guilt and shame if they find themselves feeling irritable and angry when their newborn cries, are afraid to be alone with their baby, or have obsessive thoughts about harm coming to their child. *"Maybe I can't handle being a mom"* is the fear that surfaces with every anxiety symptom. Fortunately, it's often this fear—coupled with the fierce protectiveness of motherhood—that can help us get the help we need.

> **Myth Buster**
>
> *"Postpartum anxiety is about rejecting or not wanting the baby."* Reality: women who are treated for postpartum anxiety are just as likely to become "good mothers" as those who don't suffer from it.

Way Beyond Worry

Postpartum anxiety typically rears its ugly head within a few days of delivery, although it can also come on gradually during the first year after birth. Postpartum anxiety disorders can range in severity from *adjustment disorder* to generalized anxiety disorder (GAD) to obsessive-compulsive disorder to panic disorder. From a symptom perspective, the panic disorder that develops after birth is the same as the panic disorder that develops during any other stressful period in a person's life.

Depending upon the particular disorder, symptoms may include the following:

◆ Trouble concentrating and remembering things

◆ Difficulties finishing everyday tasks

◆ Trouble making decisions

◆ Irritability and difficulty relaxing

◆ Insomnia

◆ Exhaustion

◆ Feelings of extreme uneasiness for prolonged periods of time

◆ Loss of appetite

◆ Anxiety/panic attacks

◆ Obsessive thoughts/concerns about child's health or about hurting one's child

Once again, we can see how the boundary between normal new motherhood and clinical anxiety can easily be confused. What new mother isn't exhausted? Sleep deprivation can also wreak havoc on our ability to concentrate or make decisions.

When are worries about our baby's health *obsessive?* Instead of focusing on "how much" or "how often," perhaps the question to ask in terms of when to get help is "how painful." In other words:

◆ Are you so anxious that you cannot adequately care for your baby?

◆ Are you afraid of hurting yourself or the baby to the extent that you are not sure that you can stop yourself?

◆ Are you so anxious that you cannot eat or sleep?

◆ Is your anxiety wearing you down to the point that you're starting to get depressed?

Anxiety Attack

Women who become pregnant after suffering a miscarriage often find themselves in a constant state of worry and tension over the possibility of another loss. BellaOnline's miscarriage section can be a great source of emotional support (www.bellaonline.com/subjects/6461.asp).

Answering yes to one or more of these questions suggests that we are putting too much of the burden on ourselves. In particular, when talking our feelings out with friends and family doesn't help, when our lives are becoming increasingly restricted, or when our symptoms last longer than two to three weeks, we've crossed the line from normal postpartum adjustment to postpartum anxiety. No matter what side of the line a new parent finds herself on, it's not her fault. In fact, as you're about to see, whether or not a new mother experiences postpartum anxiety is a complex, some-pieces-still-missing puzzle.

Why Me?

The verdict is in. Like postpartum depression, postpartum anxiety disorders are real, diagnosable mental conditions that impact thousands of new mothers every year. What is not as clear, though, is what causes them.

One theory is that pregnancy stimulates additional activity in certain neurotransmitters, which can trigger panic attacks. Another popular theory is that some women have a built-in sensitivity to hormonal changes that increases their vulnerability to psychological, environmental, and physiological stressors during their reproductive years. Yet others argue that the genetic vulnerability is simply a biological predisposition to anxiety and that the stress of the postpartum period is no different from the stress of any other major life transition; because full-blown anxiety is often predated by a period of life stress, a certain number of biologically prone new mothers will develop anxiety during their postpartum days. This is consistent with the diathesis-stress model we discussed in Chapter 3.

In reality, research has identified a number of risk factors th[...] postpartum anxiety. It's likely that women who develop postpart[...] some degree of biological vulnerability, which is then exacerbated b[...] after-birth stressors. The more risk factors we have, the more likely it is [...] develop postpartum anxiety. Here are the most commonly identified risk fac[...] postpartum anxiety.

Risk Factors for Postpartum Anxiety

Before Pregnancy	During Pregnancy	After Birth
History of an anxiety disorder	Anxiety or depression during pregnancy	Neonatal complications
Hormonal vulnerability (ex. PMS or previous postpartum problem)	Significant loss during pregnancy (death of loved one, job loss)	Childcare stress
Family history of anxiety disorder	Pregnancy complications	Social isolation from family, friends or spouse
Family history of postpartum depression or anxiety	Severe sleep loss during last three months of pregnancy	Difficult infant temperament
Certain personality traits (perfectionism, high need for control)	Difficult or negative labor and delivery experiences	Marital conflict
Fears/concerns about motherhood	Abrupt discontinuation of anxiety medication	Single parent
	Unplanned pregnancy	Severe sleep disruption

For example, my own family has a history of health anxiety and postpartum panic attacks. As the oldest of three children, I did quite a bit of caretaking as a child and had some ambivalence about what the role of motherhood had in store. On the other hand, I did not have a preexisting anxiety disorder and had never had much trouble with PMS.

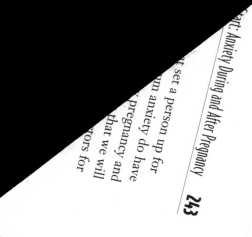

...set a person up for
...m anxiety do have
...pregnancy and
...that we will
...ors for

...regnancy-related scares and a difficult labor
.. Before delivery, I also experienced mild anxiety
... when I was in confined spaces. Post-delivery, I
... e and a healthy baby. On the downside, my oldest
... ky and didn't sleep through the night until he was

... n play a major role in postpartum adjustment.
... reak, or whose family of origin is unsupportive
... rticularly tough time adjusting to the overwhelming
... demands of new motherhood. In fact, combine a lack
of social support with a biological vulnerability and a
postpartum-free adjustment is likely to be the exception rather than the norm.

As you can see from my story, risk factors often have
a cumulative effect; they add additional weight to the
scale until the balance is tipped one way or the other.
There are those risk factors, though, that seem to
weigh more heavily in determining the odds of postpartum emotional problems. And one of the heaviest
is our emotional state during pregnancy.

Anxiety

Thyroid problems and anemia in pregnant and postpartum women can mimic psychological symptoms. Ask your doctor what specific tests have been given to rule out underlying physical causes for your emotional symptoms.

The Pregnancy Protection Myth

The joy of pregnancy. Few phrases get thrown around as much as that one. Granted, there's a lot to be both thankful for, and happy about, during pregnancy. However, over the past few years, there has been increasing recognition that for some women, pregnancy can be plagued by mood problems. The common wisdom that pregnancy hormones inevitably create a sense of elation and calm is slowly going by the wayside. Many of the postpartum emotional complications women suffer, including anxiety, may start during pregnancy.

In fact, in many cases, a woman's emotional state during pregnancy may be the best single predictor of what is to follow. Community studies consistently show that less than half of the 8 to 10 percent of new mothers experiencing either postpartum anxiety or depression were *newly* depressed or anxious; most of them had some symptoms prior to their child's birth. Twenty percent of pregnant women suffer from some type of psychiatric disorder during pregnancy, and study after study shows that health-care providers generally are not clued in.

If pregnancy can precipitate the onset of an anxiety disorder, what effect does it have on those of us who *already* have one? It depends. Women with a history of panic disorder, for example, often report a lessening of symptoms during their pregnancy. This may be due to the hormone progesterone, which increases during pregnancy. When it drops again during the postpartum period, the woman's symptoms may return.

On the other hand, about 25 percent of women with OCD will get worse during pregnancy, with some women even seeking treatment for OCD for the first time. In addition, symptoms may ebb and flow with various pregnancy stages; many women report the greatest number of symptoms during the first and third trimesters sandwiched around a three month period of relative calm.

> **On the Cutting Edge**
>
> There may be a link between calcium and reduction in postpartum emotional symptoms. In one study, women given 2,000 mg of calcium carbonate for prevention of preeclampsia (hypertension) had significantly lower incidences of depressive symptoms 12 weeks after delivery.

> **Myth Buster**
>
> "Mothers with obsessive thoughts involving hurting their babies are likely to act on them." Reality: it is extremely rare for a woman to hurt her infant.

For the anxiety sufferer anticipating pregnancy, this news can be quite disturbing. However, in this case, knowledge is power. An anxiety sufferer doesn't have to choose between motherhood and mental health. By working with her physician and mental-health professional, we can create a pregnancy plan that takes into account our personal vulnerabilities and reduces our risks.

The Panic-Free Pregnancy Plan

At first glance, it might seem depressing to consider taking special "pregnancy precautions" because of our struggle with anxiety. If so, let me propose an alternative viewpoint. Many of the steps in a good pregnancy plan will not only reduce postpartum risk factors, they will help *any* transition to motherhood go more smoothly.

First of all, take charge of your pregnancy. The greater the sense of control you have over your pregnancy-related choices and options, the less often uncertainty and anxiety will plague you. Select a medical team you trust; make sure you can ask questions of your medical practitioner and get them answered satisfactorily. Have a list of questions prepared before each OB visit. Get an early ultrasound and, subsequently, whatever testing will make you feel calmer. Research birth options and agree upon the birth plan long before delivery.

Anxiety Attack

Your pregnancy plan should take into account how much your anxiety is presently under control. If you are currently in treatment, strengthen your therapeutic relationship. If it's been a while since you've had symptoms, perhaps boost your relaxation and stress-management skills.

On the Cutting Edge

Persistent fatigue immediately following birth may be the best signal to determine whether a woman will develop postpartum mood complications, a new study suggests. Women who said they still felt extremely fatigued two weeks after having a baby were more likely to suffer from postpartum depression.

Because stress aggravates anxiety, one goal of a mentally healthy pregnancy should be to make it as stress-free as possible. Too many of us consider pregnancy as a time to complete all our household projects or beat that last sales record. We worry about getting the baby's room finished when all we really need when we leave the hospital are diapers, a few outfits, and a car seat. By the time we head into the delivery room, we're already exhausted.

Instead, consider pregnancy as a time to mentally and physically prepare for motherhood. Mother yourself. Accept help from others. Rest whenever you can. Take into account the physical demands of growing a baby and adjust your expectations of yourself. Rest whenever you can. If you can't sleep for long periods at night, take naps during the day. Even sitting in a chair with your eyes closed can provide some respite from fatigue. Eat healthfully but don't obsess about it. The average woman's diet, although not nutritionally perfect, provides far and away enough nutrients for a healthy baby, especially if you're taking a prenatal vitamin. Eat a variety of foods, but don't be too restrictive or obsessive about what you eat. Similarly, although you should generally stay away from caffeine, don't freak if you have an occasional Coke or latte; alcohol, drugs, and smoking are the real bugaboos.

Actively promote inner resilience and calm. Keep a daily journal to help you keep track of your emotions and feelings. Practice some form of relaxation, meditation, or yoga; not only do they make a measurable difference in anxiety and tension, the breath control they promote can be a powerful aid in the delivery room. In addition, while you're developing your inner calm, don't create external chaos. Avoid major life changes; it's too much to find a new job, move across the country, and find a house within a month before the baby is born.

Finally, rally your troops around you. Develop a peer support system of new and seasoned parents; the former can provide the "we're in this boat together" kind of camaraderie; the latter can help us know what to expect during our first year as a mother.

If you're in therapy, consider upping your sessions, especially during the third trimester. If you're not, getting support from a professional before pregnancy—or prior to birth—is not a bad idea. A trusted mental-health team can help you minimize risk factors by working through any unresolved issues, developing a post-hospital plan that will cut down on sleep deprivation, and developing a plan for how to handle break through symptoms during and after pregnancy.

But what should that plan *be?* Do you go off your psychotropic medication when you first see those two pink lines and white-knuckle-it through an anxiety-riddled nine months, or stay on your meds and hope for the best? Pregnant women whose anxiety worsens during pregnancy often feel caught between a rock and a hard place; on the one hand, terrified their medication could harm the fetus and, on the other, worried they won't survive without it.

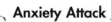 **Anxiety Attack**

Never discontinue medication "cold turkey" without talking with your doctor. Studies show that women who stopped their antidepressant during pregnancy were five times more likely to have a return of symptoms than those who decided to continue them during pregnancy.

Between a Rock and a Hard Place

Doctors used to be very hesitant to prescribe psychiatric medications to pregnant women. In fact, most pregnant women were discouraged from taking any type of medication for fear drugs and pregnancy would not mix well. However, not only can untreated anxiety during pregnancy put the mother in jeopardy, increasing research has shown that the mood of the mother during pregnancy can have long-lasting effects on her child's development. As a result, the decision to take antidepressant medication requires a careful weighing of the costs and benefits to both mother and child.

Let's first look at the potential risks of taking meds. As discussed in the preceding chapter, many of the medications used to treat anxiety fall into the category of selective serotonin reuptake inhibitors (SSRIs)—Paxil, Prozac, Zoloft, Effexor, and so on. Preliminary studies suggest that some of these antidepressants may carry a greater risk during pregnancy than others.

For example, preliminary results from two 2005 studies found that women who took Paxil during the first three months of pregnancy were 1.5 to 2 times more likely to have a baby with a heart defect as women who took other antidepressants or women who took no medication. Another study found that 30 percent of newborns whose mothers took antidepressants during the last trimester showed symptoms of withdrawal (sleep disturbances, high-pitched cry, tremor, gastrointestinal problems) after birth. None required medical treatment, and symptoms subsided within 48 hours.

To an unborn child, the risks of a mother's untreated anxiety during pregnancy can be worse. The idea that a woman's emotional state during pregnancy affects her unborn child has persisted for centuries. Called the *fetal programming hypothesis*, it theorizes that certain disturbing factors occurring during certain sensitive periods of development in utero can "program" a variety of biological systems in the unborn child. This, then, affects the ability of those biological systems to change later in life, predisposing a child to certain diseases and disorders.

In recent years, this theory has been supported by science. Stress or anxiety during pregnancy are risk factors for premature birth and growth restriction within the womb, both of which are risk factors for behavioral problems in the child. In addition, a recent study found that maternal anxiety between 12 and 22 weeks of pregnancy was a better predictor of childhood disorders at age 8 or 9 than smoking during pregnancy, low birth weight, or anxiety of the mother at the time the child developed problems.

> **On the Cutting Edge**
>
> A longitudinal study followed a group of women and children from pregnancy until the children were 7. The children of mothers, who rated in the top 15 percent for anxiety at 32 weeks into pregnancy (but not at 18 weeks), had double the risk for behavioral problems at ages 4 and 7. This was true for both boys and girls.

> **On the Cutting Edge**
>
> Doctors look for three things when testing a psychiatric medication's effects on pregnancy: the occurrence of birth defects, behavioral problems, and unusual symptoms at birth.

Obviously, whether or not to take antidepressant medication during pregnancy is a tough decision. Educating ourselves is an important aspect of feeling comfortable with whatever decision you make. Weighing the possible impact of using medication against the impact of living with anxiety through pregnancy is important to assess.

Many physicians are promoting a happy medium. Because of the risk of symptom rebound, most women who become pregnant while taking antidepressants may do well to either discontinue them gradually or continue taking them. The sweet spot between medication versus none may be to reduce multiple medications down to a single agent and use the lowest effective dose possible.

Unfortunately, just as an optimal diet and exercise routine can't guarantee that we'll never get sick, no amount of prediction or preparation is 100 percent foolproof against postpartum anxiety. Should our anxiety symptoms resurface during or after pregnancy, we will hopefully take the attitude we would if we were to suddenly develop asthma or diabetes. Rather than view our symptoms as evidence that our pregnancy plan failed, we see the work we did as giving us a head start in our recovery; again, much the same as a healthful lifestyle makes recovery from physical illness easier. And rather than search for causes or assign blame, we focus on getting the best treatment professionals have to offer.

On the Road Again to Normal

Not surprisingly, the most effective therapy for postpartum anxiety is often a combination of the tried-and-true cognitive behavioral techniques we've discussed throughout this book in combination with specific strategies to tackle the tough transition from couple to parents.

Cognitive behavioral psychotherapy for postpartum anxiety focuses on identifying and correcting inaccurate thoughts associated with anxious feelings, particularly those that center on her sense of (in)competence as a mother and her concerns over the health and well-being of her infant. In addition, depending upon her diagnosis, treatment strategies might center on halting obsessive behaviors, coping with panic attacks, or gradually approaching avoided situations.

In addition, although postpartum anxiety is not *caused* by relationship problems, it *affects* her relationships. *Interpersonal therapy* is a form of therapy that focuses on interpersonal issues that can either aggravate, or arise from, depression or anxiety. It can work wonders in helping the new mother deal with her changing role and other stressors by learning how to communicate more effectively with others. Relationship issues that often surface during the postpartum period include interpersonal disputes/conflicts over the parenting role as well as grief/anger over the sudden lack of intimacy as emotional energy is consumed by the new baby. Left unaddressed, these issues can complicate a new mother's recovery from postpartum anxiety; successfully resolved, the couple's bond strengthens and serves as a vital source of emotional support.

For the woman who is breastfeeding, concerns about the impact of medication on the baby can resurface. Whereas this decision should always be discussed with your physician, there seems to be little to worry about in terms of harm to your newborn. Only

Anxiety Attack

Check out www. postpartum.net for a wealth of information on postpartum mood disorders and a national list of postpartum support groups.

a minuscule amount of medication crosses into the breast milk during breastfeeding. If untreated anxiety is impacting the parent-child bond, deciding to start or resume medication may be easy.

Where's Dad?

Throughout this book, we've discussed how helpful supportive family and friends can be in encouraging and supporting our progress. This is especially true when anxiety intrudes during the postpartum period. Husbands are often the first to recognize that a spouse is exhibiting signs of postpartum anxiety and can be a lifeline to treatment and support. A husband's leadership in providing reassurance and emotional support, not to mention picking up the slack, can make the difference between a wife's quick recovery and months filled with unnecessary shame, self-blame, and turmoil.

Of course, the postpartum period can be tough on dads, too. More than half of new fathers feel depressed sometime during the first four months following the birth of their baby. Many factors can contribute to these feelings; worries over new responsibilities and potential loss of freedom, financial concerns, and uncertainties of being a good dad. Active involvement in a spouse's postpartum anxiety treatment can not only assure new fathers that their wives are being cared for, it can also provide a safe forum to sort through their own feelings and concerns.

Anxiety Attack

New fathers can find information and support about postpartum emotional complications (and lots of other stuff) at www.brandnewdad.com/askarmin/postpartumblues.asp.

As we've seen, postpartum anxiety can add a painful dimension to an already stressful time. Identifying and minimizing risk factors during pregnancy can reduce the odds of postpartum emotional problems, but it doesn't completely remove them. As such, for women with a history of anxiety, the best defense may be a good offense; making sure pregnancy is as anxiety-free as possible and lining up a team of professionals ready to pounce on postpartum symptoms.

On the bright side, postpartum anxiety is as treatable as anxiety during any other period of a woman's life. Early symptom recognition and good professional help can minimize the impact of postpartum anxiety on the mother, the child and the couple. In fact, some couples say that dealing with postpartum anxiety forced them to deal sooner, and more effectively, with interpersonal issues that surface among all new parents.

This chapter has been about the relationship between anxiety and pregnancy and how new mothers can get off to the right start with their babies whether or not they experience anxiety symptoms during or after pregnancy. In the next chapter, we take a look at what we can do to continue this "right start" throughout the parenting years—how we can raise resilient children and prevent anxiety from being passed from our generation onto the next.

The Least You Need to Know

◆ Feelings of anxiety and worry are common among expectant mothers, but symptoms such as panic attacks, obsessive thoughts, and an inability to complete daily tasks are symptoms of an anxiety disorder.

◆ Postpartum anxiety is often missed by both physicians and patients. Physicians either dismiss the anxiety as part of normal new mother worries or think postpartum mood problems are limited to depression.

◆ All of the clinical anxiety disorders can show up during pregnancy or after birth. The distressing symptoms are often magnified by dramatic hormonal shifts and the stress of changing roles.

◆ Understanding and minimizing risk factors during pregnancy can cut down on the likelihood of postpartum anxiety. In particular, managing anxiety symptoms during pregnancy can benefit both mother and fetus.

◆ The pros and cons of antidepressant medication during pregnancy must be carefully weighed; there are infant risks associated with untreated anxiety as well as certain antidepressant medications.

Chapter 20

Raising Hardy Personalities

In This Chapter

- ◆ Discover why anxious parents often have normal children
- ◆ Learn how broad "normal" really is
- ◆ Avoid the common pitfalls of anxious parents
- ◆ Give your child the gift of resilience

"Too many parents make life hard for their children by trying, too zealously, to make it easy for them."—Benjamin Franklin

"It is not what you do for your children, but what you have taught them to do for themselves, that will make them successful human beings."—Ann Landers

1. Normal children have problems.

2. *"Parents can help them."*—Dr. Stanley Turecki

3. *"… Even when we struggle with anxiety."*—Dr. Joni Johnston

In Chapter 10, we talked about how babies come into the world with built-in temperaments that influence how easily and how intensely they respond to the world around them. We also looked at parenting styles and how certain biological predispositions may either thrive or dwindle in response to how primary caretakers respond to them. The baby who is unusually distressed by changes in her environment, or the toddler who is stressed by situations most others would find unthreatening, isn't destined to become a fearful child or anxious teenager. And anxious parents don't have to raise anxious children.

Not only can parents help our children work with their natural temperament, we can be the superheroes of our children's psyches. We can help our children manage stress and deal with normal childhood fears. Through modeling and hands-on parenting, we can also help our children develop resilience, the strengths that allow us to prevent, minimize, or overcome the effects of adversity; the ability to connect with others, an emotional vocabulary that promotes self-awareness and empathy, and the ability to control one's behavior.

Lights! Camera! Meltdown!

From birth, Baby Jane seemed to be extremely sensitive; she cried incessantly whenever her mother took her to a certain department store with florescent lights and the slightest noise woke her from her nap. As a toddler, she insisted the tags be cut out of all her clothes. She had a harder-than-usual time adjusting to preschool and went berserk when her mom accidentally brought home a different cereal. Her mom quickly learned to avoid too many activities at once, because Jane became overly stimulated and was more prone to temper tantrums.

Highly sensitive children can be a challenge for parents. Their senses are often stronger, sharper, and more overwhelming. A loud machine or your voice can be irritating. When they cry, they fall to the floor sobbing. When they're angry, they may shriek and pound the walls.

Of course, it's often a case of the apple not falling far from the tree. Highly sensitive parents often give birth to highly sensitive children. This can make parenting quite an adventure; a child's shriek or the sensory assault of toys, shoes, and clothes all over the floor can make our own intensity rise very suddenly. We tell ourselves we should be able to comfort our child and keep our cool no matter how bombarded or irritated we feel by the noises around us. As a result, we can be tempted to ignore or deny our feelings until they overwhelm us.

And if our child is also sensitive, we may feel as though our worst nightmare is occurring. All of our lives we've been told that we're "too picky" or "too sensitive." Now our child is facing the same fate. With the best of intentions, we can parent for the wrong results, either by trying to protect her from anxiety-producing situations or by trying to "make" her be less sensitive.

How parents handle their child's sensitivity has a lot of influence over how likely the child is to develop an anxiety disorder. One reason is that such children are not only sensitive to physical stimuli, they're also sensitive to emotions. So if *you* feel anxious about their sensitivity, they begin to believe something is terribly wrong with them.

In fact, one of the best gifts a parent can give a sensitive child is a model for how their natural temperament can work in her favor. This means regulating our own sensitivity, letting it serve us in terms of being emotionally "in tune" with our child, but also knowing how to deal with our Achilles heels. Just as too much activity can send a sensitive child into a tailspin, high stimulation levels can make it very difficult for a sensitive or anxious parent to focus on a child. Know when to take a break; leave that family gathering, shopping center, or amusement park *before* you're at your limit.

If *you* have a hard time adjusting to changes or unexpected events, make your family life as organized and predictable as possible. Allow extra time to get somewhere so you don't feel rushed. Teach your children to avoid surprising you by talking about the day ahead. The more surprises you can avoid, the more energy you'll have to be there for your child. When you do get surprised—by that school nurse's call or empty gas tank—remember to pause and take a deep breath. Changes in plans can be especially tough on someone who's prone to anxiety; an empathetic reminder that transitions are hard coupled with a reminder that we can choose how to respond can help us shift gears more smoothly.

Remember Baby Jane at the beginning of this section? As Jane grew older, her mother taught her to pay attention to stress signals. She helped her see the link between her thoughts and feelings and encouraged Jane to pace herself so as not to get overwhelmed. As a teenager, Jane has age-appropriate freedom, but an unusual degree of self-awareness. However, in response to her offspring's sensitive nature, Jane's mom could have easily taken on a different role—that of the protector.

> ### On the Cutting Edge
>
> Unmanaged stress doesn't just make our lives harder; it impacts how we parent. Recent research found, when evaluating the same behaviors in their infants, highly stressed mothers viewed the babies as significantly more difficult than those whose stress was under control.

Beware the Smother Mother (Overprotectiveness)

Anxious adults often received negative consequences for being sensitive children. Some of us may have been pushed too hard or asked to handle situations that were not age appropriate, without the support or warmth we needed. Or perhaps our emotional sensitivity led a troubled parent to use us as a "therapist," sharing problems with us that were too big for us to handle. Children with this experience often engage in "reverse parenting," feeling responsible for their parents' feelings and working hard to emotionally take care of them.

Couple these memories with a parent's natural distress at seeing his child suffer, and we can easily see how we might overparent. "My child will never go through that. I'm going to be there for her no matter what." And we go about smoothing life's rough waters and letting them avoid the normal trials and tribulations of childhood.

But beware: *this doesn't do our child any favors, either.* Although we should respond to our child's nature with understanding, we should not let it become an excuse for them to avoid challenges or new situations. Being overly solicitous can unintentionally reinforce a child's belief that he *should* be afraid, that he really *can't* handle it. What you really want him to know is that his feelings are normal, that they will pass, *and* that they don't have to control him—or you.

This brings me to another potential consequence of overly focusing on our child's sensitivity or shyness—the payoff. A child who clings to his father is genuinely afraid of separation. However, if he learns that his dad is so concerned about his fear that he will do whatever he wants for reassurance, why would a child give up this special power and attention? It's normal for children to stick with what works for them even if it also creates an underlying sense of shame (my parents think there's something wrong with me) or self-doubt (there is).

Stress Relief _____

Build your child's competence by involving him in activities that contribute to a greater good, such as volunteer work or helping a kid in another class.

Of course, as our child gets older, the plusses of having our parent's attention are often supplanted by our desire for independence and control. Parents who continue to hover may find their child becoming secretive and aloof. This distance can make us worry even more, which can result in a vicious cycle of over-involvement resulting in rebellion, which, of course, confirms our need to control and protect.

So what's *good enough* parenting for a naturally sensitive child? I like the phrase, "Special care, not special worry." We accept his or her nature. We respond with empathy when she has a tough time. Whenever possible, we divide transitions into smaller steps; perhaps we stay a few minutes longer at a birthday party or walk with her to initiate play with a particular group. We help her prepare for new situations or events, investigating with her what to expect and exploring ways to make it go smoothly.

At the same time, we are cheerful, confident, and unafraid in how we take these extra steps. We're always on the lookout for signs that our child is ready to take a step toward self-reliance. This attitude—*"You can adjust to any situation and tolerate some discomfort without collapsing"*—is the most powerful factor in helping your child find her wings.

I'm Perfect and So Are You!

In Chapter 10, we talked about the link between anxiety and perfectionism. We saw how painful it can be to live under the constant pressure to be mistake free and ever more successful. It makes sense that we anxiety sufferers might take the same achievement orientation to the parenting role. If we're not careful, we can expect too much from our kids and ourselves.

For example, some of us may think that being a "good parent" means never getting angry with our child. If we have that belief, then we may respond with guilt whenever we feel angry, even when it's justified. We may then try to compensate for these very natural feelings, going overboard by giving in to our child or allowing her to talk to us in a way that is disrespectful or inappropriate.

In reality, children benefit so much from a parent who can accept, and appropriately respond to, all feelings. That doesn't mean you want to scream and rage when you are angry. It means you acknowledge when your actions and decisions were influenced by anger and correct anything that needs to be corrected. It also means helping your child accept his/her own angry feelings. "You still have to follow the rules, but it's okay to be mad at me. I know you still love me, just like I still love you, even when I'm mad."

Without meaning to, we can also direct unrealistically high expectations onto our children. We can want so much for our children that we push too much, overscheduling chores, school work, and extracurricular activities. Or our worries about our child can lead us to overfocus on the imperfect; when our fifth grader comes home with a few Bs, we start ruminating about how competitive it is to get into college and immediately phone the teacher for a "what's wrong" conference.

Anxiety Attack

Play the one-minute rule to teach give-and-take. Before taking action, saying something, or joining in a conversation or activity, the child must *stop* (for one minute), during which he is to *look* (at what others are doing), *listen* (to what others are talking about), and then *decide* to join, take action, or say or do nothing.

Concern and advice can feel like criticism or second-guessing. We may sit down with a child, for example, with the sincere desire to hear about her day. Before we know it, we find ourselves criticizing how she's handling a teacher or a friend, then arguing, and we don't know how we got there. If we do this often enough, she may start doubting herself and her ability to make good decisions—or avoiding these friendly chats.

No matter how much our children defend themselves, they take our criticisms to heart. Of course, a child's thinking isn't always clear, and there are times when we need to offer some advice, but it's possible to offer the benefit of your experience and maturity without undermining your child. For example, you can say, "I'm sure I would think/feel the same way if I were you. But have you thought about it this way?" Because it's true: if you were your child, you *would* think, feel, and even act the same way. When you say so, you convey understanding and respect, even as you offer another alternative.

The bottom line is that we don't need to protect our children by being perfect parents or creating a perfect world for them. Parents who allow their kids to find a way to deal with life's day-to-day stresses by themselves are helping them to develop resilience and effective coping strategies. As children grow, we need to slide from the control seat over to the consultant's chair. One way to maintain peace of mind as we make this transition is to know that our children have developed the ability to bounce back from tough times. Let's look at the secrets resilient children share—and every parent should know.

The Ability to Bounce Back

Resilience can be defined as those skills, attributes, and abilities that enable us to adapt to hardships, challenges, and difficulties. And guess what? Kids have them! In fact, psychologists (whom, I believe, tend to be pessimistic by nature) were astonished when they followed children who had been reared in homes rife with mental illness, alcoholism, abuse—even war-torn communities. A full half to two thirds of these children overcame all odds and lived successful, well-adjusted lives. We've all known someone who functioned much better than their "dysfunctional childhood" predicted; in fact, they even seemed somehow better or stronger because of it.

That's the kind of good news that should cause any anxious parent to sigh with relief. And the news gets even better; many aspects of resilience can be taught. The process of getting my anxiety disorder under control has certainly taught me resilience, and, I believe, made me a better parent to boot. For instance, I often try to help my children connect their thoughts to their feelings so they can learn to master their self-talk. I would like to think that I am more empathetic but less likely to rescue them from the natural consequences of their actions. And I have used some of my breathing and relaxation strategies to help a child get a "shot" at the doctor's office or prepare for a class presentation.

Just as uncontrolled anxiety can interfere with parenting, parents who take charge of their emotional distress can have a wider range of strategies and coping mechanisms to teach their child. And when we make resiliency a primary parenting goal, we're all winners: we can breathe more easily knowing our child has the strengths s/he needs, and our child can thrive no matter what life throws at him or her.

Myth Buster

"A positive attitude in the face of adversity is a state of denial." No, it isn't. Resilient people see challenge as a normal part of life and view themselves as survivors.

In looking at resilience in children, the International Resilience Project has identified three potential sources of resilience—strong and supportive external resources; a clearly defined, positive self-concept; and effective strategies for interacting with the world around him or her. These are often referred to as the "I have's," the "I am's," and the "I can's." Younger children, of course, tend to be more dependent on the "I Have's": *I have a person who loves me unconditionally, who encourages me to do things on my own, who helps me when I need it, who is predictable and sets limits, who shows me the right way to do things and behave.*

From a resilience standpoint, it matters less who that person is as much as the fact that the person is accessible to them. Parents who are struggling with an anxiety disorder often feel tremendous guilt or worry when their symptoms or avoidance interferes with their involvement in a child's life—even when it involves taking time away to get psychotherapy or other treatment. It can be reassuring to know that encouraging help and support from extended family members, healthy interests outside the home, and taking time to get professional help as needed are acts of love and can buffer a child from the potential negatives of a parent's mental illness.

The same is true for the "I am's." Resilient children are taught that they are lovable, important, responsible, and competent. They also know what they are not responsible for. Understandably, parents are often reluctant to discuss emotional issues with their children, and there are plenty of times when they shouldn't.

However, when a parent's symptoms are obvious to a child, or when they lead a parent to avoid important events in the child's life, it is better for them to have age-appropriate information than to be left to draw their own conclusions, which inevitably translate into either "I'm to blame" or "Mom doesn't care about me." On the other hand, a parent who helps her child understand that she has a problem, that she is working hard to get better, and that it's not the child's fault frees up a worried to child to focus on typical kid problems—like what to wear to school the next day.

> **On the Cutting Edge**
>
> Stress symptoms are different in children than in adults. Children commonly experience stress through headaches and stomach pains. They can also begin wetting the bed or pick up new (or regress to old) habits such as sucking their thumb.

As children get older, they rely more and more on their internal resources. We've already talked about the "I am"; the "I can" involves the child's ability to respond effectively to the world around him or her. It's here that parents can really shine, by encouraging their child's emotional awareness, by building his or her social skills and by teaching the art of self-control.

You Gotta Have Friends

Protective factors such as a good support system and a lovable, capable self-concept help a child be adaptable, better able to hit the curve balls life throws at them. They buffer children from the emotional impact of unpredictable, distressing, or new situations. In particular, the ability to connect with others—to build and maintain friendships—is perhaps the most powerful protector of all.

From the very beginning, friendships are the workshops where children design future relationships and practice negotiation with other children. Your child doesn't have to be the most popular to benefit from the stress buffer that friendship provides. It doesn't matter whether a child has a long-term best friend or short-term regular friends. All that's needed is the ability to initiate and maintain satisfying relationships. And as parents, we can help our child build social and emotional intelligence by …

- ◆ **Nurturing their emotional awareness.** From birth we can help our child develop an emotional vocabulary and gradually help him or her start connecting the dots between thoughts, feelings, and behavior. *"I can see that you're mad because I wouldn't buy that toy. It's scary to go to bed without your special blanket. It's* *frustrating when your brother keeps beating you at soccer."* Not only can we teach our child to label feelings, we can give our child permission to appropriately express both negative and positive feelings.

◆ **Promote the development of empathy and the ability to take different perspectives.** Point out how your child's actions affect other people's feelings. If she grabs a toy and another child starts crying, ask her, "Why is your friend crying? Let's see whether it helps to give her toy back."

◆ **Teach your child how to join in.** Show children there are many ways to make friends. A child can ask outright if he can play, he can offer to help with an ongoing activity, or he can invite others to join him in a new activity. This gives him a chance to practice different strategies and learn not to take it personally if one strategy doesn't work.

◆ **Teach your child to resolve peer conflicts.** Rather than swoop in to "solve" a problem, or leave young children floundering to "work it out themselves," act as a neutral facilitator. Let each child take a turn to tell her story. Ask questions that encourage them to brainstorm solutions such as "What do you think would solve the problem?"

> ### On the Cutting Edge
>
> Encourage your child's sense of humor. The kinds of jokes kids enjoy tell us a lot about their worries. For instance, potty-trained children who still have nighttime accidents usually love bathroom humor.

Anger: Help Your Child Get a Grip!

Children who develop the capacity to identify, label, and verbalize their feelings have a leg up. Not only do they communicate better, but they also have the ability to recognize and identify the intensity of their feelings, which actually helps them to regulate them. However, just like adults, anger is an emotion that can give a kid a lot of problems.

Fortunately, we anxiety survivors have an arsenal of weapons to help our children deal with intense feelings. For example, in Chapter 16, we learned to rate the intensity of a panic attack from 1 to 10. This thinking activity actually helps distract us from out-of-control feelings. This strategy can also help an emotionally intense child. Just as we learn to "observe" terrifying panic symptoms, we can teach our child to observe his or her anger and evaluate how intense the feelings are. If a child can learn to describe anger in words that capture the various rates of intensity—irritated, annoyed, furious, enraged—then she is developing a budding ability to step back and get some control over it.

Similarly, thought-stopping strategies that are useful in dealing with obsessive thoughts can also be adapted to help our child gain more self-control. It can help our child to imagine a stop sign that s/he obeys and think about a situation before responding. And just as anxiety sufferers learn to pay attention to stress signals, we can help our child identify his or her early warning signs of anger (rising voice, clenched fist, gritted teeth), so s/he has a chance to *choose* a response.

Anxiety Attack

If your child goes from calm to furious in the blink of an eye, make him an "Anger Thermometer" and assign different levels of anger to the various colors or numbers. This can help him regularly identify what thoughts, feelings and sensations signal low-level anger and what it feels like as your anger intensifies.

Finally, just as relaxation is a key strategy in anxiety management, many children find that self-calming activities are a first step in getting their anger under control. Teach your child to take a "time out" to allow the physical symptoms to subside: he can walk away, count to 10, take deep breaths, or use coping statements like, "I can handle this." When s/he has calmed down, your child can decide how to handle his or her frustration—to talk it out, to get help, or slow down and persevere.

Try Some Stress-Wrestling!

Helping our children become more emotionally sophisticated and interpersonally savvy is one way we boost our child's resilience; these are skills that come in handy during good times and bad. Another is to strengthen our child's ability to handle stress. Stress is a natural part of our child's life; we can't prevent it, but we can teach them how to cope with it.

Our child's biggest teacher will, of course, be our own behavior. Parents who fly off the handle, or become paralyzed with fear, produce children who feel insecure and lacking in confidence. On the other hand, children can handle even the most stressful situation if they understand the situation. A child who doesn't understand a situation often imagines the worst.

From birth, we parents can talk to our children about the thoughts we have about our feelings—and vice versa. As our child gets older, we can teach her to observe the connection between how s/he thinks and how s/he feels. *"When you dropped that fly ball, what did you say to yourself? What are other possible explanations? What is the evidence that these statements or true?"*

This is a novel concept for most children (and, as we saw in Chapters 8 and 9, adults, too, for that matter). However, when a child begins to be more self-aware, s/he'll notice the self-talk. Even better, s/he'll begin to see that it's not the circumstances that determine how we feel; it's what we say to ourselves about those circumstances. And that's something s/he can control.

Finally, the ability to take a mental break— by relaxing, diverting, or distracting oneself from everyday worries and concerns—can prevent a child from becoming over- whelmed by a stressful event. As any teen- ager will tell you, a set of headphones and a favorite CD can work wonders in provid- ing a mental break from the seriousness of growing up. Similarly, minimizing or deny- ing the personal impact of teasing or rejection ("I don't care; I'm still a good kid") can be useful in helping a child "diffuse" his or her feelings and create a safe place in which to plan an appropriate response.

Stress Relief _____

Help your child learn to rec- ognize and identify habits of thought with these online games. Visit www. selfesteemgames.mcgill.ca/ games/index.htm.

Distraction or denial can be great in reducing emotional discomfort when faced with uncontrollable events (much as TV watching can make the flu a little more tolerable); if we don't follow up on solvable problems that have a solution, however, we'll just feel a little better but wind up in the same place.

In this chapter, we've talked about the role par- ents can play in rearing resilient children. We've looked at the difference between a sensitive child and an anxious one and how the ways we parent can either foster self-reliance or create doubt and worry. We've also seen how we can actively encourage the skills and coping strate- gies that provide protection from the inevitable stresses and challenges our children will face.

On the Cutting Edge

New research suggests that letting a child play a video game in the operating room before anesthe- sia is administered can promote relaxation better than tranquilizers or holding Mom's hand. That's the power of distraction!

Yes, we can and should prepare our kids, by starting where they are and working forward. Sensitive kids *do* deserve special care. They don't however, warrant special worry. If we're truly going to teach our children resilience, we have to deal with our own separation anxiety. We can do this through our anxiety support groups, chats with other parents, or work with a therapist. Ultimately, we have to deal with it by doing it, so that both we and our children can see how capable they really are.

Myth Buster

"Childhood mental-health problems are really the result of poor parenting and lack of discipline in the home." Although certain parenting styles can increase vulnerability, mental illnesses often have a strong genetic component.

We also have to be realistic in terms of what we can do and what we can't. Normal children have fears and problems. The best-parented child can develop an anxiety disorder. Although we can help them, we can't always give them the care they need. In the next chapter, we'll take a look at what we can do to soothe normal childhood fears, and when—and how—to bring in the experts.

You may also decide your child needs more help than you can give. So far, we've discussed how to help normal children develop resilience. But sometimes, even with the most consistent parenting, a child's anxiety is out of the normal range. In the next chapter, we talk about how you can help that child, too.

The Least You Need to Know

◆ Anxious parents can raise normal children.

◆ Parents have a big influence over when a biologically sensitive child develops full-blown fears and worries.

◆ Overprotectiveness can be harmful to a child's mental health.

◆ Although children are naturally resilient, parents can encourage the skills and strengths that help children bounce back from adversity.

◆ Emotional awareness, good social skills, and effective stress-management strategies help a child grow up to be happy and confident.

21

Calm Down! Helping Anxious Kids Recover

In This Chapter

- ◆ Learn what childhood fears are normal
- ◆ Discover how you can help your kids overcome typical fears and worries
- ◆ Find out how much childhood anxiety is too much
- ◆ Check and see how much anxiety is impacting your child's daily life
- ◆ Identify how and when to get professional help for your child

Are youngsters more anxious these days? Well, consider some of the stressors many parents face—divorce, less access to extended family and friends, a lack of social connectedness. On top of this is our increased exposure to environmental threats such as violent crime, terrorism, child abduction, or catastrophic diseases. This increased awareness fosters both a lack of trust and an increased sense that we must always be vigilant and on-guard. The same issues that cause adults to feel anxious can unsettle youngsters, too.

If most kids are more anxious these days, then how much anxiety is *too* much? When is a fear "normal," and when is it a cry for help? In this chapter, we take a look at what amount of anxiety is typical of childhood and what is not. We also talk about how we can help our children with normal fears and what we can do when the problem is too big for us. No matter how large or small our child's problem is, though, keep this in mind: help is available.

We're All Scaredy-Cats!

Jessica, 7, has obsessive thoughts that something bad will happen to her family. She checks and rechecks the locks on the doors and windows. Inevitably, when she's finished, she worries that perhaps she accidentally left a window unlatched or a door slightly ajar. On numerous occasions, one of her parents has discovered her checking the doors in the middle of the night. And every morning there's a battle to get her out the door to school; not only does she want to check the door "just one more time," she refuses to leave unless the dolls on her shelf are perfectly arranged in a certain order.

Ryan, 13, is so nervous around other kids that he won't participate in any school activities. He has only one friend, a child he's known since preschool. He sits in the back of the room and refuses to speak aloud in class even though his grades suffer because of it. On days when the teacher goes around the room and makes students take turns answering questions, he breaks out into a sweat and can't concentrate.

Samantha, 9, is teasingly called "worrywart" by her friends and family. However, lately, her symptoms have been no laughing matter. Her mother is concerned and frustrated by Samantha's constant worrying and need for reassurance. When her dad is a few minutes late from work, Samantha is frantic and upset; she refuses to attend sleepovers or spend the night with her grandparents. She frets about every school assignment and often complains of headaches and stomachaches.

Jessica, Ryan, and Samantha are all struggling with an anxiety disorder. Even though their diagnoses are different and their symptoms vary, they have one thing in common: life is hard. For these youngsters, growing up with an anxiety disorder certainly lays to rest the myth of the happy, carefree childhood. Apparently, more and more children are stressed out while growing up; two meta studies reported in the *Journal of Personality and Social Psychology* compared thousands of children and college students from the 1950s through the 1990s and discovered that "normal" schoolchildren in the 1980s were more anxious than child psychiatric patients in the 1950s.

Let's get a few things straight. Normal kids have problems. Childhood fears are the rule rather than the exception. Most children have several fears at any given age; some studies, in fact, show that 90 percent of children between the ages of 2 and 14 are afraid of at least one thing—thunder, the dark, being sucked down the bathtub drain—you name it. It's a drag and it feels bad, but it's a normal part of growing up. In fact, some psychologists believe that these fears serve as mini-training opportunities; as children face and overcome their fears, they are developing the mental muscles they will need to tackle real-world obstacles and situations.

Children's fears often grow out of experiences that they either can't understand or perceive as threatening. Because so much of the world is new, fears can serve a protective purpose; they encourage a child to be cautious until s/he either understands a situation better or is able to cope with it more effectively. For example, a one year old may not understand why a vacuum cleaner makes such a loud noise and, as a result, is frightened by it. The most common "triggers" for normal childhood fears include the following:

Myth Buster

"Shy kids become shy adults." Reality: only 25 percent of children classified as inhibited at 2 years of age were still rated such at age 7. And 99 percent of the "shy" children were inhibited in some situations, but not in all of them.

Anxiety Attack

A hidden source of anxiety can be sleep problems. Abnormal sleep patterns (not getting enough sleep, falling asleep at school or during other activities) may result in excessive fears, anxiety, preoccupation, and daytime sleepiness.

◆ **Witnessing other people's reactions:** If you're afraid of spiders, it's likely your child will pick up on your anxiety and exhibit the same response.

◆ **A frightening event:** A 4-year-old who gets briefly separated from his dad at the park may suddenly develop separation fears. Even witnessing someone get bitten by an aggressive dog, or observing a serious car accident, can result in lasting memories that cause him to feel anxious.

On the Cutting Edge

Twenty-five percent of children involved in motor vehicle accidents may show signs of acute stress disorder, even if they weren't seriously injured; symptoms include intrusive thoughts or images and sleep difficulties.

◆ **Family disruption:** All families have disagreements from time to time, but if there is a constant air of hostility in your home, your child can absorb that tension which will translate into feelings of fear and anxiety. The loss of a parent or parents' divorce can precipitate the development of fears of separation or other unpredictable events.

Stage Fright

As we've seen, childhood fears are common and often serve a useful purpose; they encourage a child to be cautious and provide a manageable opportunity to tackle difficult emotions. Because fear is a response to real or perceived danger, it makes sense that what is perceived as dangerous will depend upon the child's developmental level and natural temperament. How children think affects what they fear; preschoolers, for instance, are often afraid of monsters under the bed, whereas an older child is likely to be afraid of real "bad guys" such as robbers or kidnappers.

The Sponge Bob character at my daughter's fifth birthday party delighted the 5 year olds—and terrified a few of the 3-year-old siblings. Here's a look at some of the common fears kids have at different stages in their childhood—and how they typically express them.

Infants

Fears: falling, being dropped, and loud noises. From 7 to 9 months until about 18 months, they're also often afraid of strangers.

Clues: crying, stiffening, and sometimes shaking.

Toddlers

Fears: strangers, separation from parents, animals, bugs, storms, sirens, large objects, dark colors, darkness, people with masks (including clowns), Santa Claus, monsters, and "bad" people such as burglars. Youngsters at this stage are often afraid of being separated from their parents.

Clues: crying, trying to avoid the person or thing they're afraid of (which can often look like a temper tantrum but which immediately ceases when the child gets away from the fear).

Preschoolers

Fears: separation from parents, being left alone or sleeping alone, and imaginary figures, such as ghosts, monsters, and supernatural beings.

Clues: crying, physical symptoms such as stomach aches or headaches.

School-Age Children

Fears: being home alone (younger school-age children may still fear separation from parents), school achievement, peer acceptance, violence, kidnapping, illness or physical injury, disasters such as floods, earthquakes, and tornados.

Clues: sleep disturbances, stomach aches or headaches, excuses about not wanting to go somewhere or do something, "jumpy," and tearful.

Adolescents

Fears: social rejection, achievement in school, whether or not they're popular, and sexual anxieties, including dating and sexually transmitted diseases.

Clues: withdrawal from parents, irritability, forgetfulness/easily distracted, over-reaction to minor changes in family routine.

Just as we do, children of all ages worry more when things change, such as moving to a new house or new school, divorce, and so on. And, as we've seen, some children are naturally more fearful than others. However, if our child's fear isn't keeping him or her from eating and sleeping, going to school, or playing with his friends, parents and children can often deal with the fears on their own.

Anxiety Attack

Children often love to hear stories about kids who have experienced similar fears. Check out www.ces. purdue.edu/providerparent/ Child%20Growth-Development/ Books_onfears_Children.htm for a list of children's books about coping with fear.

Overcoming the Fear Factor

Perhaps the biggest challenge for parents in dealing with childhood fears is in understanding how differently the world can look from our child's viewpoint. It can be frustrating to have the same child who is enthralled with fire or who is fearless in the face of oncoming traffic—realistic things we teach them to fear—become petrified by her older sister's Halloween costume or insist upon a nightly search for monsters in the closet. How tempting it can be to dismiss these fears as foolish or unimportant, or to logically explain to a 4 year old that ghosts aren't real.

We can also forget that we, too, had fears that came and went and, as a result, assign our child's age-appropriate concern with too much importance. Overreacting is a good way to teach our child that when he acts afraid, he'll be sure to get our attention. If we become anxious or worried in response to a child's fear (is something wrong with him or something wrong with me as a parent), this may up his anxiety level. Parents can unwittingly play a key role in reinforcing and encouraging normal childhood fears so that they continue long after their usefulness has diminished. Additionally, a child who is predisposed toward anxiety may tend to develop more long-lasting fears.

As with many aspects of parenting, the trick in helping our child work through his or her fear is to find the middle ground between "I'll protect you from it" and "get over it." For example, helping our children learn about what scares them (why fire trucks have sirens, why there is thunder and lightning) is a better strategy than arguing about whether the fear is legitimate or the situation objectively dangerous. Similarly, work *with* your child's beliefs; the same child who will not be convinced that ghosts or monsters aren't real might easily believe that "monster spray" will keep them away or that some ghosts are friendly.

Talk about your own childhood fears, especially what it felt like to be afraid and how you learned to cope with them. Remember how much children thrive on rituals and routine and create a sense of structure and predictability in your home. Children are also less scared when they feel they have some control over a situation, so the Boy Scout's motto, "Be prepared," is a good one for parents of a fearful child. Activities like field trips or fire drills can be stressful; ask your child what s/he expects and tell them what will happen. Take a child who's going into the hospital for a tour ahead of time; slowly introduce your dog-terrified child to some stuffed animals or a litter of puppies. Prepare your child for the next thunderstorm with a good luck charm or a calming activity such as whistling, humming, or taking deep breaths.

Don't forget to use your child's wisdom. Ask your child what would help him or her feel less afraid and encourage them to come up with ways to manage their feelings. Express pride when you notice their moments of personal courage, such as climbing the jungle gym or reaching out to a new classmate. As children grow older, you can use their intellectual maturity as well; for example, an older child can understand the difference between "probability" and "possibility," which can help them more realistically evaluate situations that provoke their anxiety.

Here are some additional strategies that can come in handy:

- Teach your child how to rate fear (just as you did with anger in the last chapter). If your child can visualize the intensity of the fear on a scale of 1 to 10, with 10 being the strongest, he or she may be able to "see" the fear as less intense than first imagined. Younger children can think about how "full of fear" they are, with being full "up to my knees" as not so scared, "up to my stomach" as more frightened, and "up to my head" as truly petrified.

> ### On the Cutting Edge
>
> Here's another reason for us parents to conquer our own anxiety. Research on children undergoing surgery found that the presence of a calm parent during the administration of anesthesia helped an anxious child; if the parent was anxious, however, calm children became more anxious and an anxious child derived no benefit at all from the parent's presence.

- Don't cater to fears. Avoiding vaccinations because a child is afraid of shots, or crossing the street to avoid a dog, reinforces that these are things to be feared and avoided. Instead, provide support and gentle care as you approach the feared object or situation.

- Find practical solutions. A nightlight in the hallway, for example, can ease a fear of the dark.

- Practice skills with your child. If your youngster is afraid of giving a speech in front of the class, encourage her to practice with you. If he's worried about his sports performance, spend time playing catch with him at home in a familiar, safe environment.

- Be reassuring and remind your child of other things or times in the past that he was afraid of but no longer fears.

- Dole out the praise for small steps in the right direction.

◆ Give your child coping strategies, such as using you as "home base" to which he can return for safety. Positive affirmations, such as "I can do this," and "I will be okay," can help your child feel less anxious in fearful situations. So can relaxation techniques such as deep breathing (imagining that the lungs are balloons that are inflating with each deep breath) and visualization (imagining himself floating on a cloud or lying on a beach).

◆ Encourage your child to exercise. This not only helps relieve stress by distracting him from what he's anxious about, but also physiologically triggers a "relaxation response." Children who are anxious often feel tired (stress can be fatiguing, and it can also cause rapid, shallow breathing which can result in feeling tired because of lack of oxygen), and so they don't feel like exercising. Exercise will improve their energy and ease their worries. If you can, join in with your kids so it will be a fun, family affair, not one more chore they "have" to do.

When Life Is Not a Breeze: Childhood Anxiety Disorders

Although all children are afraid some of the time, no child should be afraid all of the time. Some children *don't* outgrow their fears; instead, they get worse and begin to interfere with their daily lives. Although we don't know how many children develop clinical levels of anxiety, we do know two alarming facts. They are often overlooked or misjudged, and many adult diagnoses likely have their first manifestations in childhood.

Given that the lifetime prevalence for anxiety disorders in adults is about 25 percent, we can make an educated guess that there are a lot of children with a treatable mental condition who are suffering needlessly.

For example, separation anxiety disorder, an intense worry and fear about being apart from family members or individuals to whom the individual is most attached, affects approximately 4 percent to 5 percent of U.S. children between ages 7 and 11. Social anxiety disorder typically surfaces during adolescence, although it can be preceded by a period of shyness in childhood. In addition to separation anxiety disorder and social phobia, children can—and do—develop generalized anxiety disorder, panic disorder, obsessive-compulsive disorder (OCD), post-traumatic stress disorder, and specific phobias.

Symptoms of Separation Anxiety

- Constant thoughts and intense fears about the safety of parents and caretakers
- Refusing to go to school
- Frequent stomachaches and other physical complaints
- Extreme worries about sleeping away from home
- Being overly clingy
- Panic or tantrums at times of separation from parents
- Trouble sleeping or nightmares

Symptoms of Phobia

- Extreme fear about a specific thing or situation (for example, dogs, insects, or needles)
- The fears cause significant distress and interfere with usual activities

Symptoms of Social Anxiety

- Fears of meeting or talking to people
- Avoidance of social situations
- Few friends outside the family

Other Symptoms of Anxious Children

- Many worries about things before they happen
- Sleep deprivation due to worry, fear, or attempts to control these concerns
- Constant worries or concerns about family, school, friends, or activities
- Repetitive, unwanted thoughts (worries or obsessions) or actions (compulsions or avoidance of certain situations)
- Fears of embarrassment or making mistakes

- Low self esteem and lack of self-confidence

- Family conflict over seemingly mundane issues (such as going to school, a minor change in routine)

In evaluating whether or not a child has an anxiety disorder, professionals often consider four factors:

- How intensely does the child experience the anxiety symptoms; do they make her physically ill? Do her worries take up much of the day?

- How long have they lasted; anxiety that lasts longer than a month is one benchmark in looking at professional treatment.

- How age appropriate are the child's fears? Separation anxiety at 1 year is not a matter of concern; it might be if the child is 9.

- How much do the anxiety symptoms prevent the child from engaging in, and enjoying, regular activities? Is the child missing sleepovers or getting ready in the morning?

For us parents, though, our primary questions are how much emotional pain our child is experiencing and how we can help lessen it.

Are the Red Flags Waving?

Because anxious children may be quiet, compliant, and eager to please, their difficulties may be missed. We parents may be the first, or the best, ones to recognize when our child's problems are too much for him or her to manage. In looking at this checklist, the focus is on the perspective of the child—not on clinical diagnosis; what matters to parents is the amount of distress and pain our child is experiencing.

- Has your child's anxiety lasted more than one month?

- Does your child worry a lot about the future?

- Does your child often ask unnecessary questions and repeatedly ask for reassurance?

- Does your child worry excessively about a number of events and activities?

- Does your child get frequent stomachaches and headaches at school?

- Does your child have nightmares about being separated from you or excessive fears about something bad happening to you?

- Does your child seem exceedingly anxious or uncomfortable with peers, to the point that s/he avoids them?

- Does your child feel extremely nervous when she has to do something (play a sport, speak up in class) while others watch her?

- Have you noticed your child's school work or social activities declining?

- Does your child seem to make up a lot of excuses to avoid school whenever possible? ("Illnesses" that magically improve as soon as he or she is allowed to stay home.)

- Does your child throw temper tantrums to avoid certain activities or objects?

- Does your child constantly worry about things that have already happened?

- Does your child have certain rituals or routines that are extremely distressing when disrupted?

- Does your child worry to the point that she feels physical symptoms (like throwing up, dizziness, shakiness, or sweatiness)?

- Does your child redo tasks because he's never satisfied with his performance?

- Does your child constantly worry about how well she is doing at school or other competitive activities?

- Is your child consistently afraid to meet or talk to new people?

The more items you recognized in your child, the better the odds that you can benefit from the advice of a professional.

We're Alike and Yet We're Different

When it comes to anxiety in children, an educated parent is the best advocate for his or her child. Having a clear understanding of what anxiety disorders look and feel like can be a great aid in understanding when a fear is just a "stage" and when it's a warning signal. Parents who have struggled with anxiety themselves can be quick to pick up the current of fear running through a child; used wisely, our sensitivity can enable us to help our child work quickly through normal fears and get early treatment when our child's fears are excessive or limiting.

However, although anxiety symptoms are often similar in adults and children, they are sometimes expressed differently. Unlike adults, child anxiety sufferers can't manipulate their environment to avoid a frightening situation. An adult with OCD, for example, can soothe his obsessive fear of germs by showering repeatedly throughout the day. A child's compulsion to shower for hours on end may be interfered with by a parent who has to negotiate bathroom time among four children or who can't afford an extravagant water bill. The same holds true for socially anxious children, who *must* attend school and *will* be asked to read aloud, take part in a class project, or go on a field trip. As a result, in an attempt to better manipulate their environment, children with anxiety disorders may be angrier and more defiant in comparison to their grownup counterparts. Anxiety/fear can result in temper tantrums.

Similarly, anxiety symptoms in children often reflect their level of intellectual development. For instance, all children engage in magical thinking, an immature thought process that confuses correlation with causation. *I was mad at my dad and then he died; therefore, I caused his death.*

In this worldview, effects and their causes are not objectively determined, but mediated by the child's own desires; *it is raining because I am sad.* An adult with OCD who struggles with obsessive fears that harm might befall his family might repeatedly check door locks or stoves. A child with the same fears may do the same; however, s/he may also develop superstitious rituals such as avoiding cracks in the sidewalk, repeating only "safe" numbers, or obsessively arranging her room in a certain way to ward off danger.

Anxiety Attack

Pay attention to what turns a temper tantrum on and off. If your child's "fit" immediately and consistently stops when you allow him or her to avoid a certain situation or event (go to school, attend a birthday party), that's a clue that the temper tantrum was about that activity.

Stress Relief

It's hard to know how to promote self-confidence in new situations and still teach your child to be cautious of potential danger. The best defenses against the real dangers of the world are age-appropriate supervision, knowledge (safety rules, emergency procedures), and preparation (code words, how to say "no").

Helping Our Children Recover

Not only are we recognizing that many adult anxiety disorders show their face in children, we are more and more aware that the sooner an anxiety sufferer gets help, the better off s/he will be. In recognizing that a fear has gone on too long, or is taking its toll on our child's social or academic life, we can get our child the help s/he needs and prevent additional problems such as lack of friends, school difficulties, and low self-esteem. We can also prevent our child's anxiety disorder from wreaking havoc on our family or from robbing us of the joy of parenting a happy and well-adjusted child.

So what can we expect when we take that leap of faith and schedule that first appointment? We can expect our child to get better; the vast majority of children treated for an anxiety disorder show significant improvement in three to four months. We can expect our child to gradually face his or her fears. The most common (and research validated) psychotherapy approach is systematic desensitization and gradual exposure to scary situations/objects, similar to that discussed in Chapter 19. Depending upon the severity of our child's symptoms and our personal values/beliefs, we should be prepared to discuss medication.

We can also expect to take an active role in our child's recovery. We can do our homework and make sure the therapist we choose has specific experience working with children who have anxiety disorders. We can work with the therapist to make sure the messages we give our child at home are in sync with our child's treatment. We can discuss ways we can encourage our child to practice their newfound skills. We can explore ways we can simultaneously support our child, set limits on inappropriate behavior, and keep our family on an even keel. In the process, we can remind ourselves of the big picture; no matter what genetic cards our child is dealt or what life dishes up, we parents are powerful coaches in helping our children develop the coping skills to win this game called life.

And so we're back at the beginning. As we've seen throughout this book, and perhaps in our daily lives, anxiety disorders are painful. They're unpredictable. They can be disruptive.

But they don't have to defeat us. By facing our fears and actively seeking out the self-help techniques and professional intervention we need, we learn a lot about ourselves. Anxiety may be a mean teacher, but she does teach. Perhaps she has played a role in your willingness to pick up this book, an act of bravery in and of itself. If so, congratulate yourself on yet another step in your recovery from anxiety.

Anxiety Attack

When seeking a mental-health professional for your child, consider talking your concerns over with your child's pediatrician, teacher, or guidance counselor. Not only do they know you and your child well, but they should also be involved in any assessment of the problem.

Myth Buster

"If my child needs help, I must be a bad parent." No one would think less of you if your child had diabetes or cancer. A mental illness is no different. The greatest harm comes from leaving mental illness untreated. But just like physical problems, the prognosis is better when the mental-health problem is treated early.

The road to recovery is rarely easy, but it's an interesting journey. I wish I could guarantee you that there will come a time when you will *never* have anxiety symptoms again. I can't. But what I can assure you is that if you keep plugging along there will come a day when you are no longer afraid of your symptoms. There will be a day when, should it suddenly show up, you will look it full in the face and say, "You again? Well, bring it on. This time I'm ready."

The Least You Need to Know

- Worries and fears are a normal part of growing up.

- Parents can help their children overcome age-related fears by finding a balance between "get over it" and "I'll protect you."

- When childhood fears last too long and disrupt a child's daily activities, s/he may have an anxiety disorder.

- Children can be diagnosed with the same anxiety disorders that adults have. However, the expression of their symptoms can be different.

- Parents can play an active role in their child's recovery by getting the right professional help and working with the therapist to reinforce new skills at home.

Glossary

adjustment disorder A maladaptive reaction to identifiable stressful life events, such as divorce, loss of job, physical illness, or natural disaster; this diagnosis assumes that the condition will remit when the stress ceases or when the patient adapts to the situation.

agoraphobia Abnormal anxiety regarding public places or situations from which the person may wish to flee or in which he or she would be helpless in the event of a panic attack.

amygdala The part of the brain's limbic system responsible for regulating emotions and triggering responses to danger.

anxiety Apprehension without apparent cause. It usually occurs when there's no immediate threat to a person's safety or well being, but the threat feels real.

anxiety disorder An illness that produces an intense, often unrealistic and excessive state of apprehension and fear. This may or may not occur during, or in anticipation of, a specific situation, and may be accompanied by a rise in blood pressure, increased heart rate, rapid breathing, nausea, and other signs of agitation or discomfort.

assertiveness   Generally, assertiveness is characterized by behavior that enables us to act in our own best interests, to stand up for ourselves without undue anxiety, and express our personal feelings comfortably. Assertive behavior differs from aggressive behavior in that we exercise our right of self-expression without denying the rights of others.

autonomic nervous system   The part of our peripheral nervous system that controls our internal organs.

belief   Any cognitive content held as true.

classical conditioning   When an animal (or person) learns to associate a stimulus with a reinforcement or aversion. For example, bullying or teasing experienced early in life may reflexively elicit feelings of anxiety which become conditioned, creating patterns of emotional responses which carry on into adult life.

cognition   The formal word for thinking.

cognitive-behavioral therapy   A highly structured psychotherapeutic method used to alter distorted attitudes and problem behavior by identifying and replacing negative inaccurate thoughts and changing the rewards for behaviors.

cognitive distortion   Triggered by inappropriate or irrational thinking patterns, called automatic thoughts. Instead of reacting to the reality of a situation, an individual automatically reacts to his or her own distorted view of the situation. Cognitive therapy strives to change these thought patterns (also known as cognitive distortions), by examining the rationality and validity of the assumptions behind them. This process is termed cognitive restructuring.

compulsions   An irresistible impulse to act, regardless of the rationality of the motivation.

defensive pessimism   A strategy of imagining the worst-case scenarios for each situation, used by anxious people to help them manage their anxiety so they can work productively. Defensive pessimists lower their expectations to help prepare themselves for the worst. Then they mentally play through all the bad things that might happen. Though it sounds as if it might be depressing, defensive pessimism actually helps anxious people focus away from their emotions so that they can plan and act effectively.

diagnosis   Is the process of identifying a disease by its signs, symptoms and results of various diagnostic procedures. The conclusion reached through that process is also called a diagnosis.

diathesis-stress model   Involves understanding mental illness as being caused by a combination of "nature" (patient's genes, heredity) and "nurture" (family upbringing, life events, social environment). Individuals may inherit a predisposition to mental illness, and then experience a stressor that results in the emergence of an illness.

distraction   A condition or state of mind in which attention is diverted from an original focus or interest.

emotional hijacking   According to Daniel Goleman, this occurs when your planning rational mind is hijacked by your emotional response. A hijacking occurs in an instant, triggering this reaction crucial moments before the thinking brain has had a chance to fully glimpse what is happening, much less evaluate what is going on.

emotional intelligence   The ability to successfully understand and use emotions. It involves a group of skills, including the ability to motivate ourselves, regulate our moods, control our impulses and empathize with others.

exposure with response prevention   Form of behavior therapy in which clients intentionally approach situations (places, specific animals or insects, body sensations, thoughts) that make them feel fearful (the "exposure") without leaving the situation or engaging in any avoidance behaviors. The approach may be done gradually ("graduated exposure") or suddenly ("flooding"). The exposures are repeated until the person no longer feels fearful in the situation.

fight-or-flight response   The theory states that animals react to threats with a general discharge of the sympathetic nervous system, resulting in immediate physical reactions by triggering increases in heart rate and breathing, constricting blood vessels in many parts of the body. In layman's terms, an animal has two options when faced with danger. They can either face the threat ("fight"), or they can avoid the threat ("flight").

fear   An intense aversion to or apprehension of a person, place, activity, event, or object that causes emotional distress and often avoidance behavior.

fetal programming hypothesis   A theory that certain disturbing factors occurring during certain sensitive periods of development in utero can "program" set points in a variety of biological systems in the unborn child.

generalized anxiety disorder   A mental disorder characterized by chronic, excessive worry and fear that seems to have no real cause. Children or adolescents with generalized anxiety disorder often worry a lot about things such as future events, past behaviors, social acceptance, family matters, their personal abilities, and/or school performance.

habituation   The process whereby a person becomes so accustomed to a stimulus that he or she ignores it.

highly sensitive person   A term Dr. Elaine Aron uses to describe a biological sensitivity that causes the individual to process sensory information (noise, lights, emotions) more deeply and thoroughly than 80 percent to 90 percent of the people around her.

interpersonal therapy   A form of psychotherapy that targets helping a person deal with changing roles and other stressors by learning how to communicate more effectively with others.

magical thinking   The thought process whereby a person mistakes correlation for causation. For example, someone may believe a shirt is lucky if he had won a bowling competition in it. He will continue to wear the shirt to bowling competitions, and though he continues to win some and lose some, he will chalk up every win to his lucky shirt.

modeling   Learning through observation, the process by which we learn new behaviors by watching others perform them.

obsessions   A persistent, repetitive, and unwanted thought which the person cannot eliminate by logic or reasoning.

obsessive-compulsive disorder (OCD)   A problem characterized by *obsessions*, recurring unwanted thoughts which are difficult to stop, and *compulsions*, rituals of checking behavior or repetitive actions carried out in an attempt to relieve the thoughts.

operant conditioning   A process by which the results of the person's behavior determine whether the behavior is more or less likely to occur in the future.

optimism   A life view where one looks upon the world as a positive place.

overprotectiveness   A parenting style by which parents attempt to protect their child from emotional/physical harm to the extent that the child is not permitted to engage in the kinds of trial-and-error learning that are involved in developing a sense of independence and mastery.

panic attack   An intense and sudden feeling of fear and anxiety. It is associated with many physical symptoms such as rapid heart beat, trembling, rapid shallow breathing, pins and needles in the arms and hands, and feeling faint.

panic disorder   An anxiety disorder during which the person experiences recurrent episodes of intense anxiety and physical arousal lasting up to 10 minutes.

parasympathetic nervous system   The part of our involuntary nervous system that allows us to relax.

perfectionism   A learned internal motivation to strive for perfection based on the belief that self-worth is equated with performance.

personality   The unique bundle of all the psychological qualities that consistently influence an individual's usual behavior across situations and time.

personality disorder   An enduring pattern of inner experience and behavior that differs markedly from the expectations of the individual's culture, is pervasive and inflexible, has an onset in adolescence or early adulthood, is stable over time, and leads to distress or impairment.

phobia   A fear that's extreme, severe, and persistent.

postpartum depression   A complex mix of physical, emotional, and behavioral changes that occur in a mother after giving birth. It is a serious condition, affecting 10 percent of new mothers. Symptoms range from mild to severe depression and may appear within days of delivery or gradually, perhaps up to a year later. Symptoms may last from a few weeks to a year.

post-traumatic stress disorder (PSTD)   A debilitating condition that often follows a terrifying physical or emotional event causing the person who survived the event to have persistent, frightening thoughts and memories, or flashbacks, of the ordeal. Persons with PTSD often feel chronically, emotionally numb. Once referred to as "shell shock" or "battle fatigue."

procrastination   Putting off or delaying an action to a later time.

REM sleep   Sleep that is characterized by rapid eye movement, brain activity close to that of wakefulness, and a complete absence of muscle tone. Most dreaming takes place during REM sleep.

resilience   The process of, capacity for, or outcome of successful adaptation despite challenging or threatening circumstances.

risk factors   Things that increase the likelihood that you'll get a particular disease or condition.

rituals   A set of actions, performed mainly for their symbolic value. In obsessive-compulsive disorder, rituals take the form of particular mental or physical tasks that serve to temporarily alleviate anxiety.

selective serotonin reuptake inhibitors (SSRIs)   A class of antidepressants that work by blocking the reabsorption of serotonin in the brain, thus raising the levels of serotonin. SSRIs include fluoxetine (Prozac), sertraline (Zoloft), and paroxetine (Paxil).

separation anxiety   A developmental stage during which a child experiences anxiety when separated from their *primary* care giver (usually the mother). It is normally seen between 8 and 14 months of age.

separation anxiety disorder   Excessive, prolonged, developmentally inappropriate anxiety and apprehension in a child concerning removal from parents, home, or familiar surroundings.

social anxiety   Excessive fear of embarrassment in social situations that is extremely intrusive and can have debilitating effects on personal and professional relationships. Also called social phobia.

stress   A state of mental or emotional strain during which the perceived demands of the environment exceed the perceived ability/resources to cope.

sympathetic nervous system   The part of our nervous system that activates our internal organs in response to real or perceived threats.

systematic desensitization   A process whereby we gradually expose ourselves to the things/situations/events we fear the most. By repairing the feared situation with relaxation, we gradually unlearn our negative association.

temperament   The natural way a child responds to and interacts with people, materials, and situations in his or her world.

thought-stopping   The process by which you are able to cease dwelling on a bothersome thought. Effective thought-stopping techniques include replacing, substituting, or distracting oneself from the original train of thought.

trait   A stable characteristic that influences an individual's thoughts, feelings, and behavior.

values   Personal beliefs in which we have a strong emotional investment.

worry   To feel concerned or uneasy about something to the extent that it disturbs one's peace of mind.

Anxiety Resources

Websites

The internet is a wonderful resources for anxiety sufferers as long as we're informed consumers and consider the source. I've focused on those that provide fairly independent information.

Anxiety

www.anxieties.com
An excellent self-help guide.

www.ocdonline.com
Website exclusively devoted to promoting a greater understanding of obsessive compulsive disorder's (OCD) treatment and mental processes.

www.anxietybookstore.com
More than 220 books on anxiety.

www.anxietyselfhelp.com
Gives basic information about anxiety disorders as well as a chat room where people with anxiety disorders share their stories.

www.freedomfromfear.org
Screening tools, message board, and information about anxiety disorders. It also lists professionals who treat anxiety across the United States.

pacificcoast.net/~kstrong
Information and support for family members and friends of those with anxiety disorders.

www.womensmentalhealth.org
Resources for information on anxiety disorders during pregnancy.

www.webmd.com
Vast array of information about both physical and mental health issues, including information about psychological treatments, drug therapy and prevention.

www.mghmadi.org
Information on psychiatric disorders associated with women's reproduction.

www.mentalhealthchannel.net
A physician-developed, online information resource for patients and physicians.

www.nasponline.com
National Association of School Psychologists website has information and "fact sheets" for parents and teachers.

www.tourettesyndrome.net/ocd_awareness.htm
Awareness exercise showing what it's like for a child to have OCD

Stress Management

www.cmha.ca/english/coping%5Fwith%5Fstress
Sponsored by the Canadian Mental Health Association.

stress.about.com/od/?once=true&
Group of articles about stress and stress-busting techniques.

www.helpguide.org/mental/stress_management_relief_coping.htm
Expert, noncommercial information about coping with stress.

www.stressbusting.co.uk
Self-help strategies for beating stress and combating anxiety.

www.mindtools.com
Comprehensive list of tools which can help you master stress.

www.anxietyselfhelp.com
www.healingwell.com/anxiety

Health articles, medical news, doctor-produced video webcasts, community message boards and chat rooms, professional healthcare resources, email, newsletters, books and reviews, and resource link directories.

www.anxietypanic.com/index.html
Search engine for anxiety, panic, trauma, fear, phobia, stress, obsession, depression and more.

www.nami.org
National Alliance for the Mentally Ill is a nonprofit organization that serves as an advocate for persons and families affected by mental disorders.

www.algy.com/anxiety/about.php
Self-help network dedicated to the overcoming and cure of debilitating anxiety. Includes definitions, treatments, support and links.

www.socialphobia.org
Social Phobia Social Anxiety Association, a nonprofit organization, seeks to educate the public about the largest anxiety disorder—social phobia.

www.selfesteemgames.mcgill.ca/index.htm
Online games for children that promote self-esteem.

Organizations

Agoraphobics Building Independent Lives (ABIL, Inc.)
400 West 32nd Street
Richmond, Virginia 23225
804-353-3964
E-mail: ABIL1986@aol.com
www.anxietysupport.org

Agoraphobics In Motion (AIM)
1719 Crooks
Royal Oak, MI 58067
248-547-0400
E-mail: anny@ameritech.net
www.aim-hq.org

American Psychiatric Association
1400 K Street, NW
Washington, DC 20005
202-682-6220
www.psych.org

American Psychological Association
750 First Street, NE
Washington, DC 20002-4242
202-955-7600
www.apa.org

Anxiety Disorders Association of America
8730 Georgia Avenue
Suite 600
Silver Spring, MD 20910
240-485-1001
E-mail: AnxDis@adaa.org
www.adaa.org

Association for Advancement of Behavior Therapy
305 Seventh Avenue
New York, NY 10001-6008
212-647-1890
www.aabt.org

Austin Center for OCD
austinocd.com

Facts For Health
Madison Institute of Medicine, Inc.
7617 Mineral Point Road, Suite 300
Madison, WI 53717
608-827-2470
www.factsforhealth.org

Freedom From Fear
308 Seaview Avenue
Staten Island, NY 10305
718-351-1717
www.freedomfromfear.com

Hudson Valley Center for Cognitive Therapy
421 North Highland Avenue
Upper Nyack, NY 10960
845-353-3399

National Institute of Mental Health
Panic Disorder Division
1-800-64-PANIC

Obsessive Compulsive Foundation
337 Notch Hill Road
North Branford, CT 06471
203-315-2190
E-mail: info@ocfoundation.org
www.ocfoundation.org

Obsessive Compulsive Foundation of Metropolitan Chicago
2300 Lincoln Park West
Chicago, IL 60614
773-880-2035
E-mail: ocfmetchgo@aol.com
www.ocfchicago.org

Obsessive Compulsive Information Center
Madison Institute of Medicine, Inc.
7617 Mineral Point Road,
Suite 300 Madison, WI 53717
608-827-2470
www.miminc.org

Phobics Anonymous
P.O. Box 1180
Palm Springs, CA 92263
760-322-2673

Trichotillomania Learning Center, Inc.
1215 Mission Street, Suite 2
Santa Cruz, CA 95060
408-457-1004
E-mail: trichster@aol.com
www.trich.org

West Side Public Speaking and Social Anxiety Clinic
E-mail: speakeeezi@netzero.net
www.speakeeezi.com

Self-Help Books

There are hundreds of anxiety-related self-help books; the key is to pick the one that "speaks" to you. These are some of my personal favorites.

Anxiety Disorders in Adults

Antony, Martin and Swinson, Richard. *The Shyness and Social Anxiety Workbook: Proven Techniques for Overcoming Your Fears.* Oakland: New Harbinger Publications, 2000.

Baer, Lee. *The Imp of the Mind: Exploring the Silent Epidemic of Bad Thoughts.* Reissue edition. New York: Plume, 2002.

Beckfield, Denise. *Master Your Panic and Take Back Your Life.* Atascadero: Impact Publishers, 2000.

Bourne, Edmond. *The Anxiety and Phobia Workbook.* Oakland: New Harbinger Publications, 2000.

Buell, Linda Manassee. *Panic and Anxiety Disorder: 121 Tips, Real-Life Advice, Resources and More.* Second edition. Simplify Life, 2003.

Carmin, Cheryl; Pollard, Alec; Flynn, Teresa and Markway, Barbara. *Dying of Embarrassment: Help for Social Anxiety and Phobia.* Oakland: New Harbinger Publications, 1992.

Crawford, Mark. *The Obsessive Compulsive Trap.* Ventura, CA: Regal Books, 2004.

Gardner, James and Bell, Arthur H. *Overcoming Anxiety, Panic and Depression: New Ways to Regain Your Confidence.* Career Press, 2000.

Dayhoff, Signe A. *Diagonally Parked in a Parallel Universe: Working Through Social Anxiety.* Effectiveness-Plus Publications, 2000.

Hilliard, Ericka B. *Living Full with Shyness and Social Anxiety: A Comprehensive Guide to Gaining Social Confidence.* Marlowe and Company, 2005.

Hyman, Bruce M. and Pedrick, Cherry. *The OCD Workbook: Your Guide to Breaking Free from Obsessive-Compulsive Disorder*. Second edition. New Harbinger Publications, 2005.

Jordan, Jeanne and Peterson, Julie. *The Panic Diaries: The Frightful, Sometimes Hilarious Truth About Panic Attacks*. Ulysses Press, 2004.

Ross, Jerrilyn. *Triumph Over Fear: A Book of Help and Hope for People With Anxiety, Panic Attacks, and Phobias*. Bantam, 1995.

Shipko, Stuart. *Surviving Panic Disorder: What You Need to Know*. Authorhouse, 2003.

Children's Books

Pando, Nancy. *I Don't Want to Go to School: Helping Children Cope with Separation Anxiety*. New Horizon Press, 2005.

Crary, Elizabeth. *Mommy Don't Go*. Parenting Press, 1996.

Huebner, Dawn and Mathews, Bonnie. *What to Do When You Worry Too Much: A Kid's Guide to Overcoming Anxiety*. Magination Press, 2005.

Lite, Lori. *A Boy and a Bear: The Children's Relaxation Book*. Specialty Press, 1996.

Lite, Lori. *The Goodnight Caterpillar: Muscular Relaxation and Meditation Bedtime Story for Children*, Litebooks.net, 2004.

Penn, Audrey. *The Kissing Hand*. Child and Family Press, 1993.

Romain, Trevor and Verdick, Elizabeth. *Stress Can Really Get On Your Nerves!* Free Spirit Publishing, 2000.

Books on Childhood Anxiety

Chansky, Tamar E. *Freeing Your Child From Anxiety: Powerful, Practical Solutions to Overcome Your Child's Worries and Phobias*. Broadway, 2004.

Chansky, Tamar E. *Freeing Your Child From Obsessive-Compulsive Disorder: A Powerful, Practical Program for Parents of Children and Adolescents*. New York: Three Rivers Press (Crown Publishing Group), 2001.

Spence, Sue; Cobham, Vanessa; Wignall, Ann; and Rapee, Ronald M. (editors). *Helping Your Anxious Child: A Step-by-Step Guide for Parents.* New Harbinger Publications, 2000.

Spencer, Elizabeth Dupont. *The Anxiety Cure for Kids: A Guide for Parents.* Wiley, 2003.

Postpartum Anxiety and Depression

Bennett, Shoshana S. and Indman, Pec. *Beyond the Blues: Prenatal and Postpartum Depression.* Mood Swings Press, 2002.

Kleiman, Karen and Raskin, Valerie. *This Isn't What I Expected: Overcoming Postpartum Depression.* Bantam, 1994.

Misri, Shaila. *Shouldn't I Be Happy?: Emotional Problems of Pregnant and Postpartum Women.* Free Press, 2002.

Sabastian, Linda. *Overcoming Postpartum Depression and Anxiety.* Addicus Books: 1998.

Index

Q-R